A-Level Year 2

Business

Exam Board: AQA

Revising for Business exams is stressful, that's for sure — even just getting your notes sorted out can leave you needing a lie down. But help is at hand...

This brilliant CGP book explains **everything you'll need to learn** (and nothing you won't), all in a straightforward style that's easy to get your head around.

We've also included **exam-style questions** to test how ready you are for the real thing, along with a section of advice on how to pick up as many marks as possible!

A-Level revision? It has to be CGP!

Published by CGP

Editors:
Rob Harrison, Shaun Harrogate, Sharon Keeley-Holden, Ali Palin, Caley Simpson and Ben Train.

Contributors:
Paul Brockbank, Peter Gray, Nagu Rao, Adrian Murray, Jeff Harris, Angela Duffy, Alison Hazell

ISBN: 978 1 78294 353 2

With thanks to Karen Wells for the proofreading.
With thanks to Jan Greenway and Laura Jakubowski for the copyright research.

Cover photo © iStockphoto.com/Pinkypills

Clipart from Corel®
Printed by Elanders Ltd, Newcastle upon Tyne.

Based on the classic CGP style created by Richard Parsons.

Contents

Section One — Mission, Corporate Objectives and Strategy

Mission, Objectives and Strategy 2

Section Two — Internal Analysis

Financial Analysis — Balance Sheets 4
Financial Analysis — Income Statements 9
Financial Analysis — Value and Limitations 11
Financial Analysis — Ratios 12
Financial Analysis — Gearing 15
Value and Limitations of Ratios 17
Analysing Overall Performance 18
Methods of Assessing Performance 20

Section Three — Analysing the External Environment

Business and the Legal Environment 22
Employment Law 24
Business and the Political Environment 26
Business and the Economy 28
Inflation and Exchange Rates 30
Government Policy and the Economy 32
The Global Economy 34
Business and the Social Environment 36
Business and the Technological Environment 39
Business and the Competitive Environment 40

Section Four — Investment Appraisal

Assessing Investments 42
Investment Decisions 46

Section Five — Choosing Strategic Direction

Marketing Strategies 48
Positioning Strategies 50

Section Six — Strategic Methods

Business Growth 52
Business Growth — Organic 54
Business Growth — External 56
Innovation 58
Entering International Markets 62
Locating Abroad 64
Multinationals 66
International Business Strategies 68
Use of Digital Technology 70

Section Seven — Managing Change

Causes of Change 72
Managing Change 74
Overcoming Barriers to Change 76
Managing Organisational Culture 78

Section Eight — Implementing Strategy

Planning Strategy 82
Implementing Strategy 84
Network Analysis 86
Difficulties with Implementing Strategy 90
Evaluating Strategy 93

Section Nine — Maths Skills

Maths Skills 94

Do Well in Your Exams

The A-Level Exams 97
Get Marks in Your A-Level Exams 98
Worked Exam Questions 100

Answers to Numerical Questions 103
Glossary 104
Index 108

We deliberately haven't included answers to most of the questions — that's because there are lots of valid ways to give your answers. Instead, we've put in a section on how to write answers and do well. Answers to numerical questions are included though, on page 103.

Mission, Objectives and Strategy

You'll be familiar with the idea of a business's mission and objectives, but look at your Year 1 notes if you need a recap. You need to know a bit more about them though — like what influences them and how they link to a business's strategy.

Mission and Objectives are Influenced by Internal and External Factors

1) The **mission** of a business is its **overall purpose**. It's influenced by what the **owners** want the business to **achieve**, their **personal values** and **beliefs**, and what **market opportunities** there are.
2) The **objectives** of a business are the **goals** it sets in order to **achieve** its mission. **Corporate objectives** are the goals of the business **as a whole**, whereas **functional objectives** are the objectives of each **department** or **function** (e.g. marketing, finance, etc.), set to help achieve the corporate objectives.
3) Objectives can be set for **profit**, **growth**, **survival**, **cash flow** and **social/ethical** performance.
4) When setting objectives, there are many **factors** that may **influence** a business's decisions. **Internal factors** are important, as well as adapting to meet the demands of a **changing environment**, for example:

- **Ownership:** The **form** of the business and whether it's **for-profit** or **non-profit** will have a big effect on its objectives. Sole traders can pretty much **do what they like**, whereas limited companies have **directors** and **shareholders** to answer to.
- **Short-termism:** Shareholders can demand a **quick return** on their investment, which leads to **short-term objectives** to increase profit that don't necessarily **benefit** the business in the **long term**.
- **Internal environment:** The **size**, **culture** and **resources** of the business will affect its objectives — as will the **views** of the **leaders** or **management** (especially on issues such as **ethics** or **social responsibility**).
- **External environment:** **Political**, **legal**, **economic**, **social**, **technological** and **environmental factors**, as well as **competition**, influence a business's objectives. For example:

  1) Changes in the **economy** will affect whether a business aims to **increase profits** or focuses on **survival**.
  2) Consumer interest in **environmental issues** might influence a business's decision to set an objective to **minimise pollution**.

Strategies are Plans for Achieving Objectives

1) A **strategy** is a medium to long-term **plan of action** developed to achieve a business's **objectives**. A business's **corporate strategy** is based on achieving its **corporate objectives**.
2) A strategy can only be put into place once an organisation has **outlined** its aims and objectives. Businesses need to decide **what** they want to achieve before they can work out **how** to achieve it.
3) All businesses need to have a strategy. In **small firms**, these plans may not be **formally** written down. Strategies can simply be a **sequence** of business decisions made over time with the aim of reaching a particular **goal**, e.g. expanding into a new market segment.

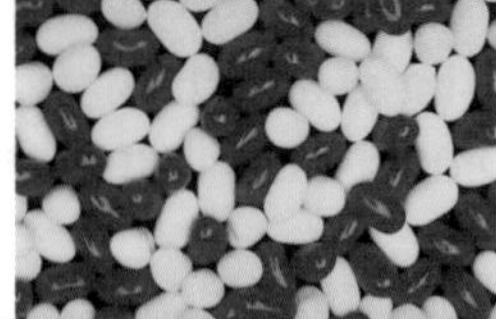
No, I said TACTICS.

4) In **larger firms**, strategy is usually more **clearly defined** because it will influence the plans of **individual departments**, such as marketing and HR.
5) **Tactics** are **short-term plans** for implementing strategy, so are more focused on **day-to-day activities**.

Functional Decision Making is based on Strategic Decision Making

1) Businesses make **strategic decisions** — they decide on **strategies** that will help the business to achieve its **corporate objectives**. Strategic decisions are **long-term**, **high-risk** decisions that determine the overall direction of the business.
2) **Functional decisions** are decisions made in **individual departments**. Departmental managers make decisions in order to **implement the overall strategy** — so they're based on the **strategic decisions** of the business. Functional decisions tend to be more **short-term** and **lower risk** than strategic decisions.

E.g. a business might have an **objective** to increase sales by 5% in one year. To do this, the business makes a **strategic decision** to expand its production capacity, so the HR department makes a **functional decision** to recruit more people.

Mission, Objectives and Strategy

Businesses use **SWOT Analysis** to make decisions about their **Future**

1) A **SWOT analysis** is a four-factor model that details the **strengths**, **weaknesses**, **opportunities** and **threats** facing a business — this helps managers to make strategic decisions.
2) The **strengths** and **weaknesses** of each department are **internal** factors that the business **can influence** (there's lots on **internal analysis** in Section 2).
3) The **opportunities** and **threats** are **beyond the control** of the business. The business has to **understand** them in order to react appropriately (there's lots on **external analysis** in Section 3).
4) **External factors** that might pose opportunities or threats include political, legal, economic, social, technological and environmental factors and competitor behaviour.

Strengths
Weaknesses
Opportunities
Threats

Example: Beasel's Tea Room is a small **tea shop** in a town-centre location. In 2014, they won an **award** in a local newspaper for "the best toasted teacake in the county". The tea shop only seats **22 customers**, but the owners have decided not to move to bigger premises because their current **location**, on a main shopping street, attracts **passing trade**. Instead, the manager has suggested that they start selling **takeaway** drinks and cakes to take advantage of their popularity. The owners are concerned about reports that a big **coffee shop chain** is planning to open a branch close to the tea shop, as they don't think they will be able to **compete** on price and may **lose business**.

Strengths: Good reputation, good location, good quality products.
Weaknesses: Small premises, cannot compete on price with chain stores.
Opportunities: Selling cakes and drinks to take away could increase their market size.
Threats: Possibility of a new competitor with lower prices.

SWOT analysis helps businesses to **Plan Strategies**

1) **SWOT analysis** is a very useful tool in developing **strategy** (see p.82-83 for more on **strategic planning**). It considers the business's **individual circumstances**, and is done in a **factual** and **objective** way.
2) In planning strategy, managers will focus on **opportunities** that build on the business's **strengths**, on **converting weaknesses** into **strengths** and on **managing threats**.
3) One advantage of SWOT analysis is that it can easily be **redone** to take into account **changing conditions** (e.g. a changing economy or unforeseen events such as floods). This means that a business can **adapt** its strategy using the new SWOT analysis.
4) SWOT analysis also lets the business know where it has a **competitive advantage** over its rivals — the business can change its **strategy** to focus on these elements.

Practice Questions

Q1 Give three internal factors and three external factors that could influence a business's objectives.

Q2 What is a strategy?

Q3 What does SWOT stand for?

Exam Question

Q1 A sandwich shop has carried out SWOT analysis and come up with the following information:
Strength — it is the only place in town that sells freshly-made sandwiches. Weakness — it is located down a dark alleyway. Opportunity — a new call centre with 100 employees is opening nearby. Threat — a local restaurant is introducing a low price lunch menu.
Evaluate how the sandwich shop could use this analysis in planning its strategy. [12 marks]

Time to SWOT up on your objectives and strategy...

That was a nice gentle start to strategy — but there's lots more to come. If you want a bit of extra practice, think about a local business and do a SWOT analysis for it (just at home — they might not appreciate it if you waltz in and start pointing out their weaknesses). Personally, I have a bit of a weakness for Hugh Jackman, but that can't be helped...

Financial Analysis — Balance Sheets

Businesses have different ways of reporting their financial information — balance sheets and income statements can be analysed to assess their performance. Luckily, that's what this section is all about. Read on to find out more...

Balance Sheets are lists of Assets and Liabilities

1) Balance sheets are a **snapshot** of a firm's finances at a **fixed point in time**.
2) They show the value of all the business' **assets** (the things that belong to the business, including cash in the bank) and all its **liabilities** (the money the business owes). They also show the value of all the **capital** (the money invested in the business), and the source of that capital (e.g. loans, shares or retained profits) — so they show where the money's **come from** as well as what's being **done** with it.
3) The '**net assets**' value (the total fixed and current assets minus total current and non-current (long-term) liabilities — see next page) is **always the same** as the '**total equity**' value — the total of all the money that's been put into the business. That's why they're called balance sheets — they **balance**.

Sally soon realised that balancing isn't as easy as it looks.

Interpreting balance sheets — Here's How It All Looks

ABC Company Ltd
Balance Sheet as at 30 March 2014

Premises			£100000
Machines			£10000
Vehicles			£15000
Total non-current assets			£125000
Inventories (stock)		£20000	
Receivables (debtors)		£10000	
Cash in the bank		£5000	
Total current assets		£35000	
Payables (creditors)	(£20000)		
Overdraft	(£2000)		
Dividends	(£10000)		
Unpaid tax	(£1000)		
Total current liabilities		(£33000)	
Net current assets			£2000
Non-current liabilities (long-term loans)			(£55000)
Net assets			£72000
Share capital			£60000
Reserves			£12000
Total equity (shareholders' funds)			£72000

Balance sheets show the financial state of affairs on one particular day.

Raw materials and finished products — things the business has spent money on, but not sold yet.

Value of products sold but not paid for yet. Money owed to the business. See p.5.

The value of non-current assets includes depreciation (see p.7) — it's what they're worth now, not when the business bought them.

Money owed by the business. See p.5.

Brackets mean a negative number.

Dividends not yet paid to shareholders.

Net current assets = current assets − current liabilities

This is the working capital available to pay for day to day spending. See p.6.

Net assets = net current assets + non-current assets − non-current liabilities.

These two figures ALWAYS balance.

The figure for reserves takes into account depreciation — depreciation is taken into account in 'net assets', so if it wasn't included here, the figures wouldn't balance.

Financial Analysis — Balance Sheets

Assets *are things the* ***Business Owns***

1) Businesses can use **capital** to buy **assets** that will generate more revenue in the future — this is **investment**.
2) Assets (like machinery and stock) provide a **financial benefit** to the business, so they're given a monetary value on the balance sheet. Assets can be classified as **non-current assets** (fixed assets) or **current assets**.
3) **Non-current assets** are assets that the business is likely to keep for **more than a year**, e.g. property, land, production equipment, desks and computers. The '**total non-current assets**' value on the balance sheet is the **combined value** of all the business' non-current assets.
4) Non-current assets often **lose value** over time, so they're worth less every year. This is **depreciation** (see p.7). Businesses should factor in depreciation to give a **realistic** value of their non-current assets on the balance sheet.
5) **Current assets** are assets that the business is likely to exchange for cash **within the accounting year**, before the next balance sheet is made. All the current assets are added together to give the '**total current assets**' value on the balance sheet.

> Current assets include **receivables** (money owed to the business by other companies and individuals) and **inventories** (or **stock** — products, or materials that will be used to make products, that will be sold to **customers**).

6) The business' **current and non-current assets** are added together, then current and non-current liabilities (see below) are deducted to give the figure for '**net assets**' on the balance sheet.

Liabilities *are* ***Debts*** *the* ***Business Owes***

1) **Current liabilities** are **debts** which need to be paid off within a year. They include **overdrafts**, **taxes** due to be paid, **payables** (money owed to **creditors**) and **dividends** due to be paid to shareholders. **Total current liabilities** are **deducted** from total fixed and current assets to give the value of 'assets employed'.
2) **Non-current liabilities** are debts that the business will pay off over several years, e.g. mortgages and loans.

Bad Debts *are debts that debtors* ***Won't Ever Pay***

1) **Ideally**, every debt owed by debtors to the business would be paid. **Unfortunately**, the **real world** isn't like that. Most debts get paid eventually, but some debtors **default** on their payments — they **don't pay up**.
2) Debts which don't get paid are called "**bad debts**". These bad debts **can't** be included on the balance sheet as an **asset** — because the business isn't going to get money for them.
3) The business **writes off** these bad debts, and puts them as an **expense** on the profit and loss account. This shows that the business has **lost money**.
4) It's important to be **realistic** about bad debts. The business shouldn't be **over-optimistic** and report debts as **assets** when they're unlikely to ever be paid. On the other hand, they shouldn't be **too cautious** and write debts off as **bad debts** when they could make the debtors pay up.

Practice Questions

Q1 What do brackets mean on a balance sheet?

Q2 What are assets? What are liabilities?

Q3 What's the difference between current and non-current assets?

Exam Questions

Q1 Which of these values would always be negative on a balance sheet?
A inventories B receivables C overdraft D share capital [1 mark]

Q2 Describe what the non-current assets of a bakery might be. [4 marks]

I'm a bit of a liability really...

If your balance sheet doesn't balance, something's gone horribly wrong. However, you won't have to actually draw up a balance sheet in the exam, so that's one less thing to worry about for now. There's more detail on all the different bits of a balance sheet over the next couple of pages, so get yourself a cup of tea and a biscuit, read on and enjoy.

Financial Analysis — Balance Sheets

Now it's time to go into a bit more detail about some of those bits on the balance sheet.

Working Capital is the Finance available for Day-To-Day Spending

1) **Working capital** is the amount of **cash** (and **assets** that can be easily turned into cash) that the business has available to pay its **day-to-day debts**. The more working capital a business has, the more **liquid** (able to pay its short-term debts) it is. See p.12 for liquidity ratios.
2) Working capital is the same as **net current assets** on the balance sheet — the amount left over when you subtract **current liabilities** (e.g. overdraft, payables and tax due to be paid) from **current assets** (i.e. cash, receivables and stock):

Working capital = current assets – current liabilities

3) Businesses **can't survive** if they don't have enough working capital. As well as generating sales, the business must make sure it **collects money** quickly to get **cash** to pay its liabilities. They need to make sure that they don't **tie up** too much of their working capital as inventories or receivables — businesses **can't** use these to pay their current liabilities until they're turned into **cash**.

Businesses need Enough Cash but Not Too Much

1) Businesses need **just enough** cash to pay short-term debts. They shouldn't have too much cash, because spare cash is great at **paying off debts**, but lousy at **earning money** for the business.
2) Businesses with a **long cash-flow cycle** need more cash, as they have to **wait** for money to come in.
3) To make money, the business needs **non-current assets** that make sales possible (e.g. machinery that produces products).
4) **Inflation** increases the costs of wages and buying/holding stock, so firms need more cash when inflation is high.
5) When a business **expands**, it needs more cash to avoid **overtrading**. Overtrading means producing so much that the business can't afford to pay its **suppliers** until it gets paid by its **customers**.

You learnt about cash flows in Year 1.

Businesses also need finance for Capital Expenditure

1) **Fixed capital** (or **capital expenditure**) means money used to buy **non-current assets** (fixed assets). These are things used over and over again to produce goods or services for sale — e.g. **factories** and **equipment**.
2) Businesses need capital expenditure to **start up**, to **grow** and to **replace** worn out equipment. They must **set aside** enough **money** to stop **non-current assets** from **wearing out**, and then they can **decide** how much **money** to invest in **growth**. This is called **allocating capital expenditure**.
3) You'll find **capital expenditure** on the balance sheet (see p.4) as **non-current assets**.

Debtors (Receivables) and Stock (Inventories) must be Controlled

1) A business needs to control its **debtors** (people who owe money to the firm). It's important that businesses make sure that their debtors pay them **on time**.
2) A company might sell millions of pounds worth of goods, but if it doesn't make sure that **payment** has been received, there'll be **no money coming in**. That means that the business is **no better off** in terms of cash flow than if it had sold nothing at all.
3) The business still has to **pay** wages, loan repayments, etc. whether its debtors have paid up or not, so businesses have to control debtors to **survive**.

Karen and Rita spent many a long hour in the debtor control room.

1) A business needs to hold suitable volumes of **stock** (raw materials and unsold products) to allow it to satisfy the demands of the market.
2) A business holding **too little stock** will **lose sales** as it won't be able to supply enough goods to the market to meet demand.
3) A business with **too much stock** has money tied up in stock instead of **working** for the company. It would be better to use the money to pay debts or wages, or invest it in new projects.
4) Businesses **predict** what the **demand** for their products will be in order to make sure that they have a suitable level of stock.

Financial Analysis — Balance Sheets

Stock is Valued at Cost or at Net Realisable Value — whichever's Lower

1) Accounting conventions say that stock values must be **realisable**. The **net realisable value** is the amount the company could get by **selling** the stock right now in its **current state** (rather than after it's been used to make a finished product).
2) The **realisable value** might be **lower** than the **cost value** (the amount the business **paid** for the stock). Or the net realisable value might be **higher** than its original cost price, if demand for the materials has increased since the business bought them — this often happens in businesses like **jewellery manufacturers**, as the price of gold and precious stones fluctuates and might go up after the business has bought them.
3) The company must record the stock value in its accounts as the **lower** value out of **cost** or **net realisable value**.

Example: A computer business buys **300 microprocessors** at **£100 each** to use in the production of laptop computers, so the **total cost** is **£30 000**. Later, the business updates the specification of the laptops and **can't use** the microprocessors it originally bought, so it has to sell them. In the meantime, **technology** has **moved on** and there are more advanced, faster microprocessors on the market. There's **little demand** for the old microprocessors, and the business would only be able to sell the old stock for **£40 each** (**£12 000** altogether). The business has to record the value of the stock as **£12 000** in its accounts, rather than the **£30 000** it originally paid.

Assets Depreciate — they Lose Value over Time

1) Most assets **lose value** over time — the **longer** the business has them, the **less** they're **worth**. E.g. if a business has been using a piece of machinery for six months, it won't be worth as much as it was when it was new, even if it's still in good condition.
2) Assets lose their value for three main reasons — they suffer **wear and tear**, they may **break down**, and they become **old fashioned** when new models or inventions come onto the market.
3) The **drop in value** of a business asset over time is called **depreciation**.
4) Although most assets depreciate, sometimes it can work the other way round and assets can **increase** in value. E.g. **property** can increase in value over time because property prices tend to rise.

Derek wondered if this meant the factory wouldn't increase in value after all.

Accounts reflect the Depreciation of assets

1) Businesses **calculate depreciation** each year to make sure that an asset's **value** on the **balance sheet** is a **true reflection** of what the business would get from **selling** it.
2) Building depreciation into each year's accounts **avoids** the fall in value hitting **all at once** when the business **sells** the asset. Spreading out the cost of the depreciation over several years is a truer reflection of the situation and allows the business to make **comparisons** between financial years more easily.

E.g. by depreciating a piece of machinery over 10 years, a business can take a tenth of the **fall in value** of the equipment (the difference between what the asset cost to buy and what managers think they'll be able to sell it for when they finish using it) into account each year. Without depreciating the asset, the business would be **understating its costs** (and therefore overstating its profits) for each year until it got rid of the asset, which would then show up as a **huge cost** on the accounts.

3) The **amount lost** through depreciation is recorded on the **income statement** (see p.9) as an **expense**. It's unusual because it isn't a cash expense — it's a recognition of the money that's been put into the asset that the business can't ever get back.

Financial Analysis — Balance Sheets

OK, now you're clued up on balance sheets, it's time to think about how to use them to assess financial performance.

Balance Sheets show the Short-Term Financial Status of the Company

1) The balance sheet shows you how much the business is **worth**.
2) **Working capital** (net current assets) is the amount of money the business has available in the short term. It's calculated by subtracting **current liabilities** from **current assets**. See p.6 for more on working capital.

The liquidity of an asset is how easy it is to turn it into cash and spend it. Cash is the most liquid asset, followed by receivables, inventories and short-term investments.

3) **Suppliers** are particularly interested in **working capital** and **liquidity**. They can look at the balance sheet to see how **liquid** the firm's assets are, as well as how much working capital the firm has. The more liquid the assets, the better the firm will be at **paying bills**. This helps them decide whether to offer the business supplies on **credit**, and how much credit to offer.
4) The balance sheet shows **sources of capital**. Ideally, **long-term loans** or **mortgages** are used to finance the purchase of fixed assets. A well managed business wouldn't borrow too much through **short-term overdrafts**, because overdrafts are an expensive way of borrowing.
5) This short-term information can help the business assess its internal **strengths** and **weaknesses**. For example, if the business has a large amount of **working capital**, they could **invest** this money in new equipment or use it to **pay off** some loans.

By Comparing Balance Sheets you can see Long-Term Trends

1) Comparing this year's balance sheet to previous years' accounts lets you pick out **trends** in company finances and evaluate the **financial performance** of the company. Looking at the "bottom line" over several years shows how the business is **changing**.
2) A **quick increase** in **non-current assets** indicates that the company has invested in property or machinery. This means that the company is investing in a **growth strategy**, which may increase its profit over the medium term — useful information for shareholders and potential shareholders, who want to see more profit.
3) Increases in **reserves** also suggest an increase in **profits** — good news for shareholders.
4) Looking at several balance sheets together also shows **trends** in how the business has **raised** its **capital**. It's risky to suddenly start **borrowing** a lot, in case interest rates rise. A company with a high value of loan capital and a relatively low value of share capital or reserves would be in trouble if the Bank of England put **interest rates** up.
5) Businesses can use long-term trends to identify their **strengths** and **weaknesses** too. If the **non-current liabilities** (i.e. long-term debts) have increased, the business might want to try and **reduce** its borrowing in the future.

Practice Questions

Q1 How do you calculate working capital?

Q2 What does 'net realisable value' mean?

Q3 What is depreciation?

Q4 Why do businesses calculate the depreciation of their assets each year?

Q5 Why would suppliers be interested in a business's balance sheet?

Exam Questions

Q1 The balance sheet for Joanne's salon shows £400 inventories (stock), £50 receivables (debtors), £150 cash and current liabilities of £120. Evaluate the short-term financial position of Joanne's business. [6 marks]

Q2 Explain why it is important for a business to control its debtors. [6 marks]

All this revision's making me feel a bit unbalanced...

There's loads to learn over the last few pages. It's all about balance — you don't want too much working capital, but on the other hand you don't want too little. The same goes for stock. Then there are debtors to chase up, and depreciation to take into account too. And then you have to walk the dog, empty the bins and make me a cake.

Financial Analysis — Income Statements

An income statement is a way of reporting profit or loss over a certain period of time (usually a year). It's a summary that shareholders and potential investors can use to assess the company's performance.

Income Statements show *Revenue* and *Expenses*

1) The income statement (also known as a profit and loss account) shows how much money has been **coming into the company** (**revenue**) and how much has been **going out** (**expenses**).
2) Revenue is **sales income** from selling goods and services. This includes **cash payments** and sales on **credit**. Expenses include the cost of **raw materials**, **production** costs, **marketing** costs, **wages** etc.
3) These figures can be used in **assessing** a company's **financial performance** — e.g. if **revenue** has **increased** by **more than** the rate of **inflation** (see p.30) since the business published its last income statement, it's often a sign that the company is **healthy**.
4) PLCs (public limited companies) have to **publish** their accounts so that they're available to **anyone** who wants to look at them — that includes shareholders, potential shareholders and competitors.

Income Statements cover a period of *Time*

1) Income statements should cover one whole accounting year. An income statement that covers **less than 12 months** can be **misleading**. High street retailers can generate **half their annual revenue** in the lead-up to **Christmas** — an income statement ignoring this period won't give an **accurate picture**.
2) Income statements can also contain the **previous year's data**, for **easy comparison**, to see what's **changed**. Some companies provide the previous five years' data. It's useful for spotting **trends** in revenue, expenses and profits, and helps whoever's looking at the accounts to see what kind of a **financial position** the business is in.

Income Statements show *Different Measures* of *Profit*

In Year 1 you learnt about **different measures** of **profit**.
Each measure shows **different things** about the company's finances.

1) **Gross profit** is **revenue** minus the **cost of sales**.
2) **Operating profit** is **revenue** minus the **cost of sales** minus **operating expenses** (or **gross profit** minus **operating expenses**).
3) **Profit before tax** takes into account any **profit** or **loss** from **one-off events**, and **other expenses** such as **finance costs**.
4) **Profit after tax** (also called **profit for the year**) is what's left after corporation tax has been paid.
5) **Retained profit** is what's left from profit after tax, once **share dividends** have been paid to shareholders.

These measures can be used to ***Assess Financial Performance***

1) **Gross profit** shows the money being made from actually **making** and **selling** products. If gross profit is **low**, **managers** need to look at ways of **reducing the cost** of making the product, or **increasing the selling price**.
2) **Operating profit** shows the money made from **'normal' business operations**. If **operating profit** is significantly **lower** than **gross profit**, it could show that the company's **operating expenses** are a **weak area**. Managers should take steps to **reduce** these expenses, e.g. by reducing **marketing costs**. However, the operating profit could reflect a big **investment** in **people**, **premises**, etc. **Banks** and **investors** will look at this figure to assess the **risk** of lending to or investing in the business.
3) Comparing **profit before tax** to **operating profit** shows if **income** or **expenses** are coming from **other activities** (e.g. selling or buying a building), rather than 'normal' activities (e.g. making and selling goods), which may **not** continue in the future.
4) **Profit after tax** tells you if the company is **profitable** or not — **shareholders** and **potential investors** will look at this figure to assess investments.
5) **Retained profit** shows how much **internal finance** the company has available to **invest**, which shows how strong its **growth potential** is.

Financial Analysis — Income Statements

Here's what an **Income Statement** looks like

Here's a **simplified** version of an income statement. Sometimes the costs and expenses will be **broken down** into different categories, but I've lumped them all together so you can see what's going on.

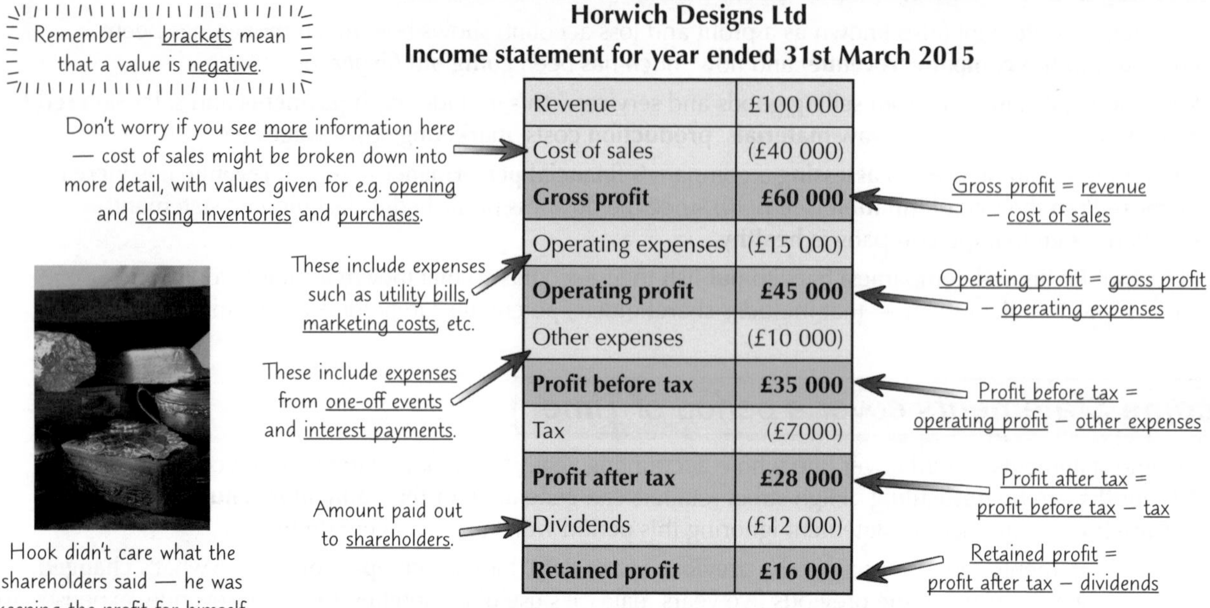

Horwich Designs Ltd
Income statement for year ended 31st March 2015

Revenue	£100 000
Cost of sales	(£40 000)
Gross profit	**£60 000**
Operating expenses	(£15 000)
Operating profit	**£45 000**
Other expenses	(£10 000)
Profit before tax	**£35 000**
Tax	(£7000)
Profit after tax	**£28 000**
Dividends	(£12 000)
Retained profit	**£16 000**

Hook didn't care what the shareholders said — he was keeping the profit for himself.

Businesses can **Choose** what to do with their **Profits**

Businesses can use their **profits** in **two** main ways:

- they can pay **dividends** to shareholders,
- they can keep the profit in the business as **retained profit**.

1) **Shareholders** usually want companies to pay **high dividends** so that they get a **good return** on their investment. If companies **don't** pay dividends, or pay very **low** dividends, existing shareholders might **sell** their shares.
2) **Retaining profit** allows the business to **spend** on things that are likely to **increase** their profits in the future — e.g. buying **fixed assets** like machinery, business premises, etc. This allows the business to **increase production**, which could lead to **increased revenue** and **profits** in the future.
3) Companies usually try to find a **balance** between dividends and retained profit — they pay a proportion of their profit to their **shareholders** and **reinvest** the rest in the business to fund **growth**.

Practice Questions

Q1 What does an income statement show?

Q2 Why can income statements that cover less than 12 months be misleading?

Q3 What is retained profit?

Q4 How can investors use income statements to assess financial performance?

Q5 Give two examples of things a business can do with its profits.

Answer on p.103.

Exam Question

Q1 In the year ending 31st March 2015, a haulage company had an annual revenue of £1 500 000 and the cost of sales was £500 000. Operating expenses were £250 000, other expenses were £100 000 and the company paid £130 000 in tax. It then paid out £250 000 in dividends to its shareholders.
Draw up an income statement for this company, including values for gross profit, operating profit, profits before and after tax and retained profit. Do you think the company has had a successful financial year? Justify your answer. [16 marks]

I'd definitely spend all my profits on ice cream...

Income statements might look a little confusing, but if you need to complete one, work down from the revenue and subtract all the different expenses to find the different profits. Make sure you know how to interpret them too.

Financial Analysis — Value and Limitations

Having just spent 7 pages telling you all about financial analysis, it's time to think about how useful it is.

Financial Analysis is Useful for Decision-Making

1) **Analysis** of the balance sheet and income statement can be really useful for **comparing** a business's current performance to its **competitors' performance**, and to its own performance in the **past**, to identify **trends** in the business's financial performance.
2) The analysis can help managers to make **decisions** based on the company's **financial strengths** and **weaknesses**. For example, they might decide to **reduce dividends** and retain more of their profits to invest in the business if the analysis shows that the business's growth has been slow.
3) **Potential investors** and **lenders** can use the analysis to **decide** if they want to **invest in** or **lend to** the business.

*Financial analysis **Doesn't Cover** anything **Non-Numerical***

1) Financial analysis **only** takes into account **financial data**. This is **useful** for **potential investors**, but it **ignores** a lot of **qualitative** (non-numerical) **data** that potential investors should also consider.
2) **Internal factors** that **don't appear** in the analysis include the **quality** of staff and products, the company's **market share**, future **sales targets**, **productivity** levels, the firm's impact on the **environment** and **customer satisfaction** (see pages 18-21).
3) **External factors** like the **economic** or **market** environment aren't reflected in the analysis either. It doesn't tell you anything about what a **competitor** might do next, or what legislation the government might pass. The development of **technology**, or potential changes to the **location** of the business (e.g. a new rail link) don't appear either. You'd need to analyse all these **external factors** to see how they might affect the business.

*The **Balance Sheet** and **Income Statement** don't tell you **Everything***

1) The **balance sheet** is a statement about one point in the **past**, which may not help predict the **future**.
2) The balance sheet doesn't give any clues about the **market** or the **economy** that the business is trading in.
3) Balance sheets value some intangible assets (e.g. a brand recently purchased by the company), but they don't value intangible assets like **staff skill**, **staff motivation** or **management experience**.
4) If bad debts are included in the balance sheet as an asset, the analysis will be misleading — see p.5.

1) The **income statement** is useful for assessing the performance of the company, but it isn't the whole story.
2) It doesn't include any information about **external factors** such as **market demand**, which would be useful in forecasting **future revenue** and **profit**.
3) It doesn't include any information about **internal factors** such as staff morale, which would be useful in determining **productivity** and therefore **profitability**.
4) In times of **inflation**, the income statement isn't so useful, because inflationary rises in price distort the true value of revenue.
5) The income statement can be **deliberately distorted**, by bringing forward sales from the next trading period and including them as part of this trading period.
6) It's best to look at the income statement and the balance sheet **together** to assess a business's finances.

Practice Questions

Q1 Give an example of why financial analysis is useful to a business.

Q2 Give two examples of non-numerical external factors that affect businesses but aren't taken into account in their financial analysis.

Exam Question

Q1 Explain why you shouldn't rely solely on financial analysis to predict a company's future performance. [8 marks]

Financial analysis never tells me anything — I can't get it to say a word...

You might think some of the stuff on this page is obvious, but it's funny how your mind can go blank in an exam as soon as you get a question like 'Why shouldn't shareholders rely solely on financial analysis to make investment decisions?'

Financial Analysis — Ratios

Ratios turn financial data from balance sheets and income statements into easy-to-understand numbers. You can use them to compare companies to each other and to assess a company's performance over time.

Liquidity Ratios show How Much Money is available to Pay The Bills

1) A firm without enough **working capital** (see p.6) has poor **liquidity**. It can't **use** its assets to **pay** for things when it needs them.
2) The **liquidity** of an asset is how easily it can be turned into **cash** and used to **buy** things. **Cash** is **very** liquid, **non-current assets** such as **factories** are **not liquid**, and **stocks** (**inventories**) and money owed by **debtors** (**receivables**) are in between.
3) A business that doesn't have enough **current assets** to pay its liabilities when they are due is **insolvent**. It either has to quickly find the money to pay them, give up and **cease trading**, or go into **liquidation**.
4) **Liquidity** can be **improved** by decreasing stock levels, speeding up collection of debts owed to the business, or slowing down payments to creditors (e.g. suppliers).
5) A **liquidity ratio** shows how **solvent** a business is (how able it is to pay its debts). The main liquidity ratio you need to know is the **current ratio**.

Current Ratio = Current Assets ÷ Current Liabilities

1) The **current ratio** compares **current assets** to current liabilities.

$$\text{Current ratio} = \frac{\text{current assets}}{\text{current liabilities}}$$

The current ratio is also called the working capital ratio.

For example, a business with **£30 000** of **current assets** and **£32 000** of **current liabilities** has a current ratio of: $\frac{£30\,000}{£32\,000}$ = **0.9375** (this means that for **£1** of **liabilities**, the company only has **£0.9375** (or 93.75p) of **assets**, which isn't great, as it means there **aren't enough assets** to cover the **liabilities**).

You could write this in ratio form as 0.9375:1 — see p.96 for more on writing ratios.

2) In reality, a business probably couldn't **sell off** all its stock. It'd also need **additional capital** to **replace** stocks — the current ratio should be **higher** than 1 to take account of this. 1.5 or 2 is considered ideal.
3) A value much below 1.5 suggests a **liquidity problem** and that it might struggle to meet its current liabilities. See above for **ways** that a company can **improve** its **liquidity**.

Return on Capital Employed (ROCE) is a Profitability Ratio

1) A **profitability ratio** shows **profit margin**. The most important profitability ratio is the **return on capital employed** (**ROCE**). It's considered to be the best way of analysing profitability and is expressed as a **percentage**, calculated by:

$$\text{Return on Capital Employed (\%)} = \frac{\text{operating profit}}{\text{total equity + non-current liabilities}} \times 100$$

The operating profit is on the <u>income statement</u>, and the total equity and non-current liabilities are on the <u>balance sheet</u>.

total equity + non-current liabilities = <u>capital employed</u>

2) The **ROCE** tells you how much money is **made** by the business, compared to how much money's been **put into** the business. The **higher** the ROCE, the **better**.
3) It's important to **compare** the ROCE with the Bank of England **interest rate** at the time, because this tells investors whether they'd be better off putting their money in the **bank**.
4) ROCE can be **improved** by **paying off debt** to reduce non-current liabilities, or by making the business more **efficient** to **increase operating profit**.
5) ROCE is just one measure of **return on investment**. Another important one is the **average rate of return** (see p.42).

Financial Analysis — Ratios

Efficiency or *Performance Ratios* show how *Efficiently* the firm is working

1) Efficiency ratios show managers and shareholders **how well** the business is using its **resources**.
2) There are **three** important efficiency ratios you need to know — **inventory turnover** ratio (stock turnover ratio), **payables days** ratio (creditor days ratio) and **receivables days** ratio (debtor days ratio). They show how efficiently the business is using its **assets** and how well managers are controlling **stock**, **creditors** and **debtors**.

1) Inventory Turnover Ratio = Cost of Sales ÷ Cost of Average Stock Held

1) The inventory turnover ratio (stock turnover ratio) compares the **cost** of all the **sales** a business makes over the year to the **cost of the average stock** held.
2) You need to know the **cost price** of everything the business has **sold**, i.e. what the products cost the firm to make. **Stock** is valued at **cost price**, so you need **sales** at cost price too. You'll find **cost of sales** on the **income statement** and **stock held** on the **balance sheet**.

$$\text{Inventory Turnover} = \frac{\text{cost of sales}}{\text{cost of average stock held}}$$

You might see 'cost of sales' written as 'cost of goods sold' instead.

For example, if a business's **sales** cost **£160 000** and its **average stock held** costs **£8000**, it has an **inventory turnover** of $\frac{£160\,000}{£8000}$ = **20** (as a **ratio**, this would be 20 : 1).

Mabel much preferred apple turnover ratios to inventory turnover ratios.

3) This ratio tells you **how many times** during the year the business **sold all its stock** — so the business above sold its stock **20 times**. A fruit and veg stall might sell their **entire stock every day**, which would give a stock turnover ratio of **365**. A property developer who took **4 months** to do up and sell each house would have a ratio of **3**. Businesses operating **JIT** (just-in-time) **production** have a **very high** ratio.
4) When you analyse this ratio, you need to judge if the business has **enough stock** to **fulfil orders**, but **not too much stock** to be **efficient**. Holding twice the stock needed might not be an efficient use of funds. The ideal turnover ratio depends on the type of the business, but companies generally aim for a higher value than in previous years or compared to their rivals.
5) The inventory turnover ratio can be improved by **holding less stock**, or **increasing sales**. Easier said than done...
6) **Aged stock analysis** lets managers make sure that old stock gets sold before it becomes **obsolete** and **unsaleable**. It lists all stock in **age order**, so the manager can **discount** old stock and cut down orders for slow-selling stock.

2) Payables Days Ratio = Payables ÷ Cost of Sales × 365

1) The payables days ratio (creditor days ratio) compares the **amount** the business **owes** to its **creditors** to the **cost** of all the **sales** a business makes over the year:

$$\text{Payables Days} = \frac{\text{payables}}{\text{cost of sales}} \times 365$$

'Payables' is a current liability on the balance sheet and 'cost of sales' is on the income statement.

For example, a business with **payables** of **£300** and **sales** that **cost £7000**, has a **payables days ratio** of $\frac{£300}{£7000}$ × 365 = **15.64 days**.

2) This is the number of days the firm takes to **pay** for goods it buys on credit from **suppliers**.
3) You can establish a **trend** over a period of time and use this trend to analyse the efficiency of the firm. For instance, if the trend is upwards it may suggest the firm is getting into **difficulties paying** its suppliers. This might be OK, but if the suppliers get the hump and decide they want to be paid **now**, it's a **problem**.
4) A business can also use this ratio to **maximise** its **cash flow**. So if the business above had an agreed credit period of **30 days**, it could take up to **2 weeks longer** to pay its debts, as it currently takes only 15.64 days.

Financial Analysis — Ratios

3) Receivables Days Ratio = Receivables ÷ Sales Revenue × 365

1) The receivables days ratio (debtor days ratio) compares the **amount owed** to a business by its **debtors** to the **total sales revenue** for the year:

$$\text{Receivables Days} = \frac{\text{receivables}}{\text{sales revenue}} \times 365$$

You'll find 'receivables' on the balance sheet as a current asset and 'sales revenue' is on the income statement.

For example, a business with **receivables** of **£1500** and **sales revenue** of **£50 000** has a **receivables days ratio** of $\frac{£1500}{£50\,000} \times 365 = \mathbf{10.95}$ **days**.

2) 'Receivables days' is the number of days that the business has to **wait to be paid** for goods it supplies on credit.
3) It's best to have **low** receivables days, because it helps with **cash flow** and **working capital**. What makes a good receivables days ratio depends on the type of business. **Retailers** tend to get paid **straight away** unless they offer credit on items such as TVs or fridges. **Medium size businesses** usually take **70-90 days** to get invoices paid.
4) You can **compare** receivables days ratios with previous months or years to look for **trends**. An **upward trend** may be because the business has offered **longer credit terms** to attract more customers. However, if it isn't monitored, the business may be heading for **cash flow problems**.
5) **Aged receivables analysis** lets managers **control receivables days**. Unpaid accounts are listed in order of how long they've been unpaid. The ones that are **most overdue** are **targeted** first for repayment.
6) **Inventory turnover** and **receivables days** are measures of **activity** — they tell you how **effectively** a business is using its **resources** to generate **revenue**.

Practice Questions

Q1 How do you work out the current ratio?

Q2 What does ROCE show?

Q3 What does the inventory turnover ratio show?

Q4 Which would have the higher inventory turnover ratio, a Porsche dealership or a shoe shop?

Q5 What's the difference between the payables days ratio and the receivables days ratio?

Exam Questions

Answers to Q1 and Q3 a) and b) are on p.103.

Q1 What is the return on capital employed of a business that has an operating profit of £50 000, total equity of £130 000 and non-current liabilities of £30 000?

A 61.54% B 16.67% C 31.25% D 20% [1 mark]

Q2 A medium-sized company is owed £7000 by its trade customers and has sales revenue of £20 000 over the year. Using receivables days analysis, evaluate how well the company controls its debtors. [6 marks]

Q3 The table below shows some financial information about a shop that sells skiwear.

Current assets	£40 000
Cost of sales	£120 000
Current liabilities	£50 000
Cost of average stock held	£80 000

a) Calculate the current ratio. [2 marks]

b) Calculate the inventory turnover ratio. [2 marks]

c) Use your results to evaluate the financial position of the company, and suggest ways in which it could improve its current position. [12 marks]

Oh look, what a lot of "lovely" ratios...

Being totally honest, these ratios are a bit of a pain in the backside. It's easy to get them mixed up, so make sure you know which one to use when. You have to be able to interpret them too — so make sure you know what the figures tell you about financial performance. Have a look at Section 9 if your Maths skills are a little bit rusty.

Financial Analysis — Gearing

If you were worried that there weren't enough financial ratios, never fear — there's still one more incredibly exciting ratio to go. Well, maybe not 'incredibly exciting' as such, but it does have an interesting name — gearing.

Gearing shows Where a business gets its Capital from

1) **Gearing** is another really important ratio. It shows **potential investors** where a business's finance has come from, i.e. what **proportion** of its finance comes from **non-current liabilities** (long-term debt), rather than **share capital** or **reserves** (equity).
2) Gearing is calculated using information from the lower part of a **balance sheet** (see p.4) — the part that shows where the money comes from. To work out the gearing, divide the amount of finance that comes from **non-current liabilities** by the **total amount** of finance in the company (from loans, shares and reserves):

$$\text{Gearing (\%)} = \frac{\text{non-current liabilities}}{\text{total equity + non-current liabilities}} \times 100$$

See p.5 for more on non-current liabilities.

3) A gearing **above 50%** shows that **more than half** of a business's finance comes from **long-term debt** — the business is **high-geared**. A gearing of **25%-50%** is fairly **standard** — **some** of its finance comes from long-term debt, but not too much. A gearing of **below 25%** shows it is **low-geared**, because **less than a quarter** of the finance comes from long-term debt.

Gearing shows how Vulnerable a business is to Changes in Interest Rates

1) The more the business is **borrowing**, the harder they'll be hit by a rise in interest rates. How much **borrowing** a business can do depends on its profitability and the value of its **assets** — the more assets the business can offer as **security**, the more money it will be able to borrow.
2) Gearing is a crude **risk assessment** that an investor can use to help decide whether to buy shares in the company. The more the firm borrows, the **more interest** it will have to pay — this may affect **profits** and the **dividend** paid to shareholders. The more the firm borrows, the more **risk** there is that the investor won't get much dividend.

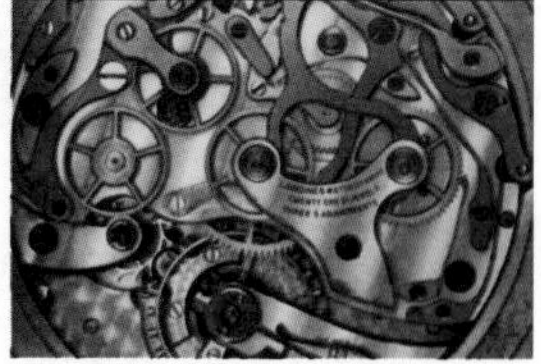

Looks pretty high geared to me.

Example

A firm has gearing of 11% — it's **low-geared**.

- This tells you that **most** long-term funds come from **shareholders**, not borrowing.
- This could be a sign that the firm is **risk averse** — it doesn't want to run the risk of spending too much money on interest payments.
- Because the firm doesn't have to spend its profits on interest payments, it can **withstand** a **fall** in profits more easily than a highly geared firm, since the firm can easily choose to **reduce** dividend payments to shareholders, unlike loan repayments, which have to be made.

Example

Another firm has gearing of 72% — it's **high-geared**.

- This tells you that **most** long-term funds come from **borrowing**.
- It's obvious that the firm is willing to take **risks** — if profits fall, or interest rates rise, the business still has to keep up with the **loan repayments** or it could **lose** the **assets** the loans are secured on (e.g. business premises).
- The company may be high-geared in order to fund **growth** (see next page), or because its directors don't want outside shareholders to **own** a large part of the business, and so they prefer to borrow money rather than sell shares.

Financial Analysis — Gearing

High Gearing has Risks and Rewards for Businesses

High gearing can be **risky**, but some businesses are willing to take these risks because of the **potential rewards**:

Rewards of high gearing for businesses

1) One benefit of **borrowing** money for the business is extra **funds** for expansion. Ideally, the loan is invested in projects or technology which **increase profits** by more than enough to pay off the loan repayments. **High gearing** can be attractive during a **growth phase**. A firm that's trying to become the market leader, and has growing profits along with a strong product portfolio, may decide to borrow heavily in order to **fund expansion** and gain a **competitive advantage**. This will **increase** the firm's **gearing**. During times of **growth**, there is plenty of **profit** even after they've paid the loan interest and repayments, so high gearing can be good for the business.
2) When interest rates are very **low**, high gearing is less risky because interest payments are lower.

Risks of high gearing for businesses

1) The **risk** to the business of borrowing money is that it might not be able to afford the **repayments** — it might not make enough profit to pay back the **loan** and **interest**.
2) Taking out loans can be **risky** even when interest rates are low, because they might **go up** later and the business will still be committed to making the **repayments**.

High Gearing has Risks and Rewards for Investors too

1) The reward (of investing money in the business) for the **lender** or **shareholder** is **interest** for lenders or a share **dividend** for shareholders (often paid out twice a year). Shareholders can also sell their shares at a **profit** if the share price goes up. Since high gearing can lead to high profits for businesses, shareholders might expect to see **large dividends** and a **big increase** in the share price compared to a low-geared company.
2) The **risk** to the **shareholder** of high gearing is that the business may **fail** if it can't afford to keep up with loan repayments. When a business goes into **liquidation**, lenders will probably get the money they're owed, but the shareholders could lose most or all of the money they've invested in the business.

Practice Questions

Q1 What is the formula used to calculate gearing?

Q2 What's meant by "high gearing"?

Q3 Changes to a business lead it to become high-geared. How could this affect shareholders?

Q4 Give one risk and one possible reward for a business of being high-geared.

Exam Questions

Q1 Calculate the gearing for a plumbing company that has non-current liabilities of £20 000 and total equity of £30 000. [3 marks]

Answer to Q1 on p.103.

Q2 Explain the risks of investing in a business which has high gearing. [6 marks]

Q3 An interior design company's gearing has increased from 48% to 54% in the last year, during a period when the economy was stable. To what extent do you think that this will benefit the company? [12 marks]

Low gearing is also helpful when driving uphill...

More ratios — good old AQA sure knows what makes A-level students happy. You can probably guess what I'm going to say — learn what gearing is for, and be prepared to use it in the exam. Exam questions might ask for a specific ratio analysis, or you might get marks for using ratios if you're asked to assess a business's financial position.

Value and Limitations of Ratios

Looking at ratios is a good way of assessing a company's financial performance, but it does have some limitations too.

***Ratio Analysis** can be very **Useful**...*

1) **Ratios** are a really good way of looking at a business's **performance** over a period of time — they can be used to spot **trends**, and to identify the **financial strengths** and **weaknesses** of the business.
2) However, these trends need to take account of **variable factors** — things which change over time, such as **inflation**, accounting procedures, the business activities of the firm and the market environment.
3) Managers can use ratio analysis to help with **decision making** — e.g. if their payables days ratio is low, they might negotiate a **longer credit period** which will **improve** the business's **cash flow**.
4) **Potential investors** can use the ratios to help them decide if they want to **invest** in the business — they may choose **not** to invest in a **high-geared business** if they think it is too risky.
5) It's also useful to **compare** ratios with **other businesses**, either in the same industry or in different industries. Ratios provide a more **meaningful** comparison when looking at **different-sized** businesses (which may have very different **profits**).

*... but it has its **Limitations***

All financial **ratios** compare figures from the **balance sheet** or **income statement**, and give you a raw **number** as an answer.

Ratios don't take account of any **non-numerical factors**, so they don't provide an absolute means of assessing a company's financial health. They have several **limitations**:

1) **Internal strengths**, such as the quality of staff, don't appear in the figures, so they won't come up in ratios.
2) **External factors**, such as the **economic** or **market** environment, aren't reflected in the figures. When the market's very **competitive**, or the economy's in a **downturn**, it's OK for ratios to suffer a bit.
3) **Future changes** such as technological advances or changes in interest rates can't be predicted by the figures, so they won't show up in the ratios.
4) Ratios only contain information about the **past** and **present**. A business which has **just started** investing for growth will have lousy ratios until the investment **pays off** — that doesn't mean it's not worth investing in.

Example of how ratio analysis can't predict changes in external factors

- Harry is interested in **investing** in XYZ Ltd. **Ratio analysis** indicates that XYZ is **performing strongly** and gives a **good rate of return** for the investor, so he decides to **buy 1000 shares.**
- Later that day, Harry talks to Sarah, who says **new EU health and safety legislation** will **ban XYZ** from making any more of its products from next year onwards. XYZ Ltd must now either **diversify** into another product/service or **close**.
- Harry doesn't feel so clever about his investment now. XYZ Ltd will need **time** and **money** to **reinvest** in a new production line so **profits will be very scarce** for the next few months. Worse still, XYZ Ltd may go **bankrupt** and he'd have shares with **no value at all**. What a nightmare.

Practice Questions

Q1 Why might comparing financial ratios to another business be more useful than comparing profits?

Q2 Give an example of an internal business strength that isn't allowed for in ratio analysis.

Exam Questions

Q1 Explain two factors that should be taken into account when comparing financial ratios for different years. [8 marks]

Q2 Ratio analysis gives information about the past and present.
Analyse the value of ratio analysis in predicting future performance. [12 marks]

Limitations of ratios — well, they can't do cartwheels for starters...

It's not possible to make 100% solid conclusions from ratio analysis alone. You need to use other data from several sources alongside ratios. It's important to consider the market that the business is trading in, and what its competitors are doing. Bear in mind that using data from the past isn't always a great way to predict the future — stuff changes.

Analysing Overall Performance

Looking at financial data is a good way of analysing a company's position — but there are many other factors that need to be taken into consideration to judge how well it's doing all round.

Non-Financial Data shows Strengths and Weaknesses in Other Areas

1) A company needs to assess its **strengths** and **weaknesses** using both **quantitative** (numerical) and **qualitative** (non-numerical) data. This is an important part of **SWOT analysis** (see p.3).
2) Analysing **non-financial data** allows a company to consider other **internal factors** (besides financial performance) that can combine to give them a **competitive advantage.** They'll look at a number of **performance measures** to see how they're doing.
3) Data is collected from each **department**, e.g. **marketing**, **human resources** (HR) and **operations**. **Performance measures** include things like:

You should have covered marketing, HR and operations data in Year 1.

Marketing

- Calculations of **market share**, **market growth** and **sales growth**.
- **Portfolio analysis** — the **products** a company has, what stage they're at in their **life cycle** and their **perceived** and **actual quality**.

Human Resources

- Calculations of **labour productivity**, **labour turnover**, **labour retention**, **employee costs as a percentage of turnover** and **labour cost per unit**.
- An assessment of **staff skills** and **qualifications**, as well as HR plans for **training** and **recruitment** — to see if these are matched to the needs of the business. **Staff morale** and methods of **motivation** may also be assessed.

Operations

- Calculations of **capacity** and **capacity utilisation**, **unit costs** and **fixed/variable costs**.
- The **age** and **condition** of any **machinery**, the operations **processes** used, etc.

4) When **analysing** the data, managers need to **ask questions** and **make judgements**. For example, if **labour productivity** has gone **down**, they need to find out **why**. If **capacity utilisation** is nearly at **100%**, they'll need to think about how the business could **expand**.
5) Managers also need to analyse how well the business is doing **overall**. For example:
   - How well are **resources** being allocated between departments?
   - Do the **organisational structure** and **culture** support the company's activities?
   - How good is the company's **image**?

Businesses can Compare their data to Other Businesses

1) Businesses can **compare** their data with data from **similar businesses** — this allows them to compare their performance with that of their **competitors**, and see where they need to **improve** (or what they're doing **better** than their rivals).
2) Making comparisons puts a business's data in **context**. For example, if its **sales growth** is **low** but a competitor's sales growth is similarly **low**, managers would be **less concerned** about the business's performance than if the competitor's sales growth was much **higher**.
3) One way of making comparisons is by **benchmarking** (see p.60). Benchmarking means looking at **successful** businesses and identifying what they do **well**, then trying to **apply** their strengths to your business. It can be done by looking at **data** (e.g. unit costs) or by looking at the **processes** they use.
4) For example, if a rival business's **productivity** is much **higher**, a business can look at what their rival does **differently** and try to **adopt** their methods.
5) The benchmark business needs to be **comparable**, so their methods will be **relevant** — for example, a **fruit juice company** could compare its **capacity utilisation** to a **fizzy drinks company** and see if there are any **methods** it can **copy** to increase its capacity utilisation. The companies are **similar** enough to compare.

Analysing Overall Performance

Businesses can look at their data **Over Time**

1) **Data analysis** needs to be **repeated** at regular intervals to allow a business to see how things are **changing**.
2) Analysis of both financial and non-financial data can be helpful to show **trends** in performance. A trend is a **general pattern** in the data values over a period of time.
3) Analysing data over time allows the business to assess its **long-term performance**, as well as its **short-term performance** — it needs to consider whether the data shows that there is a **permanent trend**, or just a **temporary change**. The business will need to take this into account when developing its **strategy**.
4) A business should try to **predict future trends** by **extrapolating** the data. This will help the business to see how likely it is that it will meet its **objectives**.
5) However, it can be **difficult** to **forecast future trends** as there are lots of **external factors** that are out of the business's control — e.g. changes in the **economy** or **government legislation**, **competitors' actions**, etc. This means there is a lot of **uncertainty** about the future.

Core Competences are **Unique Features** that make a business **Competitive**

1) **Core competences** are the **capabilities** of a business that are **unique** to that business and give it a **competitive advantage** over its rivals. They are capabilities that rivals do not have.

The idea of core competences was developed by Prahalad and Hamel in 1990.

2) They can be **any feature** that makes a business **different** — a specific piece of **technology** that allows a firm to produce items in a different way, **specialist staff training**, an **innovative production process**, an **understanding** of their customer base, etc. They can also be a **combination** of different features, or the way they work **together**.
3) It's easy to get **confused** over what's a core competence and what's not. Features that are **important** to a business but are a **standard expectation** of that type of business are **not** core competences — for example, good **customer service** is expected in a hotel, so it's **not** a core competence, as other hotels can easily offer the **same thing**.
4) Core competences are **fundamental** to the success of the business and should allow the business to **compete** in different **areas**. For example, WeightWatchers® started off as **meetings** and **support groups** — this **understanding** of how **support** helped people lose weight allowed the business to expand into **food products**, **recipe books**, **magazines** and even **electronic items**.
5) Core competences are **hard** for competitors to **copy**, which makes the business more **competitive**. They should also offer **benefits** to the consumer, so that consumers will **choose** the product over others.
6) A business should be able to **change** its core competences to meet the **changing demands** of its **market** (especially in rapidly-changing areas, such as **technology**). This will allow the business to **grow** and maintain its **competitive advantage**.
7) A business will **focus** on its core competences when developing its **strategy** (see p.82).

Unfortunately, navigation wasn't one of Captain Keith's core competences.

Practice Questions

Q1 Give an example of marketing, HR and operational data that could be considered when analysing performance.
Q2 Give two reasons why a business might compare its data with data from other businesses.
Q3 Why might businesses want to look at their data over time?
Q4 What are core competences?

Exam Questions

Q1 A company provides distance learning courses for business qualifications. Analyse how making comparisons with similar businesses could help the company to identify its strengths and weaknesses. [9 marks]

Q2 To what extent do you think it is important for a business to identify its core competences? [12 marks]

I'd give my overall performance a solid 8 out of 10...

Core competences are a bit tricky to get your head round — especially if they're made up of more than one factor. Try and think of a couple of core competences for yourself, and explain how they make the business successful. Then put on your favourite song and have a little sing and dance — trust me, it'll do you good.

Methods of Assessing Performance

There are a couple of methods of assessing the performance of a business that you need to know — Kaplan and Norton's Balanced Scorecard model and Elkington's Triple Bottom Line model. What a mouthful.

*The **Balanced Scorecard Model** gives a **Balanced View***

1) **Kaplan and Norton's Balanced Scorecard model** is used to **assess business performance** and in **developing**, **implementing** and **monitoring strategy**.
2) It uses both **financial** and **non-financial data**, including measures of **efficiency** and **effectiveness**, and links them to the overall **strategy** and **vision** of the business.
3) It looks at four different **perspectives** (covered below). For each one, managers need to consider the **objectives**, **measures**, **targets** and **initiatives** that are **key** to the **success** of their strategy (these are sometimes shown on the model, but the one below is just a **simplified** version).
4) This process involves asking **questions**, choosing **measures** of performance based on the company's **key success factors**, setting **targets**, then coming up with **ideas** on how to achieve them.
5) Managers need to be able to **balance** these different perspectives — **improvements** in one area cannot be made at the **expense** of improvements in another. However, improvements in one area will often have a **positive impact** on another area.
6) The model is **valuable** as it treats the business as a number of **dependent**, rather than independent, **functions** — this means that all **departments** need to **consider** how their actions will **impact** on others.
7) It is a **balance** between the needs of different **stakeholders**, both **internal** and **external**.
8) However, there can be **problems** when implementing this model — there's a possibility of **information overload**, potential **conflict** if one target contradicts another and **difficulty** putting the initiatives into place.

*There are **Four Different Perspectives** to consider*

The model looks at the business from **four different perspectives**.
The **analysis** for each one is tailored to the **strategy** and **vision** of the business.

The Financial Perspective

Question: "how do we create **value** for **shareholders**?"

- **Objective**: e.g. increase profitability
- **Measures**: e.g. ROCE, sales growth, etc.
- **Target**: e.g. increase ROCE by 3%
- **Initiatives**: e.g. promotional campaigns, increase efficiency of production methods, etc.

The Internal Business Process Perspective

Question: "how can we improve our **processes**?"

- **Objective**: e.g. improve efficiency
- **Measures**: e.g. capacity utilisation, unit cost, productivity, etc.
- **Target**: e.g. increase labour productivity by 15%
- **Initiatives**: e.g. try different production methods, introduce new technology, etc.

The Learning and Growth Perspective

Question: "how can we continue to **grow** and **improve**?"

- **Objective**: e.g. increase employee development
- **Measures**: e.g. labour retention, amount of staff development, etc.
- **Target**: e.g. increase labour retention by 10%
- **Initiatives**: e.g. staff training and development, changing organisational design, etc.

The Customer Perspective

Question: "what do our **customers** value about us?"

- **Objectives**: e.g. improve customer loyalty, attract new customers
- **Measures**: e.g. market share, number of new customers, brand loyalty
- **Target**: e.g. increase number of new customers by 5%
- **Initiatives**: e.g. speed up delivery times, improve quality of product, etc.

Methods of Assessing Performance

Elkington's Triple Bottom Line Model measures Sustainability

1) **Elkington's Triple Bottom Line model** is used to measure a business's performance in relation to three **overlapping** areas — **profit**, **people** and **planet**.

- **Profit**: the 'traditional' financial or economic value created by the company.
- **Impact on People**: a company's social values and the way it treats its employees and the local community.
- **Impact on the Planet**: a company's environmental values and impact on the environment.

The **overlapping** area in the centre of the diagram (where all three circles overlap) is the area of **sustainability** — this is the **ideal balance** between social, environmental and financial performance.

People
Planet
Profit

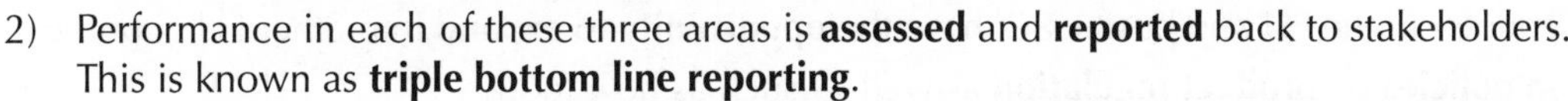

2) Performance in each of these three areas is **assessed** and **reported** back to stakeholders. This is known as **triple bottom line reporting**.

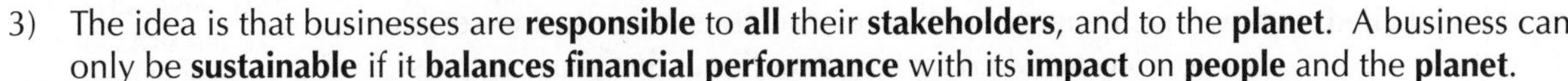

3) The idea is that businesses are **responsible** to **all** their **stakeholders**, and to the **planet**. A business can only be **sustainable** if it **balances financial performance** with its **impact** on **people** and the **planet**.

Businesses set Objectives linked to each of the Three Areas

1) To **implement** the triple bottom line model, a business sets **objectives for performance** in each of the three areas. For example, it may aim to **reduce** its **carbon footprint** by 20%, or to pay all its staff the **living wage** or more (see p.25).
2) These objectives can be used by managers to guide **strategic planning** (see p.82-83), and to monitor the strategy's **effectiveness**.
3) The business will choose a set of **measures** to assess its performance. The values of these measures can be **judged** against **pre-set targets** or by **comparing** them to the **values** for other businesses. However, it can be more **difficult** to measure the impact of the business on **people** or the **planet** than it is to measure financial performance. Some businesses now produce **environmental** and **sustainability reports**.

No, that's an elk.

4) By **assessing** its performance in these three areas, the business is more likely to **consider** its actions in each area, and alter its **behaviour** or **culture** if necessary. If **corporate social responsibility** is important to a business (see p.37), it can use the model to help it to achieve its **social** or **environmental objectives**.
5) This model is a good way of assessing **overall** performance, as it takes into account the fact that businesses might have **other objectives** than just increasing their **profit**.

Practice Questions

Q1 What are the four different perspectives managers need to consider when using Kaplan and Norton's Balanced Scorecard model?

Q2 Give one advantage and one disadvantage of using Kaplan and Norton's Balanced Scorecard model.

Q3 What are the three areas of performance measured by Elkington's Triple Bottom Line model?

Q4 Give one difficulty in using Elkington's Triple Bottom Line model to measure the performance of a business.

Exam Questions

Q1 A delivery company has a fleet of 12 vans that it uses to deliver parcels across the UK. Analyse how the company could use the triple bottom line model to set objectives and assess its performance. [12 marks]

Q2 To what extent does Kaplan and Norton's Balanced Scorecard model assist businesses in their operational effectiveness? [25 marks]

Combine the rings to summon Captain Planet...

Sorry if that reference was lost on you — it's from a 90s TV show with a really cool theme tune (which I'll now be singing all day...). Anyway, make sure you know the details of both models and how they can be used to assess the overall performance of a business. Remember, there's more to performance than just meeting the financial objectives.

Business and the Legal Environment

The UK is a member of the EU — a union of 28 independent countries, with a population of over 500 million (bigger than the US and Japan put together). The UK's membership of the EU affects its laws in a big way.

The EU is a **Single Market** — **Trade** between member states is **Easy**

1) The **European Single Market** means there are very few **trade barriers** between EU member states. Firms don't pay **tax** when they **import** goods from other EU countries, so the EU provides easy **export** opportunities for UK firms.
2) The single market **smooths out price differences** between member states. **Producers** can look for the **highest selling price** within the EU, and consumers can look for the **lowest purchase price** within the EU. When the price in part of the EU is **high**, producers **flood** that area with their product, driving **down** prices. **Low prices** attract **more buyers** to the market, pushing prices **up**.
3) The EU **customs union** means the **same customs duties** apply to all goods entering the EU — it doesn't matter which non-member country they come from, or which EU country they're going to.
4) There's **freedom of movement** within the EU for all **raw materials**, **finished goods** and **workers**. EU citizens can **work** in any country in the EU and businesses have the **opportunity to expand** into other EU countries.
5) There are **common policies** on **product regulation** as well — such as how food should be **labelled**, or how much **energy** appliances can consume. Businesses have to take these regulations into account when making **functional decisions** such as **designing products** and **packaging** — e.g. the R&D department shouldn't spend time developing a powerful vacuum cleaner as the EU **banned** vacuum cleaners of more than 1600 watts in 2014.

A common law or policy is one that's the same in all EU countries.

There are **Laws** about **Competition**...

1) **Fair competition** means companies are motivated to provide **good quality products** for **reasonable prices**. If they don't, customers will simply go **elsewhere**. Competition also encourages companies to **innovate** and develop **new products**, as well as providing customers with **choice** by **product differentiation** (see p.50).
2) In the UK, the **Competition Act 1998** sets out the laws on competition and what constitutes unfair business practices. It's the job of the **Competition and Markets Authority (CMA)** to prevent companies breaking competition laws. **EU competition law** also regulates competition across the EU. Companies breaking the laws can be given **big fines** or even be criminally prosecuted.
3) Businesses need to understand competition laws so they **don't break them** and also so they can watch out for **competitors breaking them** — they'd want to report them so the authorities could **investigate**.
4) **Competition law** means that, amongst other things:

- Businesses can't conspire to **fix prices** — where an agreement is made to keep the price of a product above a fixed amount. E.g. in the early 2000s a number of sportswear retailers were fined millions for fixing prices of football shirts.
- Businesses can't conspire with competitors to **limit production** so that higher prices can be charged due to a **shortage**.
- Businesses can't **divide up the market** to avoid having to compete. E.g. one company agrees to sell only in Europe if another agrees to sell only in Asia.

... and about **Abusing** a **Dominant Position**

1) Businesses have a **dominant position** if they have a market share of **at least 50%**.
2) Some **laws** to stop businesses **abusing** this position are:

- Dominant businesses can't demand '**exclusivity**' — that wholesalers or retailers **only** buy from them.
- They can't demand that retailers must buy a **second type of product** in order to buy the popular product they actually want (known as **tying**).
- Businesses can't sell goods at a **loss** to force smaller competitors **out of the market** (**predatory pricing**).

3) A **monopoly** is when one business has **complete control** over the market. There's **no competition** and if customers **need** the product they have to pay **whatever price** the monopoly sets. The CMA can **prevent** monopolies from occurring by stopping **takeovers** and **mergers** — this will affect the **strategy** of a business, as they will have to use **other methods** of growth to expand their business.

Business and the Legal Environment

*The **Law** protects the **Community** and the **Environment***

1) Industries which release waste into the **water** or **land** are regulated by the **Environment Agency**. Businesses have to ensure their **production processes** don't cause **unnecessary pollution**, or risk **heavy fines**.
2) Industrial processes which only release pollution into the **air** are regulated by **local authorities**. Businesses must get **authorisation** from the local council before carrying out processes which create **smoke** or make **noise**. **Environmental health officers** can force factories to **stop making noise** at night if it's disturbing **local residents**.
3) Here are some examples of specific laws and directives that affect businesses:

- The EU directive on **Waste Electrical and Electronic Equipment (WEEE)** forces businesses to increase **recycling** of waste electrical and electronic equipment, much of which previously ended up in landfill sites. Since August 2005, manufacturers have had **increased responsibility** for ensuring that goods such as computers, TVs and VCRs are **recycled** once they've come to the end of their useful life.
- The **Landfill Tax** was introduced in 1996 to **reduce the amount of waste** being dumped into **landfill** sites.
- The **EU Packaging Waste Directive** forces businesses to increase the recycling of packaging. There are **targets** for the percentage of wood, paper, glass and plastic that must be **recycled**.
- The **Climate Change Act** requires UK PLCs to report their **greenhouse gas emissions** in their annual reports. The idea is that if these are made **public**, companies are more likely to try to **reduce** them.

4) Businesses must factor in the **cost** of complying with these laws in any **decisions** they make. Decisions about the **materials** or **processes** used might also be influenced by environmental laws.
5) Some businesses are able to turn these **restrictions** into **unique selling points** of their products — e.g. by being the most **environmentally friendly** business in the market.

*The **Law** protects **Customers** and **Consumers***

Certain laws protect customers and consumers — these laws affect the **functional decisions** made by different departments. E.g. the R&D, manufacturing and marketing departments need to bear the laws in mind when **developing**, **making** and **marketing** products.

- The **Trade Descriptions Act (1968)** ensures that businesses don't **mislead** consumers with **false descriptions** on **packaging** or **advertising materials**.
- The **Sale of Goods Act (1979)**, the **Sale and Supply of Goods Act (1994)**, and the **Sale and Supply of Goods to Consumers Regulations (2002)** set out the **rights** of customers. These laws mean that goods must be **fit for their purpose** and of **satisfactory quality**.
- The **Consumer Protection Act (1987)** says that **new consumer goods** must be **safe**. There are also other, **more specific regulations**, e.g. sofa and chair cushions must be made of **fire resistant** materials.
- The **Data Protection Act (1998)** prevents the **misuse of data**. Amongst other things, it stops businesses **holding onto customer data** that they don't need and stops them from **changing** or **destroying data**.

Practice Questions

Q1 What is the European Single Market?

Q2 Give three ways that a company might break competition laws.

Q3 Why does the Competition and Markets Authority aim to prevent monopolies?

Q4 Give three examples of laws that protect consumers.

Exam Questions

Vint-Age is a manufacturer of retro radios.

Q1 Analyse how Vint-Age may be affected by the UK's membership of the EU. [12 marks]

Q2 To what extent do you think that manufacturers such as Vint-Age need to consider their environmental impact when making business decisions? Justify your answer. [16 marks]

I fought the law and the law took my profits and stopped me from trading...

Most businesses comply with the law but, sadly, there'll always be some firms who try to get away with cheating customers and selling dangerous tat. The law's there to make sure that firms obey the rules or face the consequences.

Employment Law

Employment laws aim to make things fairer for workers and stop employers taking advantage of their employees.

***Labour Laws** control what rights **Employees** have*

1) An employee has a legal right to **fair treatment** while at work, and also while looking for employment.
2) The **Equality Act 2010 protects** employees from **discrimination** based on age, gender, race, religion, disability, pregnancy, etc. These things are known as '**protected characteristics**'.
3) This Act **simplified** things by **replacing** several previous anti-discrimination acts, such as the **Race Relations Act (1976)** and the **Sex Discrimination Act (1975)**. It reflects the content of the **EU's Equal Treatment Directive**.
4) There are **two types** of discrimination — **direct** and **indirect**:

- **Direct discrimination** is treating someone **less favourably** because they have a protected characteristic, e.g. not employing someone because of a **disability**, or paying women **less** than men doing the **same job**.
- **Indirect discrimination** is when everyone is **treated the same** but it has a **worse effect** on one group of people than on others. E.g. a rule that employees must **not wear head coverings** could be indirect discrimination against some **religions**.

5) Employers have to make '**reasonable adjustments**' for workers with **disabilities**, such as installing wheelchair ramps.
6) **Parents** can ask to **work flexibly** and employers can only refuse for a **good business reason**. **Men** with young children who are **refused** flexible working could claim that it is **direct sex discrimination** if **women** with young children have had flexible working requests **approved**.

***Discrimination Laws** affect **All Aspects** of businesses*

Recruitment

- Employers aren't allowed to **state** in job adverts that candidates must be a particular age, race, gender, etc. They can't use **discriminatory language**, e.g. advertising for a "waitress" excludes men.
- Businesses are only allowed to advertise for someone of a specific age, gender, etc. if it's a **genuine requirement** of the job — e.g. a female toilet attendant for ladies' toilets.
- Businesses have to make **decisions** about who to employ without discriminating. They have to be able to **justify** why they gave a job to a particular candidate, in case an unsuccessful candidate takes them to a **tribunal** (see below).
- **Avoiding discrimination** when recruiting means that businesses will recruit a more **diverse workforce**. This means they'll have a wider range of **skills**, **talents** and **experiences** to draw upon.

Pay

- Businesses have to give male and female employees the **same pay** for work of **equal value**. They're entitled to the same **benefits** too (e.g. a company car).
- Not paying fairly can result in a fall in the **quality of work** and poor **staff retention**, as well as having to pay **compensation** and **legal fees** if taken to tribunals.

Promotions and Redundancies

- Discrimination laws mean that everyone should have the **same opportunity** to get **promoted**. For example, businesses can't just **promote older people** because they think **young people** are more likely to change jobs.
- If businesses need to make **redundancies**, they can't **deliberately select** staff who are older, disabled, etc.

Employment Tribunals** can settle **Disputes

1) If employees feel that they've been treated **unfairly** by their employers they can make a claim to a **tribunal**.
2) At a tribunal, representatives of the employer and the employee put forward their cases, and a **tribunal judge** (or sometimes a tribunal panel) decides who's in the right.
3) The employer might have to pay **compensation** or give the employee their job back in an **unfair dismissal** case.

Employment Law

Employers have to pay staff at least the Minimum Wage

1) The **National Minimum Wage** was introduced in 1999 to prevent employees from being paid unfairly low wages.
2) The minimum wage **rises** every year. From **1st October 2015**, it's £6.70 per hour for people aged 21 or over, £5.30 per hour for people aged 18-20, and £3.87 for 16 and 17 year olds. **Apprentices** get at least £3.30 per hour. In July 2015 the government announced a **National Living Wage** of £7.20 an hour for over-25s, starting from April 2016. This will replace the minimum wage for people aged 25 or over.

> The National Living Wage is **controversial** because it's **lower** than the **independently calculated** living wage. Some employers **voluntarily** pay employees the independently calculated living wage — this can **increase motivation**, **reduce absenteeism** and allows the company to market themselves as an **ethical employer**.

3) Employers who don't pay their staff enough have to **reimburse** their staff with the total amount that they've been underpaid and can also be 'named and shamed', **fined** up to **£20 000** or even prosecuted.

An Employment Contract sets out the Conditions of Employment

1) A contract of employment is a **legally-binding** agreement between the employer and the employee about what the **duties** and **rights** of the employee and the employer are, including hours, salary, etc.
2) Employees are entitled to receive a **written statement** of employment within **two months** of starting work.
3) There are some **responsibilities** that are **common** to all employers and employees, for example:

- Employees have the right to a **safe** working environment. The **Health and Safety at Work Act (1974)** states that the employer must ensure the working environment is **safe** (e.g. electrical equipment, moving machinery, etc. must be safe). Under the **Control of Substances Hazardous to Health Regulations 2002** (COSHH), businesses also have to protect employees from the risks of any **hazardous substances**.
- Employees are entitled to paid holiday. In April 2009, the **European Working Time Directive** gave full-time workers the right to **28 days** of **paid holiday** per year, including bank holidays.
- Employees have the right to **paid maternity** and **paternity** leave, although usually not on full pay. For many years, **mums** got up to 39 weeks paid leave and 13 more weeks unpaid, and **dads** got 2 weeks of paid paternity leave. However, new laws mean much of a mother's leave can be **shared** with the father.
- Employees have to **attend work** when they're supposed to, and be **on time**.
- Employees must be willing to carry out any **reasonable task** that's asked of them.

The State Pension Age is Rising

Anyone earning more than £155 a week must pay National Insurance.

1) The **State Pension** means that everyone has some money to live on in their old age. **How much** you get depends on **how many years** you've paid **National Insurance** for.
2) For years men have been able to claim state pension from 65 and women from 60, but because people are **living longer**, the age is being **increased gradually**. Due to sexual equality, by 2018 it'll be 65 for women too, then it'll rise to 68 for both men and women.
3) A new law means that employers must **enrol most employees** in a **workplace pension** and pay into it.

Practice Questions

Q1 What's the purpose of the Equality Act (2010)?

Q2 State and explain the two different types of discrimination.

Q3 How does the Health and Safety at Work Act protect employees?

Exam Questions

Q1 Analyse how discrimination laws can impact HR decisions on recruitment, wages and redundancies. [12 marks]

Q2 To what extent do you agree that employment contracts benefit the employee more than the employer? [16 marks]

Can tribunals settle disputes about whose turn it is to make the tea...

Businesses have to take all these laws into account when making decisions. For example, an employer may try to save money by only recruiting under 18s, as they have a lower minimum wage. However, if an older applicant takes the employer to a tribunal and they're found guilty of age discrimination, they might have to fork out loads of money.

Business and the Political Environment

A government policy is a plan of action to make a change — here we'll look at policies affecting businesses.

Government Policies encourage Enterprise

1) The UK government encourages entrepreneurs to set up businesses because enterprise benefits the **economy** — new businesses **increase productivity** and create **new jobs**. The government is especially keen to promote enterprise in areas that need economic **regeneration** — this provides lots of **opportunities** for new businesses.
2) Some **strategies** for this are described in the **Business Enterprise policy**:
   - **Government schemes** allow enterprises to borrow money at **low interest rates** and encourage **private investment** in businesses, e.g. the Angel CoFund. The **Enterprise Investment Scheme** is a government scheme that offers tax incentives to people who invest in small businesses.
   - To make it easier for **small** businesses to succeed, they don't have to pay **business rates** and an **Employment Allowance** means their **National Insurance contributions bill** is reduced by £2000.
   - The **Great Business website** has been launched to **advise people** on setting up and running a businesses.
   - The government is backing **initiatives** to encourage **young entrepreneurs**, e.g. the '**Tenner Challenge**', which gives young people £10 to start a business and see how much **profit** they can make in a month.

Many industries need Regulation

1) In the 1980s many state-owned firms were sold into the private sector to **improve efficiency** and make a **profit**. Examples include **British Telecom**, **British Gas**, **British Steel**, and the **water** companies.
2) Some industries are **natural monopolies** — for example, you wouldn't have several sets of rail tracks from one city to another, or several sets of water pipes and sewer pipes. When **privatising** a natural monopoly like the **railways** or **water**, the government needs to build in **regulations** to prevent the new owners from **exploiting** their position and raising prices or cutting quality.

Example: In 1989 the UK government **privatised** the ten **regional water authorities** in England and Wales by **selling assets** such as reservoirs. E.g. the water authority responsible for providing water and sewerage services to the north east of England was **taken over by** Northumbrian Water Limited.

Ofwat was created to **regulate** the industry and is mainly responsible for **setting limits** on how much companies can **charge** for water. Also, the **Drinking Water Inspectorate** was set up to **monitor** drinking water safety and quality. The **Water Industry Act 1991** sets out **laws** about the duties of the water companies and about what water can and cannot contain, etc.

3) There are lots of **regulated industries**, and the regulations affect the **decision making** of all the businesses operating in that industry. E.g. HR decisions on the number of employees needed at a residential home for the elderly would be influenced by the **Care Quality Commission**.

Infrastructure is Vital to businesses

1) The UK's **infrastructure** is made up of **physical things**, such as the **transport** network (e.g. roads, railways and ports) and **pipes** and **wires** that allow water, energy and information to move about.
2) Improvements in infrastructure are **good for the economy** as they make businesses more **productive**, e.g. by allowing people, goods and raw materials to **move about** quickly, as well as making **data transfer** through the broadband network quicker. In the short term, infrastructure improvements provide **jobs** too, e.g. in constructing roads.
3) In the UK it's mainly the **private sector** that looks after the infrastructure, but the government has **overall policies**, laid out in its annual **National Infrastructure Plan**, about what the priorities are.
4) The government also **provides money** for projects. In addition to **state funding**, the government encourages **private investment** in infrastructure projects. E.g. the **UK Guarantees scheme** means that private lenders will definitely get **repaid** if the project they're investing in fails, so there's no **risk** for them.

In 2015 the government promised £8 million to provide **charge points** at key locations across the UK for **plug-in vehicles**. These vehicles have **really low emissions**, so encouraging people to use them helps **reduce greenhouse gases**, which is in line with what the **Climate Change Act 2008** says the government has to do.

Business and the Political Environment

Government policies aim to **Protect the Environment**

1) The UK is part of the **EU's 'Emissions Trading System'**. This gives **greenhouse gas emissions allowances** to businesses such as oil refineries, power stations, airlines and many manufacturers — e.g. producers of metal, glass and paper. Companies can **trade** their allowances, giving companies an **incentive** to choose greener processes. If a company doesn't need all their allowance, they can **sell** some to a business that has run out.
2) The government also has some '**green subsidy schemes**'. For example, the **Renewable Heat Incentive** pays businesses that use **renewable energy** to heat their buildings.
3) The government and the EU **fund organisations** that encourage more efficient use of raw materials, such as the **Waste and Resources Action Programme** (**WRAP**). WRAP works with businesses to achieve a '**circular economy**' which keeps resources in use for as **long as possible**.
   As well as protecting the **environment**, it helps businesses **save money**. For example:

   > Through a **WRAP initiative**, Britvic™ launched **Robinsons Squash'd**® in 2014. These are **ultra-concentrated** tiny bottles of squash. **Less packaging** means **less environmental impact** and also reduces transportation costs.

4) The **Environment Agency** is sponsored by the government to protect and improve the environment. One of its responsibilities is to **regulate businesses** that release pollutants into water or land.
5) Businesses breaking laws will be **fined** or **prosecuted** (see p.23 for more on how **environmental laws** and **EU directives** affect business decisions). As well as operating within the law, businesses can use government initiatives to help them implement strategies to reduce their environmental impact. This can also help them to cut costs and appeal to consumers.

Political Changes can make **International Trade** easier or harder

1) **Tariffs** (import taxes) **discourage** international trade. **Removing** or **reducing** tariffs between countries provides **opportunities** for business by making international trade **easier** and **cheaper**.
   Since the **World Trade Organisation** was set up in 1995 to encourage international trade, the proportion of imports worldwide that are **tariff-free** has risen greatly.
2) **Quotas** are trade restrictions set by governments that put **limits** on **imports** or **exports**. Countries sometimes use import quotas as a way of trying to **protect** their own economies and jobs — this is called a **protectionist policy** (see p.33). Sometimes two or more countries sign a free trade agreement which **removes** (or **reduces** the number of) quotas between them to **encourage** international trade, e.g. the EU and Chile entered into a free trade agreement in 2002.
3) Since the **UK** joined the **European Union** in 1973, British **exports** to EU countries have **increased** because there are **no quotas** or **tariffs** within the EU. **Imports** from other EU countries to Britain have also **increased**. EU countries also **manufacture** to increasingly **common standards**, which makes trade more **straightforward**.
4) **Trade embargoes ban trade** with a particular country. E.g. the USA has had an embargo against Cuba since 1962 (although in 2015 the US Government began to consider lifting or relaxing it). Less extreme are **sanctions** — these are imposed for various reasons, e.g. sanctions have been placed on **Syria** by the EU and USA because of its government's **violent repressive regime**.

These political changes affect decisions about the countries a business trades with.

Practice Questions

Q1 Give three ways in which the UK government encourages enterprise.

Q2 Give an example of a regulated industry.

Q3 What is infrastructure? Give two advantages of improving it.

Q4 What are tariffs and quotas?

Exam Question

Q1 Skoob's is a new business which manufactures an innovative range of tents. To what extent do you think it is necessary for Skoob's business decisions to be influenced by government policy? Justify your answer. [24 marks]

I always thought an embargo was some kind of embarrassing illness...

You've probably gathered that the government has a lot of policies. And a lot of them are relevant to businesses. Some policies cause businesses a headache, e.g. rules on packaging and disposal, but some policies help businesses, e.g. by reducing business rates for small businesses so that they can grow more easily (which also helps the economy).

Business and the Economy

There are different ways to measure the size and growth of a country's economy.

GDP indicates the Size of a Nation's Economy

1) **GDP (gross domestic product)** is the **total market value** of **goods** and **services** produced **within** a nation over a period of time (usually a year).

GDP =	total consumer spending	+	business investment	+	government spending	+	the value of exports	–	the value of imports

2) GDP is used to measure the **economic performance** of a country, an area such as the EU, or the whole world.
3) It is calculated in **real terms**, i.e. it is adjusted so that **inflation** is ignored.

Economic Growth is the Increase in Size of a nation's Economy

1) Economic growth is an **increase** in a nation's production of **goods** and **services**.
2) It's measured as the **rate of increase in GDP**.
3) Economic growth means the same thing as "an increase in **economic activity**" — growth means there's **more demand** in the economy and **more output** to meet that demand.

Economic Growth is determined by Resources and Productivity

1) The **growth potential** of an economy depends on the **amount** and **quality** of economic **resources** available — e.g. labour and fixed assets.

Quantity and quality of labour	• **Quantity** of labour depends on **population size and age.** A problem facing the UK is its **ageing population**. The proportion of people above retirement age is **increasing** and many need **government support**. This means that fewer resources are available to **support economic growth.** • The **quality** of labour is the level of **education and training** that workers have reached. **High quality** labour enables an economy to **grow faster.** • India has the **largest youth population** in the world. It is believed that its economy could **rise dramatically** if they invest in the **education** and **health** of their young people.
Investment	• **Investment** increases the amount of **productive assets** (machinery etc. used for production). For the **value** of **productive assets** to **grow**, the **level of investment** in productive assets has to be **greater** than the amount of **depreciation** (the amount by which machines wear out) during the year.

2) Economic growth also depends on **productivity** — how hard the nation is willing or able to work.
3) **Governments** can encourage **short-term** growth by cutting taxes and interest rates. This encourages **businesses** to **borrow** money and **invest** it in production. It also encourages **consumers** to **borrow** money and **spend it** on goods, which increases **demand** in the economy.

Economic Growth has Mainly Positive Effects for Businesses

1) On the whole, **growth** in GDP means **higher revenues** and higher **profitability** for **businesses**.
2) Economic growth gives the potential for **economies of scale** (see p.52).
3) Sustained growth increases **confidence** and helps businesses **plan** for the future.
4) Economic growth affects the type of **strategic decisions** that a business makes. In periods of **sustained** growth senior managers might decide to **expand** the business, launch **new products** or try to break into **new markets**.
5) On the down side, fast growth may cause **shortages** of raw materials and skilled labour.
6) Worse still, if growth is **too fast**, it's usually followed by a **recession** — a general **slowdown in economic activity**.

Business and the Economy

Rapid Growth is usually followed by *Recession*

Very high rates of growth are usually followed by **recession**, so governments try to keep growth at a **sustainable level**. **Fiscal policy** and **monetary policy** are two ways that they do this — see pages 32-33.

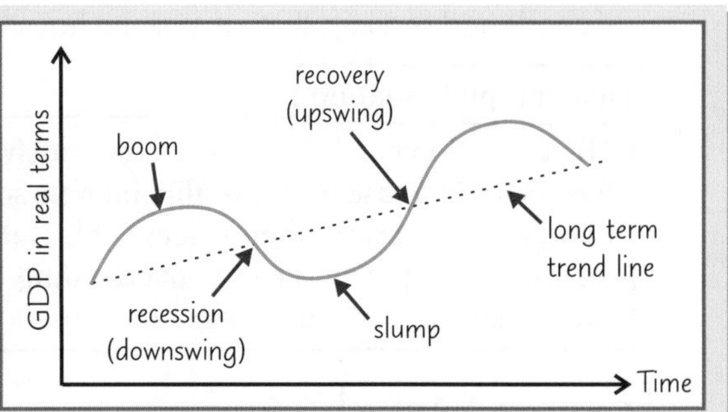

1) In a **boom**, GDP is high. As production reaches **maximum capacity**, there are **shortages**, and price increases. Shortages of skilled labour mean **wages rise**.
2) In a **recession**, incomes start to go down, and **demand** goes down. Business **confidence** is reduced.
3) In a **slump**, GDP is at a **low**. Businesses close factories and there are a lot of **redundancies**. **Unemployment** is **high**. A lot of businesses become **insolvent** or go **bankrupt**.
4) In a **recovery** or upswing period, **production increases**, and **employment** increases. People have more money to spend.
5) How much a business is **affected** by this cycle depends on the **income elasticity of demand** of its products. Businesses selling **income elastic** goods such as luxury holidays find that demand shoots **up** in a **recovery**, and dives **down** in a **recession**. Firms selling **income inelastic** goods such as staple foods **aren't affected** all that much by these changes.

Income elasticity of demand = extent to which demand depends on customer income.

Businesses deal with *Changes* in *Economic Activity Locally* and *Globally*

The state of the economy, whether local or global, influences the **decisions** that businesses make:

1) During **booms**, businesses can **raise prices**. This **increases profitability**, and it **slows down demand** a bit.
2) In a long-lasting boom, businesses **invest** in **production** facilities to increase capacity. They may come out with **new products** to take advantage of increased consumer income.
3) During **recessions**, businesses may make workers **redundant** to **save wage costs** and **increase capacity utilisation**.
4) During a **local recession**, businesses can **market** their goods elsewhere in the country — a local shop could market online. In a **national recession**, businesses can **market** their products **overseas**.
5) When a national recession or slump lasts a long time, some businesses choose to **relocate** abroad.
6) In general, **global upswings** provide growth opportunities for **everyone**, and **global recessions** are bad for **everyone**.

Practice Questions

Q1 What is economic growth and how is it measured?

Q2 What happens to production during a time of growth?

Exam Question

Q1 A business makes expensive robotic toys.
Use the graph and table to analyse whether extending its factory and investing in additional specialist machinery will increase profits in the long term.

[20 marks]

% change in GDP (6, 4, 2, 0, −2, −4, −6); 2015; — actual GDP; ------ predicted GDP

Year	2013	2014	2015
Sales (£million)	3.87	5.28	8.31

In 2008 the global economy was receding, these days it's my hairline...

Growth in the national economy is a good thing for businesses. The problems start when growth is too fast — production can't keep up, and a pleasant period of growth swings round into an unpleasant recession. Learn the ups and downs of the economy, and learn a couple of things that firms do to cope with them on a local and global scale.

Inflation and Exchange Rates

Here are two more delectable pages on how the economy affects businesses. Enjoy.

Inflation is an *Increase* in the *Price* of *Goods* and *Services*

1) The **Consumer Price Index** measures UK inflation — it tracks the prices of hundreds of goods and services that an average household would buy. There are **two types** of inflation:

Demand-pull inflation

High inflation can be caused by **too much demand** (more than the economy can supply). It happens when there's an **increase** in **disposable income** so people buy more and companies **can't supply goods** quickly enough and **increase** their **prices**. This is **demand-pull** inflation. **Excess demand** when the economy is near its full capacity is called **overheating**. **Demand-pull inflation** can actually make **profit margins** go **up**. Businesses can put up prices in response to **high demand** without their **costs** going up by as much.

Cost-push inflation

Rises in inflation can be due to **rising costs** pushing up **prices** — this is **cost-push** inflation. **Wage rises** can make prices go up — especially if productivity isn't rising. **Cost-push inflation** can make **profit margins** go **down** if businesses decide not to put up their prices.

2) When inflation is **high**, spending goes **up** temporarily — people rush to buy more before prices go up even more. If **wages** don't go up in line with inflation, however, spending goes **down** as people can afford less.
3) **Expectations** of inflation can make inflation worse. A business which expects its **suppliers** to put their prices up will put its **own** prices up to cover increased costs. Employees' expectations of rising prices makes them demand **higher wages**, so prices go up. This is the **wage-price spiral** — it's a big cause of cost-push inflation.
4) When **inflation** in the UK is **high**, it makes UK **exports** expensive abroad. UK businesses become **less competitive** globally. When inflation in the UK is **low**, UK businesses have a **competitive advantage** globally.
5) Inflation that's **too high** is bad for the economy. The Bank of England aims to keep the inflation rate within a **target range** set by the government — they do this by changing **interest rates**. It might be useful to check your Year 1 notes for a refresher on how interest rates affect demand.

Inflation affects *Business Strategy*

1) Companies producing **premium goods** are the **most** likely to be **affected** by inflation because if customers have less to spend they start to look at **cheaper** alternative **products**. Manufacturers of premium products can react by **reducing prices** (although they have to be careful not to reduce them so far that the product loses its premium image) or by investing heavily in **advertising**.
2) Periods of high inflation can be a **good time** for firms to **expand** — if **interest rates** are **lower** than the rate of **inflation** it's **cheap** for them to **borrow money** to invest in **new premises** or **machinery**. The **interest** they'd earn on their savings would be **less** than the amount prices would have gone up by in the same time, so it makes sense to **spend** rather than save. However, the Bank of England often **raises** interest rates in times of high inflation to encourage saving, so businesses don't always benefit from high inflation.

Firms compare **UK** and **foreign** interest rates. When the UK interest rate is high or volatile (fluctuating wildly), firms tend to expand into **other countries** with low, stable interest rates, as it's **cheaper** to borrow money there to invest in expansion.

3) It's harder for businesses to **plan** when inflation is **high**. They need **stable prices** in order to be able to make **accurate sales forecasts**.

Deflation is a *Decrease* in the *Price* of *Goods* and *Services*

1) **Deflation** is the **opposite** of inflation — it's when there's **not enough demand** so companies **reduce** their **prices**.
2) Deflation causes a **fall** in **productivity** because companies won't keep endlessly supplying the market with goods that nobody wants. **Lower productivity** usually means firms don't need as many workers — so deflation often leads to a **rise** in **unemployment**. This makes **demand drop** further and causes firms to **lower prices** even more.

Inflation and Exchange Rates

Exchange Rate is the *Value* of *One Currency* in terms of *Another Currency*

1) Exchange rates affect the amount of **foreign trade**.

- When the exchange rate is **high** (e.g. **more euros** to the **pound**), UK **exports** are relatively **expensive** abroad and **imports** into the UK are relatively **cheap** to buy. A **strong pound** is **bad** for UK exporters because their goods aren't competitively priced abroad.
- When the exchange rate is **low** (e.g. **fewer euros** to the **pound**), UK **exports** are relatively **cheap** for other countries (which is **good** for UK **exporters**) and **imports** into the UK are relatively **expensive** to buy.

2) A **strong pound** and **cheaper imports** mean **lower costs** for UK businesses importing raw materials from abroad, but they're **bad news** for UK manufacturers who **export goods**.
3) When a rise in the value of the pound is predicted, a business might decide to move its **production** abroad. A business can also consider **importing** their **raw materials**.
4) **Cheaper exports** should lead to increased **demand** and therefore higher **output**.

"Today's exchange rate is two sheep to the goat."

Make sure you can Convert *between* Currencies

Exam questions might ask you to use an **exchange rate** to **convert** between **two currencies**.

Example: Using an exchange rate of €1.41 to £1:

Convert €320 into pounds.	Divide: €320 ÷ 1.41 = **£226.95**
Convert £47 into euros.	Multiply: £47 × 1.41 = **€66.27**

Round your answer to 2 decimal places.

Check that your answers are sensible. The number of euros will always be higher than the equivalent number of pounds.

Exchange Rate Fluctuations create *Uncertainty*

Example: A UK manufacturer agrees a contract to sell to France, and agrees to be paid in **euros**. After the deal is made, the pound rises in value against the euro. The euro payment in the contract is now worth **fewer pounds** than before, so the UK manufacturer makes **less profit** from the contract than predicted.

Let's say that the UK manufacturer insists on being paid in **pounds** instead. When the pound rises in value, the goods are more expensive in euro terms for the French firm. They put the **selling price** up to compensate. The increase in price reduces **demand** for the goods, and there may be **less revenue** than predicted.

Some manufacturers that are based in the UK and **export to the EU** may consider **relocating** to **euro zone** countries (where the currency is the euro), so that their **costs** are in euros — the **same currency** their **customers pay in**. They may also decide to **pay UK suppliers** in euros.

Practice Questions

Q1 What is demand-pull inflation?

Q2 What type of goods are most likely to be affected by inflation? Why is this?

Q3 Is a strong pound good or bad for UK exporters? Why is this?

Q4 If 1 Australian Dollar = £0.49, convert £80 into Australian Dollars.

Answer on p.103.

Exam Question

Q1 A UK business imports components from South Korea and exports the finished products to Germany. The pound is forecast to strengthen against both the South Korean won and the euro. To what extent do you think this will influence the business decisions of the company? Justify your answer. [16 marks]

Changing interest rates — that's why we add daft stuff to our books...

The economy is pretty complicated and all sorts of things are interlinked — try to get your head around what inflation, deflation and changing exchange rates mean for a businesses. Exam questions often give you data and ask you to use it to 'analyse' why something may have happened. To get top marks you must use the figures to support your analysis.

Government Policy and the Economy

More government policies... hurray! OK, even if you're not as enthusiastic as me, you've still got to learn this stuff.

Government Policies influence the Economy

The government tries to keep the economy under control — two methods it uses are **fiscal policy** and **monetary policy**. **Taxation** is a major part of fiscal policy, so you'd best learn about that first.

Taxation Rates affect Economic Activity

1) **Individuals** are taxed on their **income**. **High** tax rates for individuals reduce consumers' **disposable income**, so people tend to **spend less** — this is bad news for businesses because it's likely to **reduce** their **turnover**. **Low** tax rates encourage people to spend, so businesses make **bigger profits**.
2) Businesses are taxed on their **profits** — sole traders and partnerships pay **income tax**, and limited companies pay **corporation tax**. These taxes are **direct taxes**. **High** tax rates for **businesses** mean that their **net profits** (after-tax profits) are **reduced**.
3) Businesses also pay **business rate** tax based on the **value** of their **premises**. The rate is the same all over the country. However, because **property values** are generally **higher** in the **South** than in the North, **businesses** in the South generally end up **paying more**. This can **reduce** their **competitiveness**.
4) Businesses want to **minimise** costs, so tax rates affect their **decisions** — e.g. where to **locate** themselves and whether to **hire** or **buy** vehicles.

Multinationals (p.66) often strategically locate their operations to countries with low tax rates — this can be controversial as many people see it as the company dodging taxes.

5) There are also **indirect taxes on spending**, e.g. VAT, taxes on pollution, tobacco and alcohol.
6) **High** tax rates **discourage** individuals from **spending**, and businesses from **expanding**. Increasing income tax **reduces spending power**, **cuts demand** and **lowers economic activity**.
7) **Reducing taxes** or giving businesses **subsidies** (financial assistance) encourages businesses to expand.
8) The effect of a tax cut or tax rise depends on the **income elasticity** of the good or service. Rises in income tax hit **luxury goods** (e.g. expensive kitchen appliances) harder than **staple goods** (e.g. petrol or bread).

Fiscal Policy changes Taxes and Spending

1) **Fiscal policy** does **two** things — it sets **tax rates** and the amount of **government spending**.
2) **Raising taxes** reduces spending in the economy, and cutting taxes increases it. **Low rates of tax** give businesses more profit, and **encourage business activity** like expansion and new start-ups.

- It's fairly easy to predict the effects of a change in **direct taxation**. Raising **income tax** reduces consumer spending, and raising **business taxes** reduces economic output.
- **Indirect taxation** is a bit harder to predict. In the **short term**, an **increase** in VAT tends to cause **inflation**, because the **higher tax** means that goods and services **cost more**. In the **longer term**, a rise in VAT **decreases** consumer spending, and **prices** have to **fall** to meet the **drop** in **demand**, so it causes **deflation**.

3) **Government spending** on social services, health, education etc. also pumps more money into the economy.

- Changing government expenditure on **welfare benefits** has a **quick** impact on the economy, because people who receive benefits will instantly have more (or less) money available to spend.
- Government spending on **infrastructure** such as roads has a **slower** effect on the economy.

4) **Fiscal policy** is really about the **balance** between tax and spending. The Chancellor of the Exchequer decides what the balance is going to be in the yearly Budget.

Fiscal Policy	When it's done	How it's done	Change in government borrowing	The effect it has
Expansionary fiscal policy	Economic slowdown / high unemployment	Cutting taxes and/or raising spending	Government **borrowing increases** (or government **surplus decreases**)	**Demand** for goods and services **increases**
Contractionary fiscal policy	Production at 100% capacity / risk of high inflation	Raising taxes and/or cutting spending	Government **borrowing decreases** (or government **surplus increases**)	**Demand** for goods and services **decreases**

5) Expansionary fiscal policy helps to **lower unemployment**. **Cutting taxes** gives people **more to spend** and increased **consumption** boosts **production** and creates **jobs**. It can cause **inflation** though, so it needs to be monitored.
6) Contractionary fiscal policy does the **opposite**. It's used to **'rein in'** economic growth to a sustainable level.

Government Policy and the Economy

Monetary Policy controls the **Interest Rate**

New monetary policy — chocolate coins... and lots of them.

1) Monetary policy means **tweaking the interest rate** to control **inflation** and **exchange rates** (see p.30-31).
2) When **interest rates** are **high**, **foreign investors** want to **save money** in **UK** banks. To do this, they **buy British pounds**, which boosts demand for the currency and makes the **exchange rate go up**, affecting **imports** and **exports**. When **interest rates** are **low**, investors prefer to invest abroad, so they **sell** their pounds and the **exchange rate falls**.
3) Interest rates are set by the Bank of England, **not** by the government — but the **Bank of England Monetary Policy Committee** bears the **government's fiscal policy** in mind when it makes its decisions.
4) Monetary policy aims to:

   1) Control **inflation**.
   2) Control the overall rate of **economic growth**.
   3) Manage **unemployment** levels (e.g. if interest rates are **low**, people have **more money** to spend and **increased demand** leads to a **rise in production** so **more workers** are needed).
   4) Influence **foreign exchange rates**.

The government must balance **Open Trade** with **Protectionism**

1) **Protectionism** is when a government protects **domestic businesses** and **jobs** from foreign competition by giving them **subsidies**, while imposing **tariffs** and **quotas** on imported products.
2) **Open** or **free trade** is when imports and exports are **not restricted**. The World Trade Organisation (WTO) (see p.27) regulates trade between member countries (almost all countries are members).
3) The **EU's Common Agricultural Policy** is an example of **protectionism**. It aims to keep farmers in business through things like **subsidies** and **guaranteed minimum prices**, as well as ensuring the EU has a **secure food supply**. It imposes **tariffs** on many imported products.
4) Open trade and protectionism have their **pros** and **cons**:

	Advantages	Disadvantages
Protectionism	Countries develop a variety of **new industries**, adding **local jobs** and **boosting economic growth**. Allows **small businesses** to grow as they don't have to **compete** with **multinationals**.	Prices of imported goods **rise** due to **decreased supply** — prices of domestic goods **rise** without a change in quality as there is **less competition**. If you **restrict** a country's trading in your country, they might **restrict your trading** in theirs.
Open Trade	Countries **specialise** in what they're good at. Countries benefit from **economies of scale**. **More choice** and **lower prices** for consumers. **Developing countries** can export goods and increase their **living standards**.	**Fewer local jobs** as multinationals expand **abroad**. Employee **skills** are concentrated around **certain jobs**. Some countries may use **sweatshops** and **child labour** to keep their costs down to **compete** internationally.

Practice Questions

Q1 What do fiscal policy and monetary policy do?

Q2 If the government raises taxes on individuals, how are businesses affected?

Q3 Give two advantages and two disadvantages of open trade.

Exam Question

Q1 Explain one way that an increase in the Bank of England's interest rate could affect a furniture retailer. [5 marks]

Political change — what's left over from government spending...

Getting the right balance between open trade and protectionism is a tricky balancing act for governments. Too much protectionism and global markets become unstable, too little and your domestic markets are at risk from competition.

The Global Economy

There have always been trade links across the world, but now it's like we're all living in one village — the global village...

Globalisation is the increase in how *Interconnected* the *World* is

1) **Globalisation** has resulted in businesses operating in **lots of countries** across the world. They can be **based** anywhere, and can **buy** from and **sell** to any country.
2) Globalisation allows businesses to make **strategic decisions** about where to get **raw materials** from, as well as where to **manufacture products** (e.g. in countries with cheaper labour).
3) Access to a **worldwide market** means businesses can benefit from **economies of scale** (see p.52), making them even more **competitive**.
4) There's more on the **opportunities** for businesses in international markets on pages 62-63.

Globalisation has *Rapidly Increased* during *Recent Decades*

There are several **reasons** for increased globalisation:

- The **internet** allows businesses to communicate between countries very quickly and cheaply. It also allows jobs to be **outsourced** across the world. E.g. if a business needs software developing, they can go to an **online staffing market** and find someone to do it, maybe in India where **labour costs** are lower.
- There's been a shift from **separate national finance markets** towards a **global finance market**, meaning it's easy to move **money** securely around the world.
- Giant **cargo ships** make it cheaper to **transport goods** around the world.
- Cheap, fast **air travel** means **goods** and **people** can move around the world easily for work.
- EU citizens can work in any other **EU country** without restrictions.
- There is **increased free trade** because of reduced tariffs, often due to the WTO (see p.27). There are various **trade blocs**, e.g. the EU and APEC (Asia-Pacific Economic Cooperation), in which the member countries have few or no trade barriers between them.

The number of *Global Brands* is *Increasing*

Huge multinational **brands** like McDonalds and Coca-Cola® can be found almost **anywhere** in the world. Some reasons for their increase are:

1) **International broadcasting** allows people to watch **television programmes** from different countries. This can create **international demand** for items in many countries. US brands like Levi's® and Coca-Cola® became popular in developing countries like India and China partly because they advertised on popular TV channels like MTV.
2) The **internet** also allows companies to market and sell their products internationally. Businesses can **sell** their products **internationally** but avoid the **expense** of setting up in foreign countries by advertising their products on **foreign websites** and offering **overseas shipping**. This allows them to create a global brand but avoids the **risks** that come with setting up a business abroad.

Businesses look for *Opportunities* in *Emerging Economies*

1) **Emerging economies** are **developing countries** with **fast growing**, but **not yet** fully developed economies. **China**, **India**, **Brazil** and **Russia** are four of the most significant emerging economies.
2) Emerging economies are a **good opportunity** for businesses as they offer **good returns** due to their **rapid growth**. **Labour** is usually **cheaper** in these countries too.
3) As jobs are created, people **move out of poverty** and a new **middle class** is formed. People are eager to spend money on **luxuries** they've never been able to afford before, creating lots of **economic activity**.
4) However, they are more **risky investments** as they're **less stable** — there might be sudden **political changes**, **currency fluctuations** or **infrastructure problems**.

The Global Economy

India and China are Important for UK Businesses...

1) China has removed its **protectionist barriers** to international trade and became a **member** of the WTO in 2001. This has provided UK businesses with more **opportunities** to **export** their products to China.
2) As **India's income** has increased, its **imports** have also increased, also providing **opportunities** for UK businesses.
3) China and India have very **large populations**, so they are both **huge markets** that can be very **profitable** for UK businesses if they manage to create **demand** for their products there.
4) Recent **economic growth** has produced many **millionaires** and even **billionaires** in China and India, so there's a lot of potential for UK companies selling **luxury products** to be very successful there.
5) UK businesses can **reduce** their **costs** by **outsourcing manufacturing** to emerging economies, or by having their **call centres** in them. E.g. average annual call centre salaries in the UK are about **£18 000**, compared with around **£2000** in India, so using Indian call centres can drastically reduce a business's costs and enable it to keep its **prices low** and stay **competitive**.

... but there are some Difficulties

1) Despite the recent economic growth, many people in China are still **very poor**. Although China has one of the world's largest economies in terms of GDP, its **GDP per person** is **below average**. In India around **25%** of people are **below** the **poverty line**. This means that the **number** of **potential customers** for any product is **reduced**.
2) The **Indian government** has put **restrictions** on **foreign businesses** investing in Indian companies. This trade barrier makes it **more difficult** for UK businesses to break into the Indian market.
3) **Language** and **cultural barriers** can prevent UK businesses from trading with India and China. These barriers are particularly difficult to overcome in **China** — in India more people speak **English**, and the **culture** is more similar to UK culture because it's a former British colony.
4) Emerging economies use **different currencies** to the UK, so UK businesses are **vulnerable** to changes in currency values (see p.31). A **strong pound** makes **British exports more expensive** abroad, which would **reduce demand** for products from UK companies in India and China.

India's trade barriers made Paul's job much more difficult.

Practice Questions

Q1 What is globalisation?

Q2 Give three reasons for the increase in globalisation.

Q3 What are the benefits for businesses in investing in emerging economies? Why is it risky?

Q4 Describe the benefits of marketing goods to China.

Exam Question

Q1 A washing machine manufacturer is considering launching products in a developing country. Some data about this country is given in the table below. Do you think that this country is a good market for the manufacturer to target? Justify your answer.

Year	2012	2013	2014	2015
GDP % growth	5.9	10.9	13.7	13.8
Exchange rate *developing country's unit of currency : £*	3.50	3.80	3.90	4.20

[20 marks]

Global economic powers are OK, but I'd still prefer super powers...

It's pretty strange to think that a few years ago India and China weren't very big players economy-wise, and now they're taking the world by storm. Makes you wonder which countries will be "global economic powers" in another few years. Anyway, no time for wondering, best get all this stuff learned and then have a choccy biccy. Yum.

Business and the Social Environment

Social concerns affect business — not the 'what shall I wear to the party' type of social concerns though.

Demographic Changes affect decision making

1) **Demographic changes** are changes in the **structure** of the UK **population** over time in terms of things like **age**, **sex** and **race** changes.
2) These changes create both **opportunities** and **threats**. E.g. the UK population is **ageing**, this is:

A **threat** — the proportion of people **available to work** (those aged 16-65) is **falling**. If businesses **can't find** enough **workers** to fill all their vacancies, it'll make growth **difficult**.

An **opportunity** — the **market size** for firms such as private healthcare providers will **increase**. Retired people often **travel** a lot — so it's good news for **holiday companies** too.

3) Demographic changes often influence a business's **decision-making**. These changes include things like:

- **More working parents** will boost the workforce, but businesses might need to provide **flexible contracts**.
- An **increase in single-occupancy households** increases the demand for **smaller houses** and for food packaged in **smaller amounts**.
- An **increase in senior citizens** might prompt a business (e.g. a cinema or a hairdressers) to offer **special rates** during weekdays, when other people are working.

4) Changes in **consumer lifestyle** and **buying behaviour** also lead to firms needing to **alter** their strategic plans.

- Consumers now use the **internet** to **research** products before buying them. Companies often send products to relevant **bloggers** to review online. This gives them **cheap, long-lasting promotion**.
- An increase in **online social networking** means this is an important means of **promotion**.
- Customers increasingly **buy things online** but are too busy to **wait in** for deliveries. So some companies use **delivery services** which drop off parcels at **convenient locations** (e.g. petrol stations) from which the customer collects them. To stay **competitive**, a business might need to consider offering this.
- Increased use of **tablets** and **smartphones** means not everyone wants **physical products**. E.g. the Camping and Caravanning Club offers a cheaper '**online membership**'. Members get access to the magazines online, rather than receiving printed copies. This **saves** the business and the customer **money** and **reduces environmental impact**.

Urbanisation and Migration affect strategic decisions

1) **Urbanisation** is an **increase** in the **proportion** of the population living in **cities**. It happened a long time ago in the UK, but it is happening now at a **fast rate** in **emerging economies**, such as Brazil.
2) This trend provides **opportunities** for companies:

- There are **new markets** with **concentrated demand** — businesses might focus on their **distribution networks** in these areas at the expense of their **wider distribution network**.
- **Infrastructure, housing** and **communication technology** will be needed, so there will be lots of **opportunities** for new and existing businesses to **expand** into these industries.
- People have access to a **higher level of education**, so the workforce becomes **more skilled** — businesses might **move certain departments** (e.g. finance) to these areas to take advantage of the **labour supply**.

3) **Migration** is the **movement** of the population from **one area or country to another**. There are currently **more** people moving **into** the UK than moving **out** of the UK.
4) Migration affects businesses because:

- When there is a **shortage of labour**, businesses **struggle** to grow. Migrants can help some businesses overcome labour shortages and allow them to **expand** into new and current markets.
- Migrants can create **demand** for **certain products** which creates **new markets** for businesses to move into, e.g. a mobile phone operator might offer cheaper international calls to **expand** its **market share**.
- However, if too many skilled people **emigrate** from a country, it can cause a '**brain drain**'. Businesses in that country will **struggle** to get skilled workers which, in the worst case, will force them to **shut down**.

Business and the Social Environment

Environmental issues affect business strategy

1) Customers, investors and the government can put **pressure** on businesses to be more **environmentally friendly** — businesses need to respond or they **risk damaging** their **brand loyalty**.
2) Businesses can choose to do **environmental audits** — these **compare** the firm's activities with those required by **legislation** and with the company's **objectives**. The outcomes can be used in **strategic planning**.
3) Businesses might decide to hire **environmental consultants** to check that they have **complied with legislation**. This will please **customers** as the business is seen to be **conscious** of its **environmental impact** — it will also please **investors** as the business is protected from **hefty fines**.
4) The government makes businesses analyse their **energy usage** and **emissions** through schemes like the **Energy Savings Opportunity Scheme** (ESOS). This forces businesses to consider the **environmental impact** when they are making **strategic decisions**.

CSR — Making the World a Better Place

1) **Corporate Social Responsibility** (CSR) is the idea that a company should go **above and beyond** what is required by **law** to help **society**, its workforce's **quality of life** and the **environment**.
2) The public are **more aware** of what companies do now than they were in the past. Companies face **pressure** to act responsibly — consumers are likely to **boycott** their goods if they don't, or simply buy from a **competitor** who they think is **more ethical**.
3) CSR has become part of **business culture** — how people **expect** things to be done in business. Companies, especially larger ones, now **publicise** how they **benefit** the environment and society.
4) Some examples of CSR initiatives are:

- **Barclays** have a two year partnership with **Teach First** (a charity aiming to recruit and train high quality teachers to teach in low income areas).
- **Marks and Spencer** work to ensure their suppliers' employees have **good working conditions**. They agree **standards** with suppliers, **visit** them regularly and **work with them** to improve conditions.
- **McDonald's Planet Champion Programme** trains employees to find ways of reducing the **environmental impact** of the company. McDonald's also runs daily **litter picking patrols**, as well as employing full time '**litter champions**' in some city centres.

CSR Costs Money but has Advantages

1) CSR should be **integrated** into a company's **operations** and **strategy** — ignoring it can lead to **long-term damage** to **profits** and **reputation**, as customers will choose more socially responsible companies.
2) Businesses implementing CSR can gain a **competitive advantage**:

- It improves **brand loyalty** and attracts **new customers** through **positive publicity** — although the public may be **sceptical** and think it's just a **PR stunt**.
- People will choose to work for firms with **good CSR records** over firms with bad ones — this means that the business will attract more **talented** applicants.
- **Employee morale** will **improve** and they will be **more motivated** to work for and stay with the company.

3) However, CSR can have its **downsides**:

- CSR has **costs**, which **shareholders** may see as a **misuse of funds** (see p.38). This can lead to them **withdrawing their investment**, or **pressuring firms** to stop their CSR activities.
- The costs may be **passed on to customers**. Most customers are prepared to pay **more** for 'socially responsible' products — however if the market is **price-sensitive** (e.g. during a recession), sales will fall.
- The expectation of CSR puts **small businesses** at a disadvantage. They are less likely to have **funds** to spare for CSR projects, or to be able to **employ** someone to organise their CSR activities.

Business and the Social Environment

Stakeholders and Shareholders don't always agree on CSR

1) Traditionally, the **decision-making process** put the **needs** of **shareholders first**, which meant that the business was concerned with its **profits** above all else.
2) Now it's considered normal for businesses to **balance** the **other stakeholders'** needs with those of the **shareholders** during the decision-making process.
3) **Corporate social responsibility** goes even further. It makes the **general public** a stakeholder and expects the business to **actively improve things** for everyone.
4) Making a **profit** is still **key** — the **survival** of the business is in the **interests** of stakeholders such as employees, suppliers and customers. In reality though, it can be **hard** to take into account the needs of **all** stakeholders:

A stakeholder is anyone with an interest in the business.

- If a company has promised to **invest** in a **local school** for the next **5 years** but its **profits fall** sharply, it has to decide which is more important — keeping **shareholders happy** or **behaving ethically**.
- Some large companies, such as Starbucks®, have been criticised in the media for **avoiding** paying **corporate tax** in the UK. They haven't done anything illegal — they've just **exploited loopholes** to **increase profits**. However, **public protests** have led to them **volunteering** to pay a meaningful amount of tax.

Carroll's Pyramid of CSR shows what Society Expects from a business

1) Carroll said that businesses have **four types** of **CSR responsibilities**. He arranged them in a **pyramid**, with each **layer** resting on the one below. The layers **shouldn't** be separated — the pyramid should be treated as a **whole**.
2) The model can be used to **analyse business decisions** and to assess whether they are made out of **necessity** (economic and legal responsibilities) or in a **voluntary** capacity (ethical and philanthropic responsibilities).

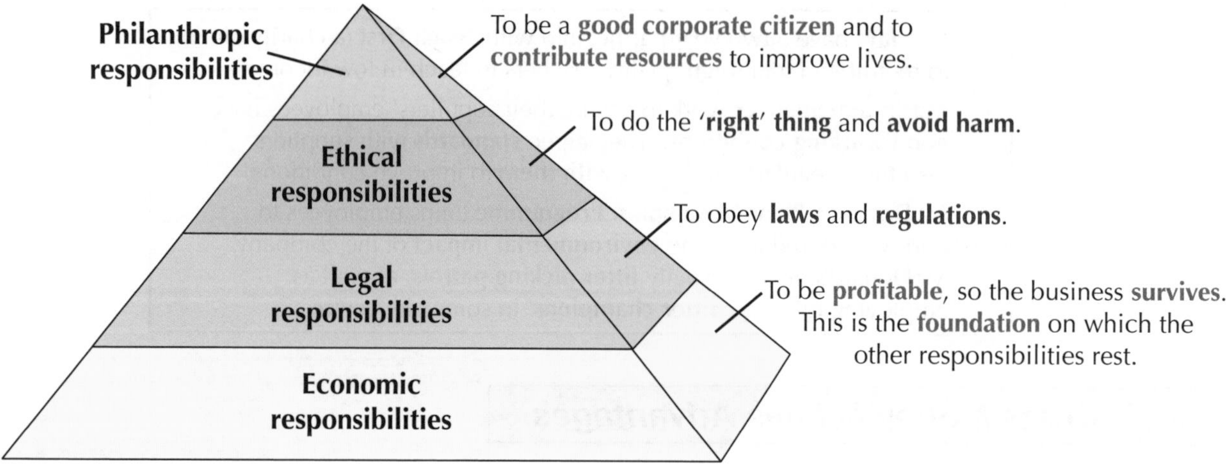

Practice Questions

Q1 Give an example of a demographic change which may affect companies.

Q2 Give two impacts of increased urbanisation.

Q3 What is CSR? Give three advantages of it for businesses.

Q4 What are the four layers of Carroll's corporate social responsibility pyramid.

Exam Questions

Q1 Analyse the possible influences on the level of CSR commitment of a medium-sized company. [9 marks]

Q2 A supermarket chain is aiming to increase its market share. To what extent should urbanisation and migration influence their strategic decisions? Justify your answer. [16 marks]

CSR — just a new TV crime series....

Corporate social responsibility has become far more important over the last few decades — lots of consumers worry about how the products they buy were made and how companies they buy from are run. On any big company's website, you'll find proud tales of how they look after the environment and all the CSR initiatives that they're part of.

Business and the Technological Environment

Stomp, stomp, stomp. That's the march of technology coming.

New Technology creates Opportunities and Threats

1) Businesses need to **monitor** the constant flow of **new** and **updated technology** to look for opportunities to **grow**, **innovate** or **improve functional areas** of the business.
2) Businesses need to decide which **opportunities** are **worth pursuing** and which are **too risky**. Here are some example of opportunities businesses can take:

- **New products** — businesses need to decide whether to **develop products** with a new technology or not. E.g. smartphone manufacturers may need to decide whether to put a new type of battery into a new phone.
- **Improving processes** — using new technology in processes can improve the business's **efficiency** and **productivity**, giving it an **advantage** over its competitors.
- **Mass customisation** — improvements to technology might mean that a business can adopt mass customisation — this can **decrease costs** and **increase revenue**.
- **Reduced barriers to entry** (see p.40) — new technology can make it **easier** for businesses to move into **new markets** — e.g. the development of ebooks means that businesses don't need a way of printing books.
- **E-commerce** — businesses are able to reach a **wider market** and **sell products** 24 hours a day.

You should remember mass customisation from Year 1.

3) Businesses need to **assess the threats** before making an **investment** into new technology. The main threat is from even **newer technology** being brought out **before** you've made your **money back** on the investment.
4) There is also a threat from **competitors** as new technology reduces the barriers to entry for **everyone** — businesses need to be wary of **new businesses** taking some of their **market share**.
5) The **growth of e-commerce** means that customers are relying much less on **physical shops**. This could mean that businesses **close stores**, leading to job **losses**.
6) Businesses that rely **too heavily** on **digital technology** will experience **decreased productivity** every time something **breaks down** — if this happens on a **regular basis**, it could put the business in **financial trouble**.

See p.71 for more on e-commerce.

New Technology can impact Different Areas of the business

1) Businesses can adopt new **Enterprise Resource Planning** (**ERP**) software (page 71) to keep track of data from **all departments** in one place. E.g. if a manager in the **production department** wants to know some **financial figures** they can look on the software rather than having to consult the **finance department**. This type of software can **increase efficiency** — however, it can lead to people **making decisions** without consulting the right people, which can have **negative impacts** on the business.

2) Instead of monitoring stock levels at **individual sites**, businesses can use **stock control systems** to monitor stock levels from a **central location**. This can **reduce costs** and **increase sales** as stock is moved to where it's **needed most**. However, the needs of **individual sites** can often be **overlooked**.

3) Adopting new technology like **Computer Aided Design** and **3D printing** during manufacturing can **reduce costs** and **improve efficiency**. However, it can be expensive to **train staff** or **employ experts**.

Practice Questions

Q1 Give five opportunities that new technology can give businesses.

Q2 Describe two ways that changes to technology can impact a company's manufacturing department.

Exam Questions

Q1 To what extent will growth of e-commerce impact strategic decisions made by a multinational company? [9 marks]

Q2 VCP Ltd is a sportswear manufacturer. Analyse how technological change may improve the competitiveness of VCP Ltd. [9 marks]

Have you been threatened by new technology? Call Jim's Solicitors now...

Businesses need to be careful that they don't miss out on opportunities to adopt key technology at the right time — a few bad decisions and competitors will gain so much of an advantage that it could be curtains for the company...

Business and the Competitive Environment

Michael Porter came up with a model that businesses could use to analyse the level of competition in an industry. As Prof Porter is considered to be the leading authority on competitiveness, he's probably worth listening to.

Porter's **Five Forces Model** shows **Influences** on an industry

1) Porter's **Five Forces model** shows an industry being influenced by **five competitive forces**.
2) It analyses the state of the market and helps managers of existing businesses to figure out the **best strategy** to gain a **competitive advantage** — it is a **decision-making** tool.
3) It can show potential market entrants how **profitable** the market is likely to be and whether it is worth getting into — and if it is, where best to **position** themselves.

1) **Barriers to Entry** — how **Easy** it is for **New Firms** to enter the market

1) New entrants to the market will want to compete by selling similar products — it's in the **interests** of existing firms in the market to make it **hard** for new firms to get in.
2) **High start-up costs** (e.g. **expensive equipment**) might deter new firms from entering the market.

Strategies to raise barriers to entry:
- **Patents** or **trademarks** (see p.61) can be used to make it harder for new entrants to sell similar products.
- Established businesses may take control of **distribution channels**. This is known as '**forward vertical integration**' (see p.56). It makes the channel **unavailable** to new entrants and makes the market less attractive. E.g. an outdoor clothing manufacturer which **buys out** or **merges** with an outdoor clothing retailer.
- Threatening new entrants with a **price war**. Large existing businesses are likely to be benefitting from **economies of scale**, so can undercut the prices of new entrants (**predatory pricing**). However, selling goods at a loss to force competitors out of the market is against **EU competition law**.

2) **Buyer Power** — buyers want products at as **Low a Price** as possible

1) **Buyers** have **more power** when there are **few buyers** and many sellers.
2) Buyers have **more power** when products are **standardised** — it's easier for firms to charge a premium price for differentiated goods and services.
3) A supplier's **main customer** can **negotiate special deals** and lower prices.

Remember, this applies to business customers, wholesalers and retailers, as well as the general public.

Strategies to influence buyer power:
- A company might **buy the supplier out** — this is '**backwards vertical integration**' (see p.56), e.g. a burger chain which buys a beef farm.
- Similar businesses could come together to form a **buying group**. They'll be buying **bigger volumes** so will be able to demand a **better deal** and so increase their profits. Buying groups help **smaller businesses compete** with large businesses.

3) **Supplier power** — suppliers want to get as **High a Price** as possible

1) **Suppliers** have **more power** when there are **few suppliers** and lots of firms buying from them.
2) If it costs customers to **switch suppliers**, then this gives suppliers more power.

Strategies to influence supplier power:
- Businesses can try to tie buyers into **long-term contracts** to make it harder for them to switch suppliers. E.g. mobile phone companies often have **2-year contracts** and lock handsets to their network.
- Suppliers can use **forward integration** to gain power — e.g. by setting up their own **retail outlets** or **buying** the retailers they supply to.
- Businesses could **develop new products** and protect them with **patents** to gain supplier power. They'll be the **only ones** selling the product, so will be able to charge a **premium** if it's a hit.

Business and the Competitive Environment

4) Threat of Substitutes — how likely consumers are to Buy an Alternative

1) The **willingness** of customers to **substitute** is a factor affecting competitiveness.
2) Relative **price** and **quality** are important — buyers are unlikely to change to a poor value product.
3) For **undifferentiated products**, e.g. washing powder, the threat is higher than for **unique products**.

Strategies to reduce the threat of substitutes:

- Businesses can make it **expensive** or **difficult** for customers to switch to a substitute (although they have to be careful not to annoy them). E.g. if you buy a Kindle™ from amazon®, you'll usually buy amazon® products to read on it as it's tricky to convert other products to the correct format.
- Customers are often **loyal to a brand** that they perceive as better. If companies can **differentiate** their product and create **brand loyalty**, they'll reduce the threat of substitutes.
- Businesses can **identify** a group of customers whose **needs** aren't quite being met and market a product designed to meet their needs **exactly**, e.g. environmentally-conscious disposable nappy users. There **won't** be any substitutes for them to buy (until other businesses notice anyway).

5) Rivalry within the industry — how much Competition there is

1) Rivalry is **intense** in a market with lots of **equally-sized competitors**.
2) Industries with **high fixed costs** are **very competitive**, e.g. parcel delivery companies which have invested in vehicles. Firms have to sell **a lot** to even cover their fixed costs. So in competitive environments, they **cut prices** to **raise demand**. Even if they're not making a **profit**, it's often hard for them to get out of the market as their expensive equipment is hard to sell on — this **increases rivalry** even more.
3) Industries producing **standardised** goods (e.g. steel, milk, flour) have **intense** rivalry.
4) Rivalry is also **intense** in **young industries** where competitors are following **growth strategies**.

Strategies to reduce the effects of rivalry:

- Some businesses try to make it **easy** for customers to switch between standardised goods. E.g. it's a **hassle** to **switch bank accounts** no matter what incentives are offered so your new bank often handles the process of switching direct debits for you.
- Businesses with a **bigger promotional budget** might do better in markets with intense rivalry.

Practice Questions

Q1 What are the five forces in Porter's Five Forces model?

Q2 How could a business raise entry barriers to a market?

Q3 What strategies might businesses adopt to improve their power as buyers and as sellers?

Q4 What type of industries have the strongest rivalry?

Exam Questions

Q1 A children's clothing manufacturer buys a high-street shop to sell its products from.
What is this an example of?

A Backward vertical integration
B Forward vertical integration
C Horizontal integration
D Product differentiation

[1 mark]

Q2 A manufacturer is entering the pet food market.
Analyse how Porter's Five Forces Model could help it to devise a strategy to maximise its profits. [25 marks]

Porter conveniently ignores the force of gravity...

... which isn't a luxury most of us have. Darn pesky gravity, making things fall down. Anyway, the Five Forces model is a rather useful tool to analyse the market and see where threats and opportunities are. Porter also came up with three generic strategies which are on page 50 — there's a lovely strategic matrix too. That'll give you a reason to go on.

Assessing Investments

Investment appraisal helps businesses decide what projects to invest in, in order to get the best, fastest, least risky return for their money.

Investment decisions must balance Risk and Return

1) Businesses often need to **invest** in order to achieve their **objectives** — e.g. if a firm's objective is to **increase sales** by 25% over three years, they'll need to invest in extra **staff** and **machinery** so that they can make the extra products they hope to sell.
2) Any situation where you have to **spend** money in the hope of **making** money in the future is **risky**, because there's always the possibility that you **won't** make as much money as you expect. Businesses like the **risks** to be **low** and the **return** (the profit on the investment) to be **high**.
3) When companies are making strategic **decisions** about how to **invest** their money (whether to launch a new product, take on more staff, relocate their call centre, etc.) they gather as much **data** as possible so that they can work out the **risk** and **reward** involved.
4) There are **two** main **questions** that businesses try to answer to enable them to make good investment decisions:
    - **how long** will it take to get back the money that they spend?
    - how much **profit** will they get from the investment?
5) There are **three main methods** that businesses can use to help them **answer** these questions and decide whether investments are a good idea: **average rate of return** (see below), **payback period calculation** (p.43), and **net present value calculation** (p.45).
6) These **investment appraisal methods** assess how much **profit** a project is going to make, and how **fast** the money will come in. The **faster** money comes in, the **less** risk in the long run.
7) All of the methods are **useful**, but they're only as good as the **data** used to calculate them.

Average Rate of Return (ARR) compares Net Return with Investment

1) **Average rate of return** (ARR — sometimes called Accounting Rate of Return) compares the **net return** with the level of investment. The net return is the **income** of the project minus **costs**, including the investment.
2) The higher the ARR, the more **favourable** the project will appear.
3) ARR is expressed as a **percentage** and calculated by: $\frac{\text{Average Net Return}}{\text{Investment}} \times 100$

Example:

	Investment	Yr 1	Yr 2	Yr 3	Yr 4	Yr 5
Project A — net cash flow	(£10m)	£4m	£5m	£6m	£7m	£5m
Project B — net cash flow	(£8m)	£3m	£3m	£4m	£6m	£6m

Numbers in brackets are negative. E.g. (£10m) means –£10m.

Net cash flow = cash inflow – cash outflow. You use this because businesses will have costs during projects, not just money coming in.

Net return (in £m) of **Project A** = –10 + 4 + 5 + 6 + 7 + 5 = **£17m**

Average net return = £17m ÷ 5 years = **£3.4m**

The investment was £10m, so **ARR** = $\frac{£3.4m}{£10m} \times 100 = \underline{34\%}$

Net return (in £m) of **Project B** = –8 + 3 + 3 + 4 + 6 + 6 = **£14m**

Average net return = £14m ÷ 5 years = **£2.8m**

The investment was £8m, so **ARR** = $\frac{£2.8m}{£8m} \times 100 = \underline{35\%}$

So managers would probably choose **Project B** because it has a higher ARR, but only just...

The pirate accountants were very fond of the average rate of return.

Assessing Investments

Payback measures the Length of Time it takes to Get Your Money Back

1) The **payback period** is the time it takes for a project to make enough money to pay back the **initial investment**.
2) The **formula** for calculating the payback period is: $\frac{\textbf{Amount invested}}{\textbf{Annual net return}}$

   For example, a £2 million project that has an **annual net return prediction** of £250 000 will reach payback in £2 million ÷ £0.25 million = 8 years.
3) Managers **compare** the payback periods of different projects so that they can choose which project to go ahead with — managers usually want to get their money back as soon as possible, so they prefer a **short payback period**.

There are Advantages and Disadvantages to ARR and Payback

Calculating the **ARR** and **payback period** can both be helpful, but they have **drawbacks** too:

	Advantages	Disadvantages
Average Rate of Return	• It's easy to calculate and understand. • It takes account of all the project's cash flows — i.e. it doesn't stop counting cash flow after a certain point, like payback period calculation does.	• It ignores the timing of the cash flows — e.g. a company might put more value on money that they get sooner rather than later. • It ignores the time value of money (see p.44).
Payback Period	• It's easy to calculate and understand. • It's very good for high tech projects (technology tends to become obsolete fairly quickly, so businesses need to be sure that they'll get their initial investment back before the products stop generating a return) or any project that might not provide long-term returns.	• It ignores cash flow after payback. E.g. two projects (project A and project B) might both have a payback period of three years. Project A will continue to provide a return of £20 000 a year after the payback period, while project B won't provide any more return after its payback period. Project A is clearly the better investment, but payback period calculation doesn't take this into account. • It ignores the time value of money.

Practice Questions

Q1 What are the two questions that businesses ask about potential investments?

Q2 Give the formula for the following: a) average rate of return b) payback period

Q3 Give two advantages of the average rate of return calculation.

Q4 Give two disadvantages of the payback period calculation.

Q5 What does ARR take into account that the payback period calculation doesn't?

Exam Questions

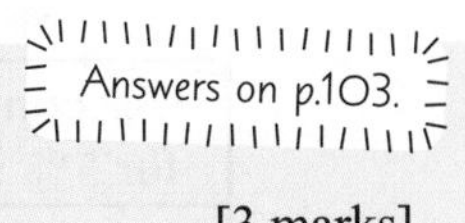

Q1 A business is investing in a new product. The initial investment is £200 000. The product will generate a revenue of £320 000 over 8 years, with total costs of £40 000. Calculate the average rate of return on the investment. [3 marks]

Q2 Priya owns a doughnut shop. She's thinking of buying a new doughnut-making machine, costing £11 000. She estimates that it will generate a net return of £3000 per year. Calculate the payback period for the new machine. [2 marks]

'Revenge of the Business students: It's Payback Time'...

Arrrr, there's nothing quite like a good average rate of return. Investment appraisal techniques are really useful for businesses, and they could come in quite handy in your Business exam if you get a question on them. So stick with it until it's all practically tattooed on your brain, and then turn over for... more on assessing investments (sorry).

Assessing Investments

Well, I know how much fun you had on the last two pages about assessing investments, so here's two more for you.

The **Future Value** of cash inflow depends on **Risk** and **Opportunity Cost**

Risk and **opportunity cost** both **increase** the longer you have to wait for money, which means that it's **worth less**. This is called the **time value of money**. If someone offers you £100 cash-in-hand now or £100 in one year's time, you'd be best off taking it **now**, because:

1) There's a **risk** that the person would never pay you the £100 after a year had gone by.
2) In a year's time the money would be worth less due to **inflation** — a general rise in prices over time. You wouldn't be able to buy as much with that £100 as you could today.
3) There's an **opportunity cost** — if you had the money now you could **invest** it instead of **waiting** for it. A high interest account would beat the rate of inflation and the £100 plus interest that you'd end up with in a year's time would be worth **more** than the £100 in your hand today, and much more than the £100 would be worth to you in a year.

Example: A bank might offer **3% interest**.

- If you put in **£100**, you'll have **£103** after a year.
- If you put in **£97.09**, you'll have **£100** after a year.

So, if you assume that you'd get an interest rate of **3%** if you invested the money today, **£100** paid to you at the **end of the year** would be worth the same as being paid **£97.09 today**. This idea is explained in more detail below.

A payment after a year or two, or three, is **always worth less** than the **same payment** made to you **today**.

Discounting adjusts the value of **Future Cash Inflows** to their **Present Value**

1) **Discounting** is the process of **adjusting the value of money** received in the **future** to its **present value**. It's done so that investors can **compare like with like** when they look at the cash inflows they'll receive from projects. £4 million this year **isn't the same** as £4 million in five years' time, and it's not wise to **pretend** that it is the same.
2) **Discounting** can be seen as the **opposite** of **calculating interest**. It's done by **multiplying** the amount of money by a **discount factor**. This discount factor is like the opposite of a bank interest rate. Discount factors are **always less than 1**, because the value of money in the future is always less than its value now.
3) **Discount factors** depend on what the **interest rate** is predicted to be. **High** interest rates mean that the future payments have to be **discounted a lot** to give the correct present values. This is so that the present value represents the **opportunity cost** of not investing the money in the **bank** where it would earn a nice **high interest rate**.

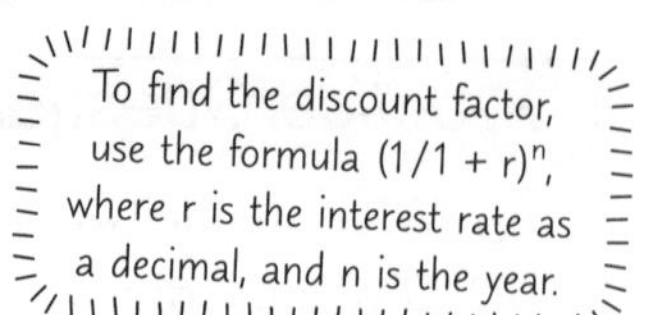

Year	0	1	2	3	4	5
Discount Factor for 5% interest	1	0.952	0.907	0.864	0.823	0.784
Present Value of £1000	£1000	£952	£907	£864	£823	£784

Year 1 discount factor = 1/1.05 = 0.952. Year 2 discount factor = $(1/1.05)^2$ = 0.907. Year 3 discount factor = $(1/1.05)^3$ = 0.864.

Present value of £1000.

4) As you might expect, when **interest rates** are predicted to be **low**, the future cash inflow doesn't need to be discounted so much. There's **less** opportunity cost.

Assessing Investments

Net Present Value is used to Calculate Return

1) **Discounted cash flow** (DCF) is an investment appraisal tool that uses the **net present value** (**NPV**) to calculate the **return** of the project.
2) **Net present value** is the **value** of the project assuming all future returns are **discounted** to what they would be worth if you had them **now**, which is **always** less than their face value (because of inflation and lost interest).
3) If you end up with a **negative NPV**, that means that the business could get a better return by putting their money into a **savings account** rather than going ahead with the project. Businesses will usually only go ahead with projects with a **positive NPV** — projects that are going to **make them money**.
4) The **downsides** of discounted cash flow are that it's a bit **hard to calculate**, and that it's difficult for businesses to work out what the **discount factor** ought to be, because they don't know what the bank interest rates are going to be in the future. The **longer** the project is set to last, the **harder** it is to predict the discount factor.

Here's an Example of Discounted Cash Flow

Project A has an initial investment of **£10m**, and **project B** has an initial investment of **£8m**.
The **expected rate of interest** is **10%**. The discount factors are given in the table below.

Project A	Net Cash Flow	Discount Factor (10%)	Present Value
Year 1	£4m	0.909	£4m × 0.909 = £3 636 000
Year 2	£5m	0.826	£5m × 0.826 = £4 130 000
Year 3	£6m	0.751	£6m × 0.751 = £4 506 000
Year 4	£7m	0.683	£7m × 0.683 = £4 781 000
Year 5	£5m	0.621	£5m × 0.621 = £3 105 000
Total Present Value of Net Cash Flows			£20 158 000
Net Present Value (Total minus Investment)			£20 158 000 – £10m = **£10 158 000**
Return ((Net Present Value ÷ Investment) × 100)			(£10 158 000 ÷ £10m) × 100 = **101.6%**
Project B	**Net Cash Flow**	**Discount Factor (10%)**	**Present Value**
Year 1	£3m	0.909	£3m × 0.909 = £2 727 000
Year 2	£3m	0.826	£3m × 0.826 = £2 478 000
Year 3	£4m	0.751	£4m × 0.751 = £3 004 000
Year 4	£6m	0.683	£6m × 0.683 = £4 098 000
Year 5	£6m	0.621	£6m × 0.621 = £3 726 000
Total Present Value of Net Cash Flows			£16 033 000
Net Present Value (Total minus Investment)			£16 033 000 – £8m = **£8 033 000**
Return ((Net Present Value ÷ Investment) × 100)			(£8 033 000 ÷ £8m) × 100 = **100.4%**

Net cash flow = cash inflow – cash outflow.

The return gives a percentage, so that two different projects can be compared more easily.

Working out the NPVs shows that **both** projects are **worthwhile**, because both have a **positive NPV**.
The **return** on both projects is **more** than 100% — so they more than **double** the investment.
Project A gives a **slightly better** return than **project B**.

Practice Questions

Q1 How do you calculate the net present value of a net cash flow?

Q2 What does it mean if a project has a negative net present value?

Exam Question

Q1 Explain the benefits of finding the net present value. [4 marks]

Discounts? Brilliant — I love a bargain...

Another tricky couple of pages here. Over halfway through the section though, so try to summon up the energy to learn these two pages, and then there's just two more to go. Discounting future income is a bit of a weird concept to get your head around at first, but it really makes sense for businesses to do it, so keep going over it until you're sure you've got it.

Investment Decisions

The last few pages have covered techniques that analyse the numbers involved in an investment. But there are loads of other, non-numerical factors to consider too.

Non-Numerical, Qualitative *factors affect* ***Investment Decisions***

The **investment decisions** made by managers are based upon a range of numerical data and **quantitative** methods. But managers must also put the decisions into a **qualitative** context, based on **internal** factors and market **uncertainty**.

Business Objectives and Strategy can Influence Investment Decisions

- An investment appraisal recommended purely on **financial data** may not fit in with the **objectives** of a firm. Many businesses will only make an investment if the project will help them **achieve** their objectives.
- For example, a business that aims to produce **low cost products** for a large mass market (e.g. teaspoons) would be **unlikely** to invest as much in **research and development** as a high-end technology business.
- **Human resources** investment takes away from short-term profit, so a firm with the objective of **maximising** profit for shareholder dividends would be unlikely to invest too highly in staff development. On the other hand, a business which aims to produce **high quality**, high-tech products would invest in **skilled staff**.

Corporate Image can Influence Investment Decisions

- **Good corporate image** brings **customer goodwill** and **loyalty** in the long term, and the firm may consider this more important than **short-term rate of return** on investment. Investment decisions that create **bad publicity** and **damage** customer loyalty will damage profits in the **long term**.
- A firm with a green, **environmentally friendly** image would avoid investments that would damage the environment. Some firms incorporate **environmental costs** into their investment appraisals.

Phil had spent all morning perfecting his corporate image.

Industrial Relations can Influence Investment Decisions

- Investments which result in a **loss of jobs** may be turned down, even if they show a good rate of return.
- **Loss of jobs** affects **staff morale**. Cost of **redundancy payments** should be factored into the decision. Trade unions may **strike** over job losses, which would affect **productivity**. **Corporate image** may also be damaged.

There's ***Always Risk*** *and* ***Uncertainty*** *involved in* ***Investments***

1) Businesses can use all the investment appraisal methods on the last few pages, but that **doesn't** mean that a **new project** will necessarily be successful just because they expect it to be — there's **always** a **risk** involved in investing in a new project.
2) All investment appraisal methods are based on **predictions** about how much **income** they can generate from investments. It's very **difficult** to **accurately** predict what's going to happen in the future, so businesses **can't** always **rely** on their predictions. E.g. a business might work out that the **payback period** of a machine is four years, based on a predicted income from the investment of £8000 a year — but the investment could end up only generating £3000 a year, so their payback period calculation would be **completely wrong**.
3) Market environments are always **uncertain**. Circumstances might change **unexpectedly**, and this could have a negative impact on the business. **Exchange rates** may alter, **sales** may decrease, **customers' tastes** may change, **competitors** may become stronger, the **cost** of **raw materials** may increase, etc.
4) Any change in the **circumstances** that businesses based their investment **predictions** on can mean that their predictions are **no longer valid**. E.g. if a business works out the net present value based on an interest rate of 6%, but the interest rate actually goes up to 9%, their net present value results will be **inaccurate**.
5) Every firm has a **different attitude** to **risk** — some firms are happy to take **big risks** that might lead to **big financial rewards**, but other firms prefer to **play it safe** and go for **less risky** investments.
6) It's often a good idea to have a set of **investment criteria** — conditions that need to be **met** for an investment to be **approved**. These could include anything, such as expected **return**, **job** creation, or **environmental** targets.

Investment Decisions

Sensitivity Analysis tests Assumptions that decisions are based on

1) Most decisions rely on certain **assumptions** about future events. For example, an **investment decision** might be based on the assumption that the **price** of raw materials will increase by **8%** over the next three years, and that **sales revenue** will increase by **3%** each year. All the assumptions put together makes a **scenario** for the future called the **base case**.
2) **Sensitivity analysis** looks at the base case and **considers** what would happen if you **alter** the assumptions, for instance if the price of raw materials increases by **10%** or **15%** instead.
3) The most simple method analyses factors **one at a time**. Analysing more than one factor at a time can be very **complicated**, but can be done with specialist **software**.
4) A business can use this information to **evaluate** the **risk** of an investment — if they could cope with raw materials going up in price by 10% but not by 15%, they need to decide whether it's worth the risk, or if they could take **extra measures** to reduce the risk.

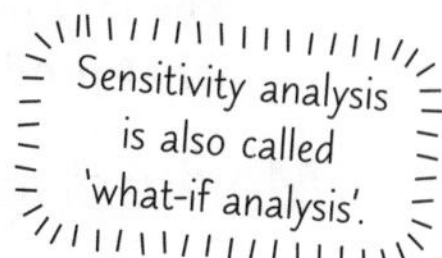

Example

The owner of a music shop is considering **investing** in larger premises. Her **research** suggests that **operating** in the new premises will cost **10% more** than the current premises, and that **passing trade** will **increase** by **3%**. She decides to use **sensitivity analysis** on these two factors.

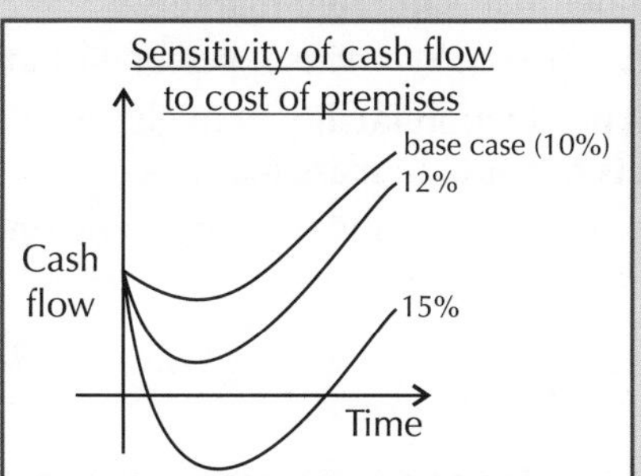

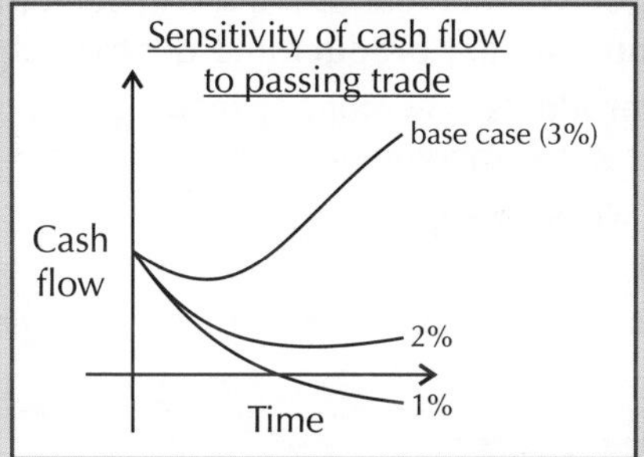

- The top graph shows that if the cost of operating in the new premises is **12%** more, it isn't that different to the **base case**. But if it costs **15%** more, then the shop will have a significantly **reduced** cash flow, even going **negative** for a period.
- The bottom graph shows that having a **2%** increase in passing trade has a **big effect** on the cash flow compared to the base case, and having a **1%** increase leads to a negative cash flow.
- The owner of the shop could decide that the **risk** is too great, and not invest in the premises. Or she could decide that it is worth the risk, but only with **precautions**. For example, she could **negotiate** with the estate agent and energy suppliers to prevent the cost of premises from increasing too much, and make the shop front more **appealing** to keep passing trade at a suitable level.

Practice Questions

Q1 How can industrial relations influence investment decisions?

Q2 Why can't businesses rely completely on their predictions?

Q3 What are 'investment criteria'?

Q4 What is a base case?

Q5 How does sensitivity analysis work?

Exam Question

Q1 Analyse the value of sensitivity analysis in investment decisions. [9 marks]

My take on sensitivity analysis is to call my boss names and see if he cries...

The stuff on these pages is pretty important in business. A company doesn't just launch straight into an investment with no considerations — it'll want to look at all the different risks and uncertainties and figure out if the investment is worth it. And you've reached the end of this section. Bravo — treat yourself to a little rest. Have a biscuit, or a cuppa (or both...).

Marketing Strategies

North. No, west. OK, how about north-west? Oh, that's not what you mean by choosing strategic direction. Whoops.

Strategic Direction is guided by the Marketing Strategy

1) **Strategic direction** is the **general path** a business takes, based on its **mission** and **achieving its objectives**.
2) The strategic direction influences how a **business's strategy develops** and affects **all areas** of the business.
3) **Key factors** in setting strategic direction are the choices of **which markets** to compete in, **what products** to offer and **which direction** the business should **grow** in.

Marketing Strategy decides on Markets and Products

The **markets** that a business plans to compete in and the **products** it plans to offer are influenced by **market research** and **analysis** as well as **internal skills** and **resources**. Here are some **important factors** that influence these choices:

Markets

- **Type of product** — the products that a business offers will impact its **choice of market**. Certain products are more suited to **B2B** (business-to-business) markets than **B2C** (business-to-consumer) markets, **niche** markets than **mass** markets, etc.
- **Level of competition** — businesses will favour markets where there is a **low level of competition**. They will also prefer to compete in **growing markets** rather than **saturated markets**.
- **External factors** — e.g. **political**, **social**, or **economic factors** could create opportunities in certain markets.
- **Internal resources** — e.g. if a business only has a **small production facility**, it might be more inclined to choose to compete in **niche markets** rather than **mass markets**.
- **Attitude to risk** — businesses that take **big risks** are more likely to compete in **new** and **unknown markets**.

Products

- **Research and development** (R&D) — a company with a **strong** R&D department can develop **new**, **innovative** products to sell (see p.58-59).
- **Competitors** — businesses need to **react** to the actions of rival companies. If a competitor has launched a new, successful product, they might choose to **develop** a **similar product** in order to compete.
- **Technology** — changes in technology could affect the **products**. A company making TVs will need to develop **smart TVs** to keep up with the rest of the market.
- **Finances** — businesses that have **healthy finances** and **working capital** can afford to spend more money **developing new products**.
- **External factors** — just like the **choice of market,** products are influenced by different external factors, like social, economic or environmental factors.

There are Different Options for Strategic Growth

A chap called Igor Ansoff came up with **four** different **strategies** that a business can use to **grow**. These strategies set the **direction** for business growth and strategy development.

1) **Market penetration** means trying to **increase** your **market share** in your **existing market**. E.g. if a company makes washing powder and currently has a 25% market share, it might try to achieve a 30% market share using **sales promotions**, **pricing strategies** and **advertising**. This strategy works best in a **growth market**. It **doesn't work well** in **saturated markets**, where demand for the product has stopped growing.
2) **New product development** is selling **new products** in your **existing markets**. It's best when the market has good **growth potential** and the business has high market share, strong R&D and a good **competitive advantage**.
3) **Market development** (or **market extension**) is selling **existing products** to **new markets**. It can be done through **repositioning** — this means that a business focuses on a **different segment of the market**. They need to **research** the target market segment and work out how they can **adapt** their product or promotion to suit the needs of a different set of consumers. This might involve creating a **new advertising campaign** or **promotion** which **targets** a different audience. Businesses can also target different market segments by using **new channels of distribution**, e.g. using **e-commerce** to sell **directly to consumers** rather than selling through a **retailer** or **agent**.
4) **Market development** can also be done by **expanding** into new geographical markets to exploit the same market segment (e.g. in a different country — see p.62-63).
5) **Diversification** means selling **new products** to **new markets**. Diversification is a **very risky** strategy, as it involves moving into markets that the business may have **no experience** of. It's used when a business really needs to reduce their dependence on a **limited product range** or if **high profits** are likely, which **reduces** the **risk**.

Marketing Strategies

Ansoff's Matrix is used to decide on a *Growth Strategy*

1) **Ansoff's matrix** is a tool for comparing the **level of risk** involved with the different growth strategies. It helps **managers** to decide on a direction for **strategic growth**.
2) The **advantage** of Ansoff's matrix is that it doesn't just lay out potential strategies for growth — it also forces managers to think about the **expected risks** of moving in a certain direction.
3) One **disadvantage** of the matrix is that it fails to show that **market development** and **diversification** strategies also tend to require **significant change** in the **day-to-day workings** of the company.
4) **Product development** is less risky than diversification, but it works best for firms that already have a strong **competitive advantage**.
5) **Market penetration** is the **least risky** strategy of all — so **most firms** opt for this approach to start with.
6) Some people believe that Ansoff's matrix **oversimplifies** the **options** available for growth. For example, **diversification** doesn't have to be **completely unrelated** to what the business does currently. It might be a **safe option** to diversify by moving into your **supplier's business**, as you know there's a **guaranteed market** for that product.

Markets \ **Products**	Existing	New
Existing	Market penetration	Product development
New	Market development or extension	Diversification

Increasing Risk →

Increasing Risk ↓

Example: KFC® International Market Development

KFC®'s expansion from the USA market to the UK market is an example of **market development**. KFC® began operating in the USA in 1952 and extended their market by opening an outlet in Preston, UK in 1965. This was the **first American fast food chain** to open in the UK. There are now over 750 outlets across the UK and Ireland. These outlets were run as a **franchise** by an **independent company**, KFC GB Ltd, until it was bought by PepsiCo in 1986.

Ansoff's matrix shows that KFC®'s market development strategy is the result of taking an **existing product**, their fast food business model, and developing it in a **new market**, the UK. This is a **safer** option than **diversification**, particularly since the UK had no other fast food chains in 1965 so there was **no competition**.

Practice Questions

Q1 Give two internal and two external factors that affect marketing strategies.

Q2 What does a market penetration strategy involve?

Q3 What is diversification?

Q4 What are the four areas of Ansoff's matrix?

Exam Questions

Q1 Which of these is the least risky growth strategy?

A market penetration B product development C market development D diversification [1 mark]

Q2 A company is considering developing a new product to sell in their existing market.
Explain the advantages and disadvantages of new product development as a growth strategy. [6 marks]

Q3 Organoats is a company that makes organic porridge. They currently just sell plain porridge oats, which are selling well. By considering the Ansoff matrix, analyse the different marketing strategies the company could implement in order to grow. [16 marks]

Ansoff's Matrix — bet Keanu wouldn't want to star in that one...

Marketing strategies probably won't save the world but they can be pretty useful for businesses who want to plan for the future. And knowing about them won't help you win the war against intelligent robotic lifeforms or help you escape from virtual reality but they just might come in useful when you're sitting your A-level Business exams.

Positioning Strategies

In Year 1 you learnt about how businesses position themselves in the market. Well, here are some positioning strategies.

Positioning Strategy *is an important* ***Strategic Choice***

1) **Strategic positioning** means choosing how to **compete** with the other businesses in the market. A business's **positioning strategy** is part of the marketing strategy — the choice influences the **general direction** a business **develops in** and affects **all areas** of the business.
2) **Different positioning strategies** work for **different companies**. It is important to choose the right strategy — it should play to the company's **strengths** and give them a **competitive advantage**. The wrong positioning strategy can be **disastrous** — **value** products with too **high** a price and **luxury** products with too **low** a price will **fail**.
3) The positioning strategy chosen will be **affected** by a number of things. The **product** itself will be very important, as will the state of the **economy**. The company's **image** and **resources**, along with its **mission**, are important too.

Businesses want to have a ***Competitive Advantage***

1) If a business has a **competitive advantage**, customers see an **advantage** to buying **its products** compared to its **competitors' products** — competitive advantages are often gained through a firm's **core competences** (p.19).
2) Porter identified **two types** of **competitive advantage**:

Cost advantage

1) A business can get a **competitive advantage** by selling a similar **product** at a lower cost than its rivals.
2) **Low-cost airlines** like EasyJet and Ryanair use a "no frills" strategy to keep their costs at a **minimum** — they use cheaper airports like Luton and cut out travel agents' fees by using online booking.

Differentiation advantage

1) Selling **better products** at the same or a slightly higher price creates a **competitive advantage**.
2) Offering a product that consumers see as **different** from competitors' products can make consumers think it's **better**. This is called **product differentiation**.

3) Having a **competitive advantage** is great for a company — they'll either sell a **high volume** of products at a **low price** and make a **large profit**, or they'll be able to sell enough products at a **high price** to make a **large profit**.
4) A competitive advantage can also build **brand loyalty** — customers **associate** the particular advantage with the **brand**, which makes them **more likely** to choose that brand in the future.
5) However, **holding on** to your competitive advantage can be **tricky**. Maintaining **low cost production** might be difficult. **Competitors** can **lower** their **prices** or **copy** your **unique features**. **Consumer tastes** can change, and a changing **economy** can alter the demand for luxury or value products. Businesses need to continuously monitor both **internal** and **external factors** in order to **keep** their advantage.

Porter *suggested* ***Three Generic Strategies*** *to* ***Gain Advantage***

These three strategies are **competitive strategies** based on the strengths of **low costs** and **differentiation**.

Cost Leadership

1) **Cost leadership** strategy calls for the **lowest cost of production** for a given level of quality. **Big firms** with **large** and **efficient production facilities**, benefiting from **economies of scale**, can use this strategy.
2) In a **price war**, the firm can maintain profitability while the competition suffers losses. If prices **decline**, the firm can stay profitable because of its **low costs**.

Differentiation

1) **Differentiation** strategy requires a product with **unique attributes** which consumers value, so that they **perceive** it to be **better** than rival products. Unique products allow businesses to charge **premium prices**.
2) Businesses that are **innovative**, have **strong branding** and offer **quality products** can benefit from this strategy.
3) Risks include **imitation** by competitors and **changes in consumer tastes**.

Focus

1) **Focus** strategy concentrates on **niche market segments** to achieve **either** cost advantage or differentiation.
2) This strategy suits firms with **fewer resources** who can target markets with specific needs. A firm using this strategy usually has **loyal customers**, making it very hard for other firms to compete.

Positioning Strategies

Porter's **Strategic Matrix** helps decide on a **Competitive Strategy**

1) Porter's **strategic matrix** helps a business choose its **positioning strategy** based on its **competitive advantage** and its **market scope**. A business can place itself in a particular section depending on whether it's aimed at a **broad** or **narrow market** (also known as a niche market and whether it offers **cheaper** products than competitors or **unique**, **quality** products.
2) For example, in the jewellery market, Accessorize sells products to a broad market at relatively low prices, so it would be placed in the **cost leadership** section of the matrix. Tiffany & Co. sells high-quality products at premium prices, focusing on a narrow market, so it would fit into the **differentiation and focus** section.

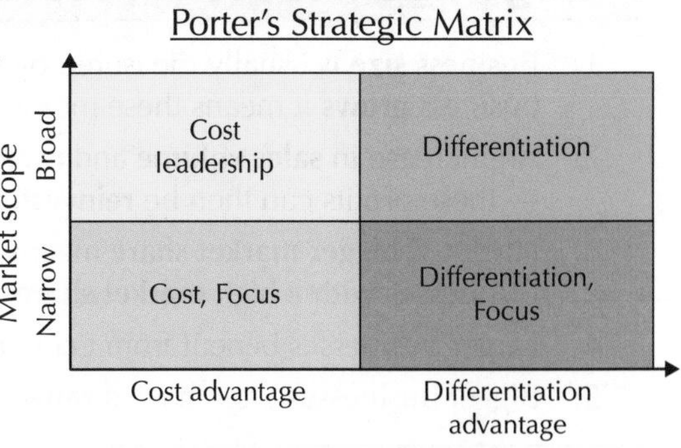

Bowman's Strategic Clock shows **Pricing** and **Differentiation Strategies**

1) **Bowman's strategic clock** shows different **positioning strategies** based on different combinations of **price** (from low to high) and **perceived added value** or **benefits** (also from low to high). It shows that some positioning strategies are likely to be **more successful** than others.
2) It can be used to analyse the **competitive position** of a company. It's **similar** to Porter's strategic matrix above, but goes into a bit more **detail**.
3) Position 1 corresponds to a strategy of low price products with low added value — this will only be successful if the products sell in a **high volume**.
4) Position 2 corresponds to the **cost leadership** section of **Porter's strategic matrix**.
5) Position 3 is the **hybrid** area — **modest prices** with a relatively **high** perceived added value.
6) Position 4 corresponds to the **differentiation** section of Porter's strategic matrix, and position 5 corresponds to the **differentiation and focus** section.
7) Positions 6-8 (the grey area) combine a **high price** with fairly **low** perceived added value. Unless a company has a **monopoly** (see p.22), if it adopts these positioning strategies it will ultimately **fail**.

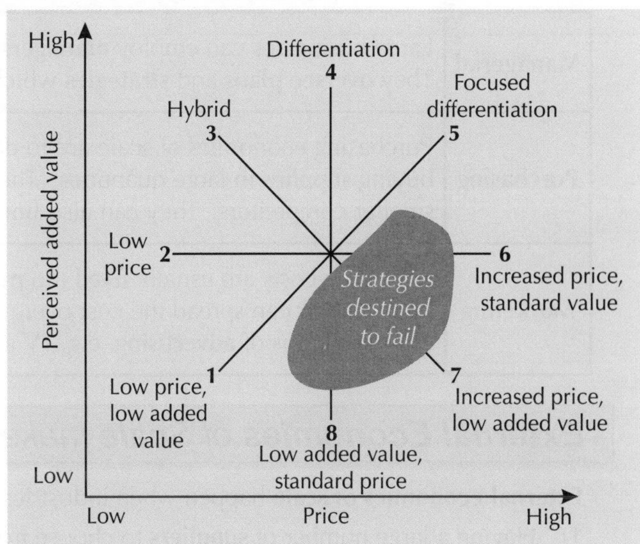

Practice Questions

Q1 Explain one way a company could lose its competitive advantage.
Q2 Describe Porter's generic strategies.
Q3 What are the four areas on Porter's strategic matrix?
Q4 Where is the hybrid position located on Bowman's strategic clock?

Exam Question

Q1 The Norfolk Wales ice cream company sells luxury organic ice cream. To what extent do you agree that the company has chosen a 'differentiation' positioning strategy? [12 marks]

What time is it Mr Bowman — time for your strategy to fail...

I know, I know — it's a bit of a weird clock that only goes up to 8 o'clock. And they might as well have labelled that grey area between 6 and 8 as 'DOOM' or 'WARNING: HERE BE MONSTERS'. But other than that, it's OK really. 3, 4 and 5 are the only ones with funny names, so if you learn them, you'll be laughing all the way to the exam.

Business Growth

A business might pursue a strategy of growth so that it can reap the rewards that come with being a bigger business...

Large Businesses** are **More Stable** than **Small Businesses

1) Business **size** is usually measured by **revenue**, **profit**, **market share**, **number of employees** or **assets**. When a business **grows** it means these measures are increasing — growth can be **organic** or **external** (see p.54-57).
2) An increase in **sales volume** and **revenue** will likely mean bigger **profits** for the business — these profits can then be **reinvested** back into the business to **stimulate more growth**.
3) Having a **bigger market share** means that the business has more **influence** over the market. Businesses with a **high market share** can use their influence to **control prices**.
4) Larger businesses benefit from **economies of scale** and **economies of scope** which means **lower unit costs**.
5) Bigger businesses often have a **range of products** or **services**, so they can cope better if the **market changes**.

Economies of Scale** mean bigger is **Cheaper

Economies of scale mean that as the scale of production **increases**, the **cost** of producing **each item** (the unit cost) **decreases**. **Internal** economies of scale increase efficiency **within** a firm, and there are several different types:

Technical	Technical economies of scale are related to **production**. Production methods for **large volumes** are often more **efficient**. Large businesses can afford to buy better, more advanced **machinery**, which might mean they need **fewer staff**, and **wage costs** will **fall**.
Managerial	Large businesses can employ **managers** with **specialist skills** to manage specific departments. They **oversee plans** and **strategies** which can result in work being done more **quickly** and **efficiently**.
Purchasing	Purchasing economies of scale are to do with **discounts**. Big businesses can negotiate discounts when buying **supplies** in large quantities. They can get bigger discounts and longer **credit periods** than their smaller competitors. They can also **borrow money** at lower rates of interest than small businesses.
Marketing	Marketing costs are usually **fixed** (no matter how many units are sold), so a business with a **large output** can spread the cost over more units. A **large** business can also afford more **effective** forms of **advertising**, e.g. TV adverts.

***External Economies** of **Scale** make a **Whole Industry** or **Area** more efficient*

External economies of scale happen when industries are concentrated in **small geographical areas**.

1) Having a large number of **suppliers** to choose from gives **economies of scale**. Locating near lots of suppliers means firms can **easily negotiate** with a **range of suppliers**, which tends to **increase quality** and **reduce prices**.
2) A good skilled local **labour supply** makes an industry **more efficient**. This is most important in industries where training is **expensive** or takes a long time. For example, **software development** firms in California's "Silicon Valley" know that plenty of people who are **qualified** to fill their vacancies already live **within driving distance**.

*The **Experience Curve** — the **More** you do something, the **Better** you get*

As a business **grows** and increases its **sales volume**, it will begin to **produce more** products. Workers will get **more experienced** and **more efficient** at making the products, which will cause the **cost per unit** to decrease.

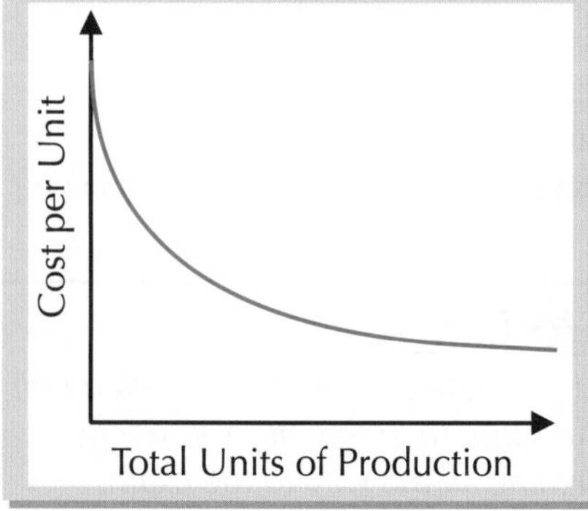

1) In general, the **production** of any **goods** or **services** will follow the experience curve. As the **total units produced** by a business **increases**, the **cost per unit decreases** at a **constant rate** — e.g. if the total units produced doubles, the cost per unit might decrease by 20%.
2) The main reason for this effect is that as workers get more **practice** and **experience** at making the products, they become **more productive**.
3) **Efficiency increases** as **total units produced increases** — workers develop better ways to make the product, including wasting **fewer materials**, taking **less time** and becoming better at using **technology** and **machines**.

Business Growth

Economies of Scope mean More Variety is Cheaper

1) **Economies of scope** arise when a business produces **multiple products** instead of specialising in one.
2) It's **cheaper** for **one business** to produce **many products** than it is for **many businesses** to produce **one product** each.
3) A business that already has **people** and an **infrastructure** in place will be **more efficient** at producing an additional product than a new business, specialising in only that product, will be. They are able to **expand** the **production department** without having to expand **other departments** in the business, so **unit costs decrease**.
4) Existing businesses are also able to benefit from **brand loyalty** — people already know the company's brand, so they are more likely to buy other products that they make.
5) Economies of scope allow businesses to charge **lower prices** due to **lower unit costs**. This gives them a **competitive advantage** over other businesses and can force rivals out of the market.

Diseconomies of Scale — being bigger can be Bad News, too

1) **Diseconomies of scale** make **unit costs increase** as the scale of production increases. They happen because large firms are **harder to manage** than small ones.
2) It's important to keep all departments working towards the **same objectives**. **Poor coordination** makes a business **less efficient**. In a big firm, it's hard to **coordinate** activities between different departments.
3) **Communication** is harder in a big business. It can be **slow** and **difficult** to get messages to the right people, especially when there are **long chains of command**. The **amount** of information circulating in a business can increase at a faster rate than the business is actually growing.
4) It can be hard to **motivate** people in a large firm. In a **small** firm, managers are in **close contact** with staff, and it's easier for people to feel like they **belong** and that they're working towards the same aims. When people **don't feel they belong**, and that there's **no point** to what they're doing, they get **demotivated**.
5) Diseconomies of scale are caused by problems with management. Strong **leadership**, **delegation** and **decentralisation** can all help **prevent diseconomies** of scale and keep costs down.

Businesses may become Smaller — this is called Retrenchment

1) **Retrenchment** may be necessary in order for a business to remain **profitable**. The need for retrenchment is often due to **diseconomies of scale**, **declining markets**, **economic recession** or **improved competitor performance**.
2) **Retrenchment** means that the business will have to **downsize** in some areas. This can be achieved by:

- **Cutting jobs** — if **sales** are decreasing, a business will need to **decrease** its **wage bill** by cutting jobs.
- **Reducing output** — if a business is selling **fewer units** it has to **reduce** its **output** and **capacity**.
- **Withdrawing from markets** — businesses might choose to **stop selling products** in **less profitable markets**.
- **Splitting the business up (demerging)** — it's easier to **manage** and **control** a smaller business, so a large business might **split up** into several smaller ones and focus on making each one **profitable**.

3) Retrenchment affects **workers** — if it is done in lots of **little steps** over a **long time**, then workers may not be too badly affected. However, if a business has to **retrench quickly** (e.g. during a recession), the impact on workers is **significant** — it can lead to **decreased productivity** which might make the problem even worse.

Practice questions

Q1 Outline three benefits of growth to a business.

Q2 Give two internal and two external economies of scale.

Q3 What is retrenchment?

Exam Questions

Q1 Explain the advantages of economies of scale for a manufacturing business. [5 marks]

Q2 A retail business is growing rapidly. Analyse the possible benefits and drawbacks of this growth. [12 marks]

Tea and retrenchments will be served at the end of this section...

Make sure you can tell your economies from your diseconomies and your scale from your scope when you're learning this stuff. You can even put the experience curve into practice — the more business you revise, the better you'll get at it.

Business Growth — Organic

If a business is a success and demand for its products is high, it may decide to implement an organic growth strategy.

Organic Growth is when a business Grows From Within

See p.48-49 for more on the different directions of strategic growth.

1) Expansion from within a business is known as **organic growth** (or internal growth) — a business can come up with **strategies** to sell more products, make new products, increase market share, expand into new markets, etc. in order to **grow**.
2) Businesses that grow organically are often able to **finance** their growth (increased capacity, new premises, more staff, etc.) by **reinvesting profits** into the business.
3) Businesses find it easiest to grow organically when the **markets** they are in are **growing quickly** and when they are **outperforming** their competitors, enabling them to increase their **market share**.
4) Organic growth is **slower** and **more gradual** than **external growth** (i.e. mergers and takeovers — see p.56), which means that it's easier for the company to **adapt** to growth.

Advantages of Organic Growth over External Growth	Disadvantages of Organic Growth compared to External Growth
• Can maintain current **management style**, **culture** and **ethics** of the business. • **Less risk** as it's expanding what the business is good at and it's usually **financed using profits**. • It's easy for the business to **manage** internal growth and **control** how much the business will grow. • Less disruptive changes mean that workers' **efficiency**, **productivity** and **morale** remain high.	• It can take a **long time** to grow a business internally and it can take a while for the business to **adapt to big changes** in the market. • **Market size** isn't affected by organic growth. If the **market isn't growing**, the business is **restricted** to increasing its **market share** or finding a **new market** to sell products to. • Businesses might miss out on **opportunities** for more **ambitious growth** if they only grow internally.

Growing in Size brings its Own Problems

1) Large companies can suffer from **diseconomies of scale** (see p.53) — any further growth will result in them **losing money** and the only solution may be **retrenchment**.
2) Growing companies find it more difficult to **manage cash flow** — they need to **invest** in **infrastructure** and **assets** but also have enough cash available for the **day-to-day expenses** of the business.
3) Fast growth increases the risk of **overtrading** — increased **demand** means the business needs to buy more **raw materials** and employ more **people**. This **reduces** the amount of **working capital** available to pay the bills, and the business runs the risk that they'll go bust before they have the chance to get paid by their customers.
4) When a company grows in size it will often change from a **private limited company (Ltd)** to a **public limited company (PLC)**. This can make running the company more complicated:
   - The **original owners** lose some control to new **shareholders** which can affect strategy (see p.92).
   - Becoming a **PLC** can make managers more **short-termist** as shareholders seek a **quick return** on investment through **dividend** payments.
   - Once a company becomes a **PLC**, it's more open to being **taken over**. Anyone with enough money could buy enough of its shares to take a **controlling interest**.
5) Businesses have to avoid growing so much that they **dominate** their market and become a **monopoly** (see p.22) — companies can be penalised by the **Competition and Markets Authority (CMA)** if they **damage competition** in a market.
6) Business owners may choose to **restrict** growth or **retrench** for the following reasons:
   - They may want to **maintain the culture** of a small business.
   - The business will become more **complicated** to manage as it gets bigger.
   - Growth requires the business to **secure additional financial resources**, which can be complicated.
   - They may not want to put too much **strain** on their **cash flow** position.

Being bigger was very bad news for Jerry — his wife banned him from eating pies.

Business Growth — Organic

Greiner's Model of Growth describes different *Phases of Growth* over *Time*

The Greiner Model shows that each **phase of growth** is followed by a **crisis**.

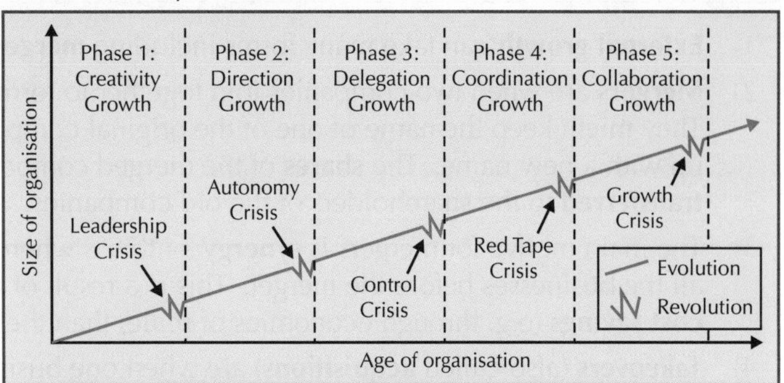

Phase 1 — Creativity → Leadership Crisis

When a business is starting up it is often **very creative** and everyone in the business can **share ideas** easily. Once the business gets to a certain size, there is a need for **strong leadership** to give the company **direction** and **structure**.

Phase 2 — Direction → Autonomy Crisis

Leaders set up a formal **organisational structure** with defined **departments** and **roles**. As employees become **more experienced** they will want **more say** in decisions, and the business will be **too big** for **senior managers** to **manage everything**. So more **autonomy** through **delegation** is needed.

Phase 3 — Delegation → Control Crisis

More **power** and **responsibility** is **delegated** down to middle-managers and the organisational structure may become **decentralised**. Leaders may try to regain some **control** in order to have a more **coordinated business** that is **optimising** its use of the **resources** available.

Phase 4 — Coordination → Red Tape Crisis

As **control is regained** by senior managers, certain decisions become more **centralised** and **new procedures** to **coordinate** different areas of the business are implemented. However, there can be **too many procedures**, which will **decrease efficiency** as people are constantly **waiting for decisions** to be **made** and **approved**.

Phase 5 — Collaboration → Growth Crisis

To continue growing, some **formal procedures** are replaced by **collaboration** between departments and teams. More focus is put on **communication** and **information management** (see p.75). At this point the company might **struggle** to **grow internally** and may have to consider **external growth** (see p.56).

Franchising allows established businesses to *Grow Quickly*

1) A **franchise** is an **agreement** (contract) which allows a new business to use the **business idea**, **name** and **reputation** of an **established business**.
2) The **franchisor** is the established business which is willing to **sell**, or **license**, its idea, name and reputation. The **franchisee** is the business which **buys** into the franchise. They usually pay the franchisor an **initial fee**, plus **ongoing payments** — usually a **percentage** of their **revenue** or **profit**.
3) Franchising allows the franchisor to **grow quickly** as most of the **costs** and **risks** are taken on by the franchisee. For example, through franchising, SUBWAY® **increased** the number of its fast-food restaurants in the UK & Ireland from **100** in 2002 to **over 2000** by 2015.
4) Franchising can have **some risks** for the **franchisor**. If just one of their franchisees has **poor standards** and gets a **bad reputation**, then it will affect the reputation and profits of the franchisor.

Practice questions

Q1 Give three advantages and three disadvantages of organic growth.

Q2 According to the Greiner Model, what are the five phases of growth?

Q3 What is franchising?

Exam Questions

Q1 Stu's Soda Co. is a fast-growing new business that brews and sells fizzy drinks. By referring to Greiner's Model of Growth, analyse the potential problems that the business might face as it grows. [9 marks]

Q2 Analyse the reasons why a fast-food restaurant might want to restrict the growth of the business. [12 marks]

Organic Growth is better for the environment but 100% more expensive...

"To grow or not to grow?" That's the question all businesses need to ask themselves. You should learn the pros and cons of organic growth and know the phases of Greiner's model as well as the hairs on your knuckles... just me then?

Business Growth — External

Businesses can also grow externally — an external growth strategy often means working with other businesses.

External Growth can help Businesses to Grow Quickly

1) **External growth** can take many forms including **mergers**, **takeovers** and **ventures**.
2) **Mergers** are when two companies join together to form one company. They might keep the name of one of the original companies, or come up with a new name. The **shares** of the merged company are **transferred** to the shareholders of the old companies.

Demergers are the opposite of mergers — they're when a business splits into parts. This is an example of retrenchment (see p.53).

3) The main motive for mergers is **synergy** — this is where the business after the merger is **more profitable** than all the businesses before the merger. This is a result of the **merged business** generating **more revenue** or **cost savings** (e.g. through economies of scale) than the **independent businesses** could between them.
4) **Takeovers** (also called **acquisitions**) are when one business buys enough shares in another so that it has **more than 50%** of the total shares. This is called a **controlling interest**, and it means the buyer will **always win** in a vote of all shareholders. Takeovers can be **agreed** or **hostile**:

- **Hostile takeovers** occur when one **public limited company (PLC)** buys a **majority** of the shares in **another** PLC against the will of the directors of that company. It can do this because the PLC shares are **traded** on the stock exchange and **anyone** can buy them. The company will encourage existing shareholders to sell them the shares by offering a **premium** — an extra payment on top of the value of the shares.
- **Agreed takeovers** happen when shareholders or other types of owners such as sole traders **agree** that they'll sell the business to someone else. This is usually because the owners believe it would benefit the **survival** of the business.

5) **Ventures** are **small businesses** or **projects** that are set up by **existing businesses** in the hope of making a **profit**. They are often set up to try and **meet needs** that are not being met in the **current market**. If **more than one** business invests then it is called a **joint venture**.
6) In a joint venture, businesses **share their resources** but there is **no change of ownership** for the businesses involved. When the joint venture is **terminated**, bills are paid off, profits are shared and the businesses remain **separate**.
7) A joint venture can be a good way to set up a **new business** if you don't have the **capital** to do it yourself — it can also be a good way for businesses to **access markets** in **different countries**.
8) A venture often involves a lot of **risk** to the business setting it up — a joint venture is often **preferable** because the **risk can be spread** among the businesses involved.

External Growth can be Horizontal, Vertical or Conglomerate

1) **Horizontal integration** happens when a firm combines with another firm in the **same industry** at the **same stage** of the production process (e.g. two suppliers). It's a very **common** type of takeover or merger. It **reduces** the **competition** in the market — for example, the Morrisons supermarket chain bought out Safeway to extend its branch network and reduce competition.
2) **Vertical integration** occurs when a firm combines with another firm in the **same industry** but at a **different stage** of the **production process**, e.g. a retailer taking over a manufacturer or distributor.
3) Vertical integration can be **forward** or **backward**.

- **Forward vertical integration** is when a business combines with another business that is **further on** in the production process. For example, a manufacturer merging with the **outlets** where its products are sold gives the manufacturer **direct access** to the retail market and they can then **control** what is sold and exclude competitors' products.
- **Backward vertical integration** is when a business combines with another business at an **earlier stage** of the production process. For example, a retailer taking over its suppliers allows them to **control production** of their supplies so they can be sure that supplies won't be **disrupted**.

4) **Conglomerate mergers** are between **unrelated** firms — they aren't competitors of each other, and they aren't each other's supplier or customer. **Pure conglomerate mergers** are between totally unrelated firms. **Product extension mergers** are between firms making **related products** (e.g. hairbrushes and hairspray). **Geographic market extension mergers** are between firms in the same industry, but competing in **different geographic markets**.

Business Growth — External

External Growth Methods *are used to* ***Gain Resources***

External growth is **much quicker** than organic growth and can rapidly increase the **capacity**, **workforce**, **technology**, **skills** and **assets** available to a business. It can also increase the **market share** of the business, which will **directly increase sales**. The **reasons** and **motives** for growth will **influence** the type of **external growth** a business chooses.

1) Some businesses want to **diversify**, so they **combine** with an **existing business** operating in the market they want to **enter**. They **gain** from the **experience** of those employed by the business they combine with.
2) Businesses can **reduce** the amount of **competition** they face through **takeovers** or **mergers** with companies that **operate in the same market**.
3) Businesses who want to move into **another country** will often combine with companies who already **operate** and have **established infrastructure** in that country.
4) Companies in the same industry may combine so that they can benefit from **economies of scale** and **economies of scope** (see p.52-53).
5) In the car industry, companies such as Ford, Peugeot, BMW and General Motors have bought out car manufacturers overseas. They can **switch production** from country to country where **labour costs** may be lower but the **expertise** already exists.
6) If businesses **lack** certain **technology** or **expertise** needed to develop **new products** and **processes**, they might consider combining with a business that **already has** the technology and expertise required.

External Growth *can be a* ***Risky Strategy***

1) There can be **tensions** between the staff of merged businesses as they try to **establish** their **status** in the new organisation. It will also take **time** for staff to **learn** new procedures — which may lead to **poor customer service**.
2) Some parts of the new organisation may need to be **sold off** or **closed**. This could mean additional **redundancy costs**, which will **reduce profitability**.
3) Businesses involved in mergers and joint ventures may have **different objectives** and **cultures**. This could lead to **clashes on important issues** and **inefficiency** which may result in **diseconomies of scale**.
4) When one business buys another, it takes on all the **liabilities** of the other business — this could include things like **compensation claims** for long-term disabilities suffered by **ex-employees** of the other business.
5) The **Competition and Markets Authority** investigates whether a proposed merger will **restrict competition** in the marketplace. If this is found to be the case the government can **stop** the merger from taking place or place **restrictions** on it. The finance used to **plan** the merger would then be **wasted**.
6) If a takeover is part of a **diversification strategy** (see p.48), the purchasing business will have **limited experience** in the new industry and it will take time to **learn** how it works. Mistakes would **reduce profitability**.
7) When companies **expand overseas** they should consider the **different laws**, **languages** and **cultures** of the host country. Just because a growth strategy is **successful in one country** doesn't mean it'll be **successful in another**.

Practice Questions

Q1 What's the difference between a takeover and a merger?

Q2 Explain what a joint venture is.

Q3 Define the terms 'horizontal integration', 'vertical integration' and 'conglomerate merger'.

Q4 Give four reasons why a business might base its growth strategy on external growth.

Exam Question

Q1 In 2009 Deutsche Telekom owned T-Mobile UK and Orange SA owned Orange UK. They announced that they were going to merge T-mobile UK and Orange UK in a joint venture to form EE. Analyse the possible benefits and drawbacks of this joint venture for both Deutsche Telekom and Orange SA. [24 marks]

External Growth Strategy: Seek immediate medical advice...

There are quite a few different terms to learn on these pages — mergers, ventures, horizontal integration, vertical integration... Try not to get too bogged down with it all — all the terms are quite descriptive, so you'll probably find they're not too hard to remember once you get going. Just don't have nightmares about hostile takeovers.

Innovation

Businesses need to come up with new ideas if they want to stay ahead of the competition...

Innovation comes in the form of New Ideas, Products and Processes

1) Innovation means thinking of a **new idea** and putting it into **action**. This could be in the form of a **new product** or a **new process**.

> **Product Innovation** — making **new** goods/services or **improving** existing ones. E.g. car manufacturers are constantly innovating **new features** to put on their latest models.
>
> **Process Innovation** — putting in place new or improved **production** and **delivery methods**. E.g. in 2007, amazon® introduced amazon Prime to the UK, which provides unlimited **one-day delivery** for an **annual fee**.

2) New ideas can come from **anywhere** in the business, but many businesses have a **Research and Development** (R&D) department that drives innovation.
3) Businesses are always looking for ways to innovate as it can help them to stay ahead of **competition**, expand their **markets** and increase their **market share**.
4) The **pressure to innovate** is greater in some industries than others — e.g. in the technology industry businesses need to constantly innovate **new products** or they will **fall behind** their competitors.

Innovation can be Risky but is often the best way to make Big Profits

Some industries are particularly **fast moving** and need to **constantly** develop new products. However, **innovation** can have **benefits** and **drawbacks** for a business:

Benefits of Innovation	Drawbacks of Innovation
• Businesses can initially charge **higher prices** for innovative products and services before their **competitors** bring **similar products** to market. • Being innovative can be good for a firm's **reputation** — if they've been the **first to launch** exciting **new products** in the past, people will naturally be **interested** in their **future products**. • Innovations in **processes** can help **add value** to existing products and services. • Businesses with lots of innovative products can take advantage of **economies of scope** (see p.53).	• Innovation can be a **very costly** and **time consuming** process — businesses risk running out of money if they **invest too much** into R&D and don't get the products to market **quickly enough**. • Businesses can end up **wasting resources** by developing something customers **don't want**. • Businesses might not be able to produce the new product on a **large scale** at a **low enough cost** — there is no guaranteed **return on investment**. • Businesses risk ruining their reputation if the innovative product is **poor quality**.

Innovation affects Functional Areas of the business

FINANCE R&D for innovative products is **expensive**, so the finance department might need to raise extra **working capital** to pay for it.

OPERATIONS Innovation in **production methods** might mean that the **operations department** has to set some of its budget aside to spend on **expensive new machinery**. They will also need to organise **training** for employees to get them **up to speed** with the **new methods**.

MARKETING The amount of **market research** a company does is **increased** when researching a new idea — the **risks** and **costs** are **high**, so they need to be sure customers want or need the product. Innovative products require changes to the **marketing mix**. E.g. marketing might use a different **pricing strategy** (usually **skimming**) for an innovative product. **Promotional activity** increases too — there's often a lot of **PR** (public relations) activity when a new product is launched.

HUMAN RESOURCES Innovation can mean there's a change in **staffing needs** — if a company suddenly decides to focus heavily on R&D they might need more **skilled staff**. HR also needs to make sure that the business has the right **culture** for innovation to thrive. In a culture where staff are **scared** of the consequences of **failing**, workers are unlikely to want to take risks. HR needs to find ways of **encouraging** employees to take **risks**, e.g. by **rewarding** people who try **new things**.

Innovation

New Product Development (NPD) has Six Stages from Idea to Launch

The **Research and Development** department can turn **raw ideas** gathered through **market research** into **innovative** new products using the **new product development** process.

1) Idea

The business comes up with **new ideas**, explores and **develops existing ideas** or **modifies competitors' ideas**. New ideas can come from **brainstorming** in a group, from **employee suggestions** or from **R&D department meetings**. New ideas are also discovered through **market research** finding out what consumers want, or from customers submitting requests to a firm. Businesses can sometimes also use **already patented ideas** (for a fee).

2) Analysis and Screening

The business wants to see if the product can be produced and sold at a **profit**. All aspects of the idea are investigated — whether there's a **potential market** for it or not, based on market research, whether the **technology** and **resources** exist to develop it, whether a **competitor** has an existing patent on a similar idea. At this stage, a **prototype** may be made to see what the product will be like.

3) Development

The **R&D department** develop a **working prototype**. They test it **scientifically**, and tweak the design to make the **functional** design (how it works) and **aesthetic** design (how it looks, feels — or smells and tastes if it's a food) as good as possible. This is the real "meat" of research and development.

4) Value Analysis

The business tries to make the product good **value** for money. This means balancing the **function**, **features** and **appearance** of a product with the cost of **making**, **warehousing** and **distributing** it — the goal is to make a product that is **good value** for both **business** and **consumer**.

5) Test Marketing

This is where the marketing department gets involved again.

The business sometimes sells the new product in a **limited geographical area**, and then analyses **consumer feedback** on the product, price and packaging. This allows **modifications** to be made before a wider launch.

6) Launch

A successful launch requires **enough stock** of the product to be distributed across the market. It also needs an effective **promotional campaign** in place to **inform** retailers and consumers about the product and **persuade** them to buy it.

The new product launch certainly went with a bang.

Practice Questions

Q1 What is the difference between product innovation and process innovation?

Q2 Give two reasons why innovation is risky.

Q3 Give two ways that innovation can involve the marketing department of a business.

Q4 Outline the six stages of new product development.

Exam Question

Q1 Evaluate the need for, and risks of, innovation in a digital technology firm. [20 marks]

R&D — not to be confused with R&B, which can also be fast-moving...

Hey, all those amazing new products have to come from somewhere. Just think, there are research and development eggheads beavering away as we speak, to come up with something utterly amazing that we'll all rush out to buy.

Innovation

As well as the work of the Research and Development department, there are other ways that businesses can innovate.

Kaizen** can be a **Continuous** form of **Innovation

1) The **kaizen** approach to innovation is by encouraging employees to improve the **way they work** and the **processes** they use all the time. Over a long period of time these small kaizen changes can **add up** and lead to **innovation.**
2) Another important part of kaizen is to give workers some control over **decision making**. Whenever there's a problem, workers are encouraged to ask '**why?**' until they get to the root of the problem. This creates a **working environment** in which **innovation** can thrive.
3) The **benefits** of using kaizen to drive innovation are that the company doesn't have to spend lots of **time** and **money** on research and development, and the processes become **more efficient** all the time.
4) However there are many **downsides** to only relying on kaizen for innovation. For example, the kaizen approach probably **won't** lead to **innovative new products** as workers aren't really encouraged to think about the **wants** and **needs** of the customer.
5) The kaizen mindset also means that workers are focused on making **small changes** to their **own job** rather than thinking about **big changes** they could be making to the **whole process** — this means that big innovation leaps are rare.

*Some businesses **Encourage Employees** to become **Intrapreneurs***

1) **Intrapreneurship** is when employees **within a business** are encouraged to **solve a problem** by coming up with **innovative new ideas**.
2) Businesses allow intrapreneurs to take risks and experiment with lots of different ideas until they find the **most productive** and **effective** way to complete a task — their solution can then be implemented across the **whole department** or **company**.
3) An advantage of intrapreneurship is that it is done **alongside** the intrapreneur's regular role, so the company isn't **wasting money** employing someone just to try new things. Even if the intrapreneur **doesn't find a solution** to the problem, they will still have **produced some work** along the way.

Examples of intrapreneurial innovation

- Intrapreneurship can lead to **innovation** of the **technology** used by the company. For example, in a publishing company, an intrapreneur might investigate different publishing **software** in order to find the most efficient type for making a book — this software could then be implemented across the whole editing department.
- Intrapreneurs can also come up with **innovative goods and services** during their experiments and research. E.g. Google™ allows its workers time to be **creative** and work on **personal projects** — one of the biggest successes to come out of this is Gmail™.

Benchmarking Learns** from **Other Businesses

1) Benchmarking studies **other businesses** with excellent **quality standards**, and aims to innovate by **adopting the same methods**. Companies can sometimes do this by joining **benchmarking groups**, where firms agree to **share information** about their way of doing things.
2) Businesses can **benchmark internally** — they can study activities in efficient departments and use what they learn to **innovate processes** in other departments.
3) It's also possible to benchmark across **different industries** — e.g. in 2010, Tesco introduced **Click+Collect** to their **UK supermarkets**, which let customers **order online** and pick their groceries up **at the store** without having to **leave their car**. This was benchmarking of the popular **drive-though service** offered at **fast-food restaurants**.
4) Benchmarking tends to **motivate** staff. It's more encouraging to **introduce** a process or a product that you've already seen working **successfully** somewhere else than it is to introduce something **unknown**.
5) Another advantage is that it provides **early warnings** to businesses about **technology** or **methods** that might allow their competitors to **overtake** them.
6) A downside to benchmarking is that it won't directly lead to **new products** — **competitor products** are likely to be protected by a **patent** or **copyright** (see next page) and you need to be careful what ideas you take from them.
7) Another downside is that **processes** can't always be transferred between different **corporate cultures** — what works for one company might not be **suitable** for another company with a **different culture**.

Innovation

Original Ideas are business Assets that can be Protected by law

Businesses and individuals who produce **original work** and earn an income through it need to **protect their ideas** from being copied by others. This is known as protecting the **intellectual property** of a business or individual and it can be done in several ways, depending on what is being protected:

1) A patent is a way of registering and protecting a new invention

- If you have a new invention, you can apply for a **patent** from the **Patent Office** (a government agency that checks that an invention is unique and original enough to be issued a patent). You can get patents for your **product** and the **method** for producing it. No one else can copy it unless you give them a **licence** — and you can **charge** for the licence.
- Patents allow businesses to maintain the **unique features** of their products for as long as the patent lasts. They do not have to worry about **competitors copying** their exact invention.
- The more **general** a patent is the better — if a patent is **very specific** then it is very **easy** for **competitors** to tweak the invention and get around the protection that a patent offers.

2) Trademarks (™) protect logos, slogans, etc.

- If you want to protect your business's **name**, **logo** or **slogan**, you can register it as a **trademark** (™) so that nobody else can use it.
- For example, the McDonald's golden arches logo is the **intellectual property** of McDonald's International Property Company Ltd and it can't be used by any other company. McDonald's promote a certain **brand image** — if the logo was used by other companies, McDonald's **reputation** might be damaged. McDonald's might also lose **profits** if consumers went to another restaurant by mistake because it had the same logo.
- It can be **difficult** to register some slogans as a trademark — especially those that **don't include** the **company's name**. McDonald's were able to trademark the slogan "I'm lovin' it" because of its distinctiveness (they might have been less successful if they'd tried to trademark the phrase "I love it").

3) Copyright gives protection to written work and music

- It's **illegal** to reproduce other people's work without their permission.
- Authors and musicians or their publishers receive **royalties** (payment) every time their work is published or played on the radio.
- Any **original writing, music, video, images** and **photos** are **automatically protected** under UK copyright laws.

Copyright only protects against some things... karate protects against everything.

Practice Questions

Q1 How can a kaizen approach to work lead to innovation?

Q2 Give two advantages of intrapreneurship.

Q3 What is benchmarking?

Q4 What are the advantages of a business applying for patents for its products?

Exam Questions

Q1 Which of these would prevent another business from copying your logo?
A benchmarking B copyright C a patent D a trademark [1 mark]

Q2 Paul Newby wants to innovate the processes of his business by benchmarking against similar firms. Explain the benefits of doing this, as well as some of the problems he might encounter. [9 marks]

Q3 Snack4now is an online retailer that makes and delivers snacks to homes and offices. Analyse the effects that adopting a culture of kaizen and intrapreneurship will have on Snack4now's innovation. [16 marks]

Benchmarking — the defence method favoured by lazy footballers...

Kaizen, intrapreneurship and benchmarking allow businesses to become more innovative without investing loads of money into research and development. Companies need to be careful when they're benchmarking though — certain processes and products will be protected under patent laws so they'll have to ask permission if they want to copy them.

Entering International Markets

Businesses can gain advantages through targeting, operating in and trading with international markets.

International Markets** offer businesses **Growth Opportunities

Moving into international markets is called internationalisation.

1) Businesses can **increase** their market size by **selling existing products** in **new countries** (this is a **market development strategy**, see p.48) — the **bigger the market**, the **more** they're likely to sell and the higher their **revenue** will be. E.g. Tesco have nearly saturated the UK market, but they can still **increase** the size of their market by **targeting other countries**.
2) Businesses can **extend** the **life cycle** of their products by launching them in **new countries** as the product enters **maturity** in its home market. This is common with cars — businesses can sell models that are **old-fashioned** in the UK to **developing countries** like India.
3) Businesses can **reduce costs** by getting their **raw materials** from countries with the **cheapest** prices. Businesses can also buy **components** from **overseas** countries at cheap prices and then put the **final product** together in the UK — this is called **global sourcing**.
4) **Operating** in **developing countries** with **low wage rates** can also reduce costs (e.g. by relocating factories).
5) If the UK economy is in **recession**, businesses can secure revenue by trading in international markets — e.g. by **exporting** to a **growing economy**.

*Many factors affect the **Attractiveness** of **International Markets***

1) Size of the Market

- Countries with **large populations** and **developing markets** (such as China and Brazil) can be attractive prospects for businesses as **markets** will be **bigger** there. However, they also need to consider the **population demographics** when assessing the **size** of the market — e.g. a pharmaceutical company might specifically **target** countries with **ageing populations**.
- The **wealth** of the population will also affect the size of a business's **potential market**. For example, a designer clothing company is more likely to open outlets in Switzerland where wages are **generally high** than in Bangladesh where wages are **generally low**.
- The availability of **technology** can also affect the size of the market — e.g. internet streaming services such as Netflix won't enter countries where the **internet isn't readily available** or **connection speeds are low**.

2) Political and Economic Factors

- Businesses entering **international markets** need to take into account the **laws** in the country they are entering — **employment**, **environmental** and **tax laws** can all affect the **profitability** of a business.
- Businesses also need to consider **political controls on trade** through **tariffs** and **quotas** (see p.27).
- Businesses would prefer to enter a country with a **stable political environment** — if there is **political unrest** in a country, a business might **wait** until the problem is **resolved** before entering the country.
- Fluctuations in **exchange rates** (see p.31) make the cost of international trade **unpredictable**, so it's difficult for businesses to accurately **forecast** revenue and profits.

3) Cultural, Ethical and Environmental Factors

- Businesses will find it **easier** to trade with countries with **similar cultures** and **languages** to the one that they already operate in. It's more difficult to **trade** with countries when there are **language** and **cultural barriers**.
- Cheap labour can make certain countries attractive for businesses, however businesses need to be careful that they are not **exploiting workers** — this is very **unethical**, and can lead to consumers **boycotting** the company if its unethical practices come to light.
- Businesses might take into account the **damage** that their activities might do to the **environment**. Getting **raw materials** from abroad is often **cheaper**, but **transporting** them from one country to another causes lots of **pollution**. **Distributing** finished products to other countries also causes **pollution**.
- Businesses can **exploit** the lack of **environmental restrictions** in other countries to gain **cheap resources**, e.g. through deforestation. However, **ethical companies** will choose a more **sustainable source**.
- Countries that have **fewer restrictions** on the buying and selling of **certain products** can be appealing to some businesses. For example, **weapons manufacturers** can make money by selling **missiles** and other **weapons** abroad, but selling weapons to countries that are seen as a **security threat** is unethical.

Entering International Markets

Methods of **Entering International Markets** have different amounts of **Risk**

Importing and Exporting

- Businesses can easily enter **international markets** by **importing** or **exporting** goods and services. This means **buying from** or **selling to** companies and consumers in **other countries.**
- Businesses **importing** from other countries will benefit from **greater variety** and **cheaper prices.** Businesses **exporting** to other countries will benefit from an **increased market size**.
- However, putting the **infrastructure** in place for **importing** or **exporting** can be **expensive** — these costs will **decrease the value added** unless the **price** of the product is **increased**.

Licensing

- Businesses can also get **foreign firms** to produce their products **under licence** (e.g. another firm makes the product, but the **original company's name** is on the product) — this is known as **licensing**.
- An advantage of this method is that the **business benefits** from the **infrastructure** foreign firms already have in place — they can **make money** without having to do very much work and with a very **low amount of risk.**

Alliances

- Businesses can join forces with similar companies **abroad**, combining **local knowledge** with a product that has already proved **successful** in their own country — this is called an **alliance**.
- Alliances can **spread out** the **costs** and **risks** and help businesses **overcome trade barriers** (see p.64).
- The **main drawback** is that the business **loses some control** over their venture into that country.

Direct Investment

- **Direct investment** is when a business **takes over** or **merges** with a business in a **different country**.
- The **main benefit** of this is that it allows the business to **enter markets quickly** and already have an **instant share of the market**. The business doesn't need to invest in establishing its **name** and **reputation** in the new country.
- Direct investment can also **reduce the risk of failure** — the business benefits from the **knowledge** and **experience** of the **local market** and **culture** provided by the business it joins with.

Entering International Markets can **Impact** all areas of the business

Internationalisation can affect the decisions and activities of **different departments** within the business.

1) HR may start recruiting people who can **speak multiple languages** so they can **communicate more effectively** within the **business** and with their **customers** — they might also have to help current employees **relocate** abroad.
2) The finance department will have to put methods in place for dealing with **fluctuating exchange rates** as goods are bought and sold in **different currencies**.
3) Marketing may have to split into separate **international** and **national departments** as products will be **priced** and **promoted differently** depending on the country they are being marketed in.

Practice Questions

Q1 Give five reasons why a business might enter an international market.

Q2 What political and economic factors could affect a business's decision to expand into a country?

Q3 Give four methods of entering international markets.

Q4 What effect could entering a new international market have on the marketing department of a business?

Exam Questions

Q1 Analyse the external factors affecting a mobile phone operator starting to enter African markets. [9 marks]

Q2 The Golden Spud Company is a fast-food restaurant, specialising in jacket potatoes, based in the UK. Evaluate the different methods they could use to enter the French market. [20 marks]

If only you could form an alliance before entering your exam...

You'll need to learn the reasons and methods for businesses entering international markets. Then it's the same old story of learning the factors affecting their strategy and thinking about the knock-on effects to functional areas of the business.

Locating Abroad

Firms can locate some or all of their business abroad in order to gain advantages when trading or producing goods.

Producing Abroad *can be a way of* ***Cutting Costs*** *or* ***Increasing Revenue***

1) Locating abroad can reduce costs

- One of the main reasons why companies choose to move **production** overseas is that they can often pay **foreign workers** much **lower wages** than they would have to pay their UK employees. Some companies have been accused of not paying foreign workers enough to live on — this is **unethical**.
- The cost of **land** and **office space** also tends to be **cheaper** overseas, especially in emerging markets. **Utilities** like water and electricity might also be cheaper abroad.

2) Locating abroad is a way of targeting new international markets

- Locating a firm close to the overseas market makes it easier to spot **local market trends**.
- The company is able to absorb more **local knowledge**, which means it's less likely to make **expensive marketing errors** and it might even spot new market **niches**.
- Locating close to a **new international market** will also make **distribution** of products to the market **easier** and **decrease** the company's **distribution costs** to that market.

3) Locating abroad helps companies avoid trade barriers

- Some countries create **trade barriers** in order to **protect** domestic companies from **foreign competition**. These barriers might be things like **taxes** or **restrictions** on sales of goods from abroad.
- Locating part of a business **within** a country with trade barriers helps companies **get round** these penalties.
- Trade barriers can protect **domestic** industries from international competition, causing them to become **inefficient**. This could mean that a **foreign** company that locates in a country with trade barriers will have a **competitive advantage**, because it's likely to be more efficient.

4) Locating abroad has been made easier by improved transport and communication links

- The **price** and **availability** of **air travel** means it's **easy** for people to **travel** between overseas locations.
- Trading overseas has also been made easier because countries with **emerging markets** are **investing** heavily in **infrastructure**. This means that they have better **road and rail networks** and **ports** than they had in the past.
- Doing business overseas has also been made easier by **technological** developments. Businesses can communicate internationally by **email** and **video-conferencing** — so people don't have to leave the UK.

Offshoring *means* ***Moving*** *parts of a business to* ***Cheaper Countries***

1) Many businesses locate some of their **departments**, such as their call centres or payment processing departments, **overseas** — this is called **offshoring**.
2) The countries that firms move to most often are **China**, **India**, **Malaysia**, **Mexico** and **Indonesia** — these countries all offer much **cheaper labour** than the UK.
3) Although offshoring is a good way to **cut costs**, it's not always good for a company's **image**. The **media** and **trade unions** often criticise companies for **UK job losses** caused by offshoring.

Staff loved the new off-shore department.

Re-shoring is when a business moves departments back to its country of origin

- Some businesses are **moving departments back** to the UK in reaction to changing **customer attitudes**.
- Customers are **more aware** of a business's overseas activities than they used to be — businesses that are seen to **treat overseas staff poorly** will get a **bad reputation** and face a **backlash** from their customers.
- Re-shoring allows a business to **improve the quality** of its products and processes as **manufacturing** is easier to **monitor** and **control** if everything is made in the same country.
- Re-shoring also means that **distribution** to the home market is **cheaper** and **more efficient** as products don't have to be shipped all over the world — businesses can offer a **better delivery service** to their customers.
- Sometimes the **low wages** of overseas labour are still **too appealing** for companies — however, as the **wage gap** between UK workers and oversees workers **decreases**, more and more companies will begin to **re-shore**.

Locating Abroad

Certain countries can offer **Benefits** to **Specific Departments**

1) As a result of offshoring, some countries have become **specialised** in providing certain skills or services.
2) Countries that **specialise** in particular areas will attract lots of business from **overseas companies**. This creates a **competitive environment** in that country which can lead to even **cheaper prices** and **better services** being offered.

- **India** specialises in **communications** (e.g. call centres) and **IT services**, so they can offer competitive **prices** and a pool of suitably **trained workers**. Businesses might choose to take advantage of this by moving their **customer service department** to India.
- **China** and **Brazil** have lots of **cheap** and **skilled labour** — some businesses have moved their **manufacturing departments** to these countries to take advantage of this. Their products are made for relatively **low labour costs** but often to quite a **low standard** as they focus on volume rather than quality.
- **China** also attracts lots of **Research & Development** departments as they relocate to be closer to the manufacturing department and to take advantage of the **skilled low-cost labour** and **infrastructure**.
- The **Philippines** has a lot of **young university graduates** with very **strong work ethics** and very good **digital communication infrastructure**. Some businesses have begun moving their **IT departments** to the Philippines to benefit from the **people** and **technology** that they already have in place.

3) Countries that offer specialised services do run into **problems**. Workers may lose **motivation** as the majority of **available jobs** are in the **same industry**, or the size of the industry may lead to **diseconomies of scale**. There's also a risk that **another country** will find a way of providing the skills or service even **more efficiently**.

Locating Abroad has **Non-Financial Benefits** and **Costs** to a business

1) **Non-financial benefits** and **costs** are the **positive** and **negative impacts** a business has on the **outside world**. These benefits and costs don't have a **direct impact** on the business's **profits** but they can affect its **reputation**.
2) Before making any **decisions** about locating abroad, businesses need to consider the **impact** that they are going to have on the country they are **moving into**.
3) The non-financial benefits of locating abroad are that the company will create **new jobs** in that country, which can increase people's **income** and **standard of living**. Companies also **invest** in the host country by paying for factories, roads, etc. to be built, and by paying **taxes** to the local government.
4) However there are **non-financial costs** of locating abroad too — it will lead to a **loss of jobs** and **investment** in the original country. It can also have negative impacts on the country they're moving into — **overseas workers** can be **exploited** if they aren't protected by **employment laws** and there may be a **rise in pollution**.
5) Although it can be difficult to put an **exact financial value** on these costs and benefits, companies should still **weigh up** the impact that these issues have on their **reputation** before making any decisions.

Practice Questions

Q1 Describe four advantages of locating abroad.

Q2 Explain the terms 'offshoring' and 're-shoring'.

Q3 Give two advantages of offshoring your IT department to a country that specialises in IT services.

Q4 Outline the non-financial costs of relocating a business abroad on the country you're leaving.

Exam Questions

Q1 Ulverston Broadband Co. have a call centre based in India.
Analyse the reasons why they might choose to re-shore their call centre back to the UK. [9 marks]

Q2 Flimby Gadgets Ltd manufactures innovative digital gadgets and plans to relocate its manufacturing department to Brazil. Analyse the benefits and drawbacks of doing this. [16 marks]

Offshoring communication — sending messages in bottles...

I don't think it's that difficult to understand why companies might like to locate abroad. After all, who wouldn't rather stare out of the window at a sunny beach rather than at a rainy, grey town centre? Make sure you know the benefits that re-shoring can bring too — have you ever tried to get your hands on a decent pork pie or scotch egg in Brazil?

Multinationals

Multinationals are businesses that are based in more than one country. A bit like those annoying celebrities who have holiday homes in various exotic locations. Multinationals aren't quite as glamorous though I'm afraid.

Multinationals are located in *More Than One Country*

1) A **multinational company** is a business that has **branches** or **departments** in more than one country. Its **head office** will be based in **one country** and it will coordinate its **global activities** from there. It will also have **offices** or **factories** in **other countries** that offer services or produce goods.
2) Multinationals are able to utilise the **different locations** of their factories in order to **produce goods** in the most **cost-effective way** — this has increased the overall level of **international trade**.
3) Some of the largest multinationals now have **annual turnovers larger** than the **GDP** (gross domestic product — see p.28) of some countries. This means these businesses have a lot of **economic power**.

Multinationals can *Benefit Developing Countries...*

1) Multinationals **increase employment opportunities** for the populations of countries where they're based.
2) Multinationals **increase** the local **standard of living**. Although they get paid less than workers in developed countries, the employees of multinationals in developing countries often receive **better pay and conditions** than employees of **local companies** in the developing country.
3) **Inward investment** into the host country increases because multinationals **spend money** on building the **factories** and **infrastructure** (roads, etc.) that they need. This is called **foreign direct investment** (FDI).
4) Multinationals cause **economic growth** for each country they expand into. The GDP of the host country increases as a result of **additional spending** in the economy on things like **increased travel** into the area and **demand for hotel rooms** from visiting businesspeople.
5) Multinationals locating in developing countries will **pay taxes** to the **local government**. This results in increased **government income**, which might be spent on projects such as **schools** and **hospitals**. Payments by multinationals to local governments might include:
   - taxes on the **purchase of land**,
   - taxes on the **wages** of local employees,
   - taxes on **profits** they make,
   - taxes on products **exported** abroad.
6) **Ethical multinationals** try to benefit the countries they locate in by paying **fair wages** rather than exploiting workers — see below. This **increases costs**, but if businesses highlight the fact that they trade ethically then consumers may be willing to pay slightly higher prices for their products.

... but they can also Exploit Developing Countries

1) Some multinational businesses may **exploit developing countries** in order to **maximise** their **profits**.
2) Some multinationals base their production in countries with **low wages** to **reduce** their **costs**. They might set up **sweatshops** — factories where employees work long hours in difficult and sometimes dangerous conditions for minimal payment.
3) A multinational might locate in a country with **less strict employment laws** in order to reduce costs by employing **child labour**, making employees work **long shifts**, or not providing the correct **safety equipment**.
4) Multinationals sometimes sell **products** which **don't** quite **meet** EU or American **safety standards** to developing countries.
5) A multinational might extract large quantities of **unsustainable natural resources**, i.e. oil, gas or minerals. It might also fail to redevelop the landscape when there's no more to extract. In a developed country a company would be required to **minimise** its **environmental impact**, but in some developing countries, **environmental laws** are **less strict**, and multinationals might take advantage of this.
6) The **governments** of developing countries might **overlook unlawful behaviour** by multinational businesses because they **rely** on the **tax income** they generate, so they won't want the business to relocate away from their country.
7) Many multinational companies are increasingly committed to **Corporate Social Responsibility** (see p.37), so **exploitation** is **less common** than it used to be.

Confusing 'sweatshop' and 'sweetshop' when you're looking for a job could have disastrous consequences.

Multinationals

Multinationals also locate in *Developed Countries*

1) Developed countries often have **stable** and **growing economies** — this can be attractive for a multinational as there will be plenty of **potential customers** to sell their products to.
2) Instead of just **selling their products** in a developed country, multinationals often **set up factories** in them — this can help them to keep their **distribution costs low**.
3) **Producing** goods in the country where they're sold also helps companies to **avoid** some **taxes**.
4) Many global multinationals have **factories** and **distribution centres** in at least one country that is a member of the European Union (EU). This allows them to **sell** their products to all EU countries without having to pay **import tax**. For example, Toyota and Honda (both Japanese car manufacturers) have **factories** in the UK for **distribution** within the EU.

Multinationals are subject to Political, Economic and Legal Restraints

1) As multinational corporations operate in **many different countries**, each with its own **laws**, governments sometimes **coordinate** their approaches to **control** and **manage** the activities of multinationals.
2) The **European Union** has tried to **standardise employment laws** such as equal opportunities and health and safety standards to ensure that multinational corporations within the EU have to meet **minimum standards** wherever they locate. This is known as **harmonisation**.
3) Governments sometimes use **protectionist policies** like **tariffs** and **quotas** to protect their own economies (see p.27).
4) **Pressure groups** sometimes try to **influence government policy** on multinational organisations. They try to persuade governments to put **tighter controls** on how multinationals from one country operate in **other countries** (e.g. to stop multinationals from using child labour in foreign countries).
5) **Transfer pricing** is when a multinational business buys and sells products between parts of the company based in **different countries** — it can make it very difficult for governments to **control** the **taxes** a multinational pays. Transfer pricing can be used to make all the **profits** appear to belong in a country with very **low tax rates**, which **reduces** the amount of **tax** a multinational pays. However, this might **conflict** with any **Corporate Social Responsibility** (CSR) code the business has.

Not that kind of legal restraint...

Practice Questions

Q1 What is a multinational?

Q2 Give two possible benefits to the country that a multinational expands into.

Q3 State three ways in which multinationals might exploit developing countries.

Q4 Give two reasons why a multinational would locate in a developed country.

Q5 How can governments manage the activities of multinationals?

Exam Questions

Q1 Analyse the extent to which governments can control multinationals. [9 marks]

Q2 To what extent do you agree with the statement "multinationals locate their manufacturing plants in developing countries in order to increase employment levels and provide economic support for the countries through payment of taxes"? [16 marks]

Mini skirt, turtleneck, straw hat and sandals — I'm a bit of a multifashionable...

You've probably noticed that most location decisions for multinationals are based on one thing — money. You need to learn why companies locate parts of their business in developed or developing countries (it often comes down to saving money one way or another). You should also understand the benefits and drawbacks for the developing countries.

International Business Strategies

There are different strategies for managing international businesses. The choice of strategy will depend on how important it is for the business to reduce its costs and be able to adapt to the local market.

Multinationals** can be difficult to **Manage Effectively

This year's grand multinational was off to a chaotic start.

1) The **management strategies** needed to run a **multinational** are very **different** from those needed to run a **domestic business.**
2) Multinationals are very **complex** — different parts of the business are subject to the **laws**, **culture**, **economy** and **markets** of the country they operate in.
3) For example, if a multinational only operates in countries with **similar laws**, **cultures** and **market conditions** it may be able to take a **centralised** approach to management. However, a multinational that operates across countries with very **different laws**, **cultures** and **market conditions** may have to take a **decentralised** approach to management.

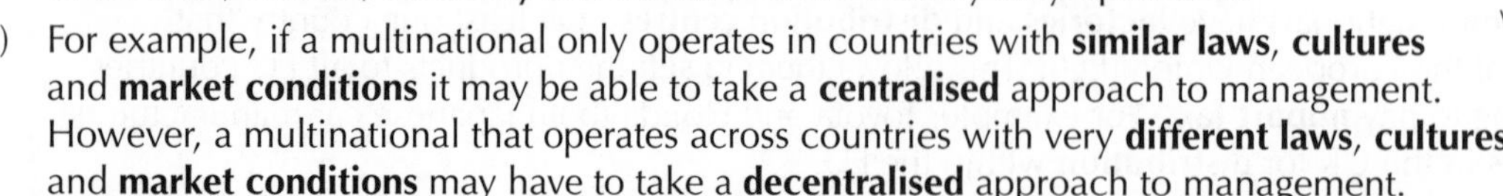

4) **Bartlett and Ghoshal** proposed that a multinational could adopt one of **four different strategies** for management, depending on the nature of the business and the needs of its markets.

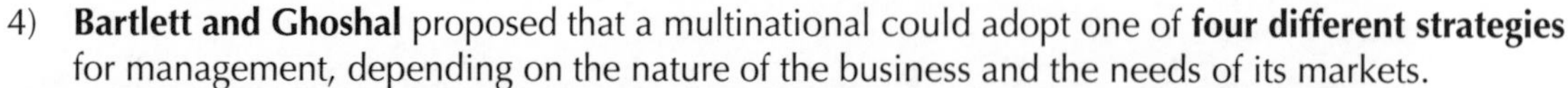

Bartlett** and **Ghoshal's International Business Strategies

The **four international business strategies** outlined by Bartlett and Ghoshal are shown on the grid below. The level of pressure for **local responsiveness** (e.g. adapting products for different locations) and the level of pressure to **reduce costs** through **global coordination** can be used to help a business **decide on a strategy**.

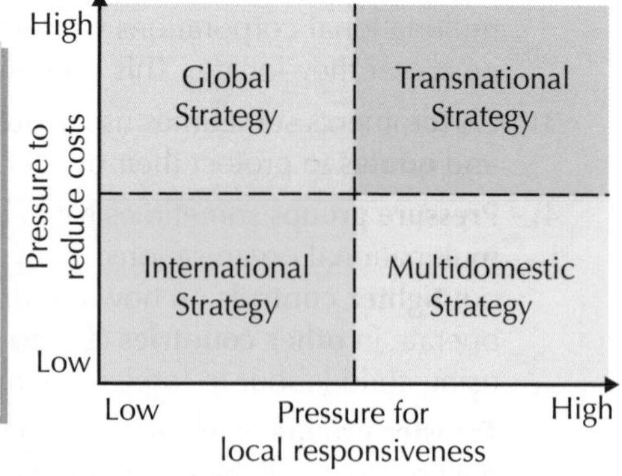

International Strategy

- If the **demands of markets** in other countries are **similar** to the demands of the home market, the pressure for local responsiveness is **low**. If pressure to **reduce costs** through global coordination is also **low**, then an **international strategy** is adopted.
- The business structure will remain very **centralised** with most of the **research**, **big decisions** and **development** being carried out at **head office**. These decisions can then be implemented in the parts of the business that are **located abroad**.

Multidomestic Strategy

- When the demands of the **different markets** are **very different** and there is **little pressure** to reduce costs through global coordination, a **multidomestic strategy** should be implemented.
- The business structure becomes **decentralised** and the business operates as if it were lots of **independent companies** each running itself. Most **decisions** are made **locally** to meet the **local needs**.
- **Different branches** of the business will **look** and **work differently** — products will be **adapted** and **promoted** to suit the **local markets**, and **knowledge won't be shared** between the separate branches.

Global Strategy

- A **global strategy** is used when the demands of the different markets are similar and global coordination of the business could **reduce its costs significantly**.
- The business structure will be **centralised** and it will **coordinate operations** across countries to take full advantage of **economies of scale**.
- Products will remain **standardised** and innovation and development will take place at a **central location**, with **knowledge** and **resources** being passed on to the **different branches**. A business may decide to only sell **specific products** in certain countries rather than its **full range**.

Transnational Strategy

- When pressure to reduce costs and meet local needs are **both high**, a **transnational strategy** is best.
- The focus of a transnational strategy is on **developing knowledge** and **ideas locally** and **sharing them globally** in order to benefit the **whole business**.
- The business structure will be a balance between centralisation and decentralisation, where the **responsibilities** passed down to each branch of the business are based on its **experience** and **capabilities**.

International Business Strategies

Management of Different Functions becomes more *Complex*

When a company becomes a multinational, its functional areas will need to change. This may result in them being **spread** across **different locations**, **increasing in size** or just adapting to **new challenges** facing the business.

FINANCE

1) If **finance** remains based at a **central location** then staff will have to adapt to work with **different currencies** and ensure that the different **branches** of the company have a **healthy cash flow**.
2) Trade laws **limit** the **amount of money** that multinationals can **take out** of a country's **economy** — finance will need to **comply** with the **trade laws** of the different countries.
3) They also need to know and understand the **tax laws** in different countries so that they can provide **detailed analysis** of **expansion opportunities** and point out any **risks** of planned expansions.
4) Due to the **complexity** of multinationals, **financial functions** might be spread across different locations. For example, the financial functions that apply to the **whole business** (e.g. making budgets, managing debts and managing assets) might be done at a **central location**, while **functions** that are specific to **certain branches** (e.g. purchasing and day-to-day cash flow) might be done at the **different branches**.

MARKETING

1) If products have been **adapted** to **meet the needs** of **local markets**, marketing will need to have different **campaigns** and **strategies** to **promote** the different products.
2) If products are **standardised**, then marketing may still need to adapt their **promotional message** to appeal to the different markets. E.g. in developed countries they might highlight the **ethical nature** of the product, whereas in **developing countries** they might emphasis the **functionality** of the product.
3) Depending on the **type of product** that a company sells, marketing campaigns may need to be adapted to take into account the different **advertisement laws** in a country.

OPERATIONS

1) If the business is producing **standardised global products**, the different **manufacturing facilities** will need to be **coordinated** — they will all need to work in the **same way** using the **same materials** and **machinery** in order to make products that are all up to a **consistent standard**.
2) If the products are being **adapted** for the different **local markets** then it's **less important** that the **manufacturing** facilities are **coordinated** — it's more important that each one runs **efficiently**, even if that means **independent facilities** using **different processes**.

IT

1) **IT functions** will often be carried out at **each branch** of the business in order to manage the **day-to-day** IT problems that are specific to that branch's **machines** and **IT systems**.
2) If the business is trying to adapt to **local markets**, **IT** might need to create, manage and update **several different websites** which may result in the department **expanding**.

Along with the difficulties faced within **each functional area**, multinationals will also face **culture clashes** and **language barriers** across the whole business. This will be a bigger problem if the business structure is **centralised** as they will need to think about how **decisions** will **affect** and **be communicated** to all the branches of the business.

Practice Questions

Q1 Why are multinationals harder to manage than domestic businesses?

Q2 According to Bartlett and Ghoshal when should businesses use an international strategy?

Q3 Explain the difference between a global strategy and a transnational strategy.

Q4 How might a company's marketing department be affected by the choice of international business strategy?

Exam Questions

Q1 A multinational cardboard box manufacturer operates in 28 different countries. Evaluate the four different strategies suggested by Bartlett and Ghoshal and suggest which one is best for this company. [16 marks]

Q2 Analyse the effects that a transnational strategy will have on the functional areas of a business. [9 marks]

Cooking and hoovering — yet another example of a multidomestic strategy...

Multinationals can be managed in a variety of ways — make sure you know the difference between international, multidomestic, global and transnational strategies. You'll also need to learn when businesses should use each strategy.

Use of Digital Technology

Digital technology is changing all the time and it is up to businesses to change with it. If businesses don't embrace digital technology, they risk missing out on great opportunities to grow their business.

Businesses face Pressure to Update their Digital Technology

1) New digital technology is constantly being **developed** and businesses must decide which developments will provide them with the **greatest return on investment** and which will have the **greatest impact**.
2) If businesses make the **correct decisions** and adopt the **right technology** at the **right time**, they can **grow rapidly** and gain the **upper hand** on competitors.
3) However, if businesses make the **wrong decisions** or they are **too late** to take up new technology they may **lose ground** to their competitors and might never be able to gain that **market share** back.

Digital Technology can lead to Innovative New Products

1) The research and development department can incorporate **up-to-date digital technology** in new products — these **innovative products** have a chance to revolutionise the market and make the business a lot of money.
2) Digital technology can offer **small upgrades** to existing products to keep the business ahead of its competitors. For example, smartphones are always being **upgraded** to offer better cameras, more powerful processors and a wider variety of features — these small upgrades allow the business to **retain its market share**.
3) The internet allows businesses to **monitor updates** to digital technology on a **global scale**. E.g. an R&D department in the UK might see an invention in Japan and find a way of incorporating it in their own product.

Disadvantages of Digital Technology for Innovation

- It is often **very expensive** to develop new products that are based on **new digital technology** — if these products never make it to market then the business has **wasted a lot of money**.
- New technology hasn't always been **fully tested**, so if a business chooses to use it in their product they are running the risk of their product having **lots of bugs** and **not working properly**.
- Problems with digital technology can be **difficult to diagnose**, customers can get **frustrated** with a company if they can't get products to work properly.
- Businesses run the risk of the new technology not catching on. E.g. Sony® brought out their first **MiniDisc player** in 1992 but it was **too expensive** and never really sold very well.

Digital Technology can make the Production Process more Efficient

1) New technology can lead to changes in the way that **products are made** — this can result in positive changes, e.g. **better quality products**, **increased capacity** and **increased efficiency**.
2) Businesses need to **weigh up** whether the expense of implementing new digital technology in the **production process** is actually going to be **profitable** in the **long-term**.
3) It can take a **long time** to apply new technology to the process — by the time you've implemented it and got the process **running efficiently** again, there may be **better technology** available.
4) To use new technology efficiently, staff often require some **specialised skills** — they will need to be **retrained** so that they have the skills required to interact with the new technology. This means that efficiency will fall until staff are properly **up to speed** with the **new processes**.
5) If a business introduces **too much** new technology to their production process, staff will become **overwhelmed** and **resistant** to the **changes**.

Examples of Digital Technology in Production

- The introduction of **3D printing** means that businesses are able to produce **prototypes** of their new products **quickly** and **cheaply** — it's also much easier to tweak aspects of the product than it was previously.
- Developments in software have made it easier to keep track of **inventory** and **deliveries** from suppliers, which allows the production process to run much more smoothly and efficiently.
- The introduction of **more machines** has resulted in business shifting away from **labour-intensive production**. This saves the business a lot of money in **wages** but can have a **negative impact** on the **company's reputation** and the **workers' morale**.

Use of Digital Technology

Digital Technology has given businesses New Opportunities

1) **Improvements** in digital technology have allowed businesses to gather **big data**. Big data describes the vast quantities of data businesses can collect from a range of sources, e.g. **social media**, **loyalty cards**, **etc**. Some companies **buy** big data from other businesses.
2) Big data can then be **analysed** using computers and specially designed **digital software** to spot correlations and trends — this analytical process is know as **data mining**.
3) Data mining can make sense of big data and supply **useful information** on **customers** and **competitors** to the **functional areas** of the business. For example, the R&D department can use this information to develop new products, the marketing department can use it to inform decisions about the marketing mix and the finance department can use the information when making cash-flow forecasts.

E-commerce provides lots of new opportunities for businesses

1) Improvements in digital technology have resulted in **e-commerce** becoming the primary way for some businesses to **trade goods and services**. This means that businesses don't need to invest as much money in **stores** as they can reach a much **bigger customer base** through a **website**.
2) The growth of e-commerce has given businesses **greater access** to **international markets** — businesses can translate their website into **different languages** and offer **worldwide delivery** in order to expand their markets.
3) **Manufacturers** can use their **own website** or **online market places** to sell **directly to consumers** rather than selling through an **agent** or **retailer** — this allows them to keep **all** of the **revenue** for themselves.
4) Companies such as amazon® **keep track** of the **online order history** of their customers. This allows them to **make personal recommendations** to customers that they know will be interested.
5) Business are able to **interact more directly** with their customers through **social media**. This means that businesses can regularly update customers about **improvements** to their goods and services.
6) Businesses are able to deal with **customer complaints** more **efficiently** by switching from **telephone services** to **live online assistance** — this means that **a customer service assistant** can deal with **many customers** at once.
7) However, customers also have access to this technology — they are able to look up **reviews** of a **product** and find **prices** of **similar products** within seconds. This means that the **products** and **prices** a business offers have to be **genuinely competitive**. E.g. they can't gain an advantage by being the only DIY shop in town.

Enterprise Resource Planning (ERP) can benefit every department

1) Enterprise Resource Planning is **business management software** that allows a business to **monitor activities** in **every department** through the **collection** and **interpretation** of data.
2) It can help the **HR department** to track the **work rates** of staff to see who needs **extra training** or when **productivity drops** — e.g. in a supermarket, managers can monitor the scan speed of their checkout operators.
3) The **finance department** might use data from previous infrastructure changes to budget for upcoming changes.
4) It helps the **marketing department** to keep track of how well their promotional products are selling and to **compare sales** before and after **promotion**.
5) It can be used to track **stock levels**, **distribution networks** and **productivity** in order to see how well the **operations department** is functioning and if any improvements are needed.

Practice Questions

Q1 Give two disadvantages of using brand new technology in new products.

Q2 Give two examples of how the production department of a business can use new technology to improve efficiency.

Q3 What is data mining?

Q4 How can ERP benefit the functional areas of a business?

Exam Question

Q1 Analyse the advantages and disadvantages of using digital technology to advertise and sell products. [9 marks]

Digital technology has more uses than annoying celebrities on Twitter...

You need to understand the value of digital technology to a business and know how all departments can benefit from adopting and updating their technology. You should also consider the risks to departments of too much technology.

Causes of Change

Businesses need to keep an eye out for change and the things that cause it. Doing this helps them to act before they end up in trouble, or allows them to adapt various aspects of the business to make the change work to their advantage.

Change can be caused by Internal and External Factors

When the business environment changes, managers must **change** the way the business is run to suit the new **circumstances**. They might change **staffing levels**, **location** and **product range** or they might start **spending** more on **research and development**, staff **training** and **new machinery**. There are **internal factors** (within the business) and **external factors** (outside the business) that cause firms to make changes:

Internal Factors

- A change in **leadership/management** often leads to further changes. If the director of a company leaves or is replaced, the new director may have different ideas about how the business should be run, which could lead to changes in the **organisational culture** or **structure** of the business.
- **Better than expected performance** could lead to a decision to expand the business, in order to take advantage of the increased profits. **Poor financial performance** may lead to changes such as **retrenchment** (see p.53), i.e. cutting down or reorganising in order to save money.
- If there are **changes** to the **staff**, it could mean that the business no longer has the required **skills** and further changes need to be made. The company might go through **recruitment** or **retraining**, or **outsource** their work.
- **Business growth** can lead to other changes. For example, a business expanding into **international markets** may have to adapt its **product range** to match the needs of customers in other countries.
- The **type** of business can influence the amount of change. For example, if a business is **innovative**, it may keep coming up with **better methods** of doing things, so the business may **continually change** to use these new methods. More **traditional companies** might prefer to stick to the old, **tried** and **tested methods**.

External Factors

- The availability of **new technology** can cause change. Businesses might change their production methods if new technology means production can be **faster** or **cheaper**. New technology can also lead to **shorter product life cycles** — companies have to **change** and **update** their products **frequently** if they want to **stay ahead** of the competition.
- If consumer **tastes** change, the business might need to alter its **product range** to fit in with changing demand.
- If the **economy slows**, people will have **less disposable income**, so product prices may need **reducing**.
- Changes in the **law** can affect the way businesses are run — e.g. government restrictions on pollution may force businesses to alter their **methods of production** or change to a **local supplier**.
- Changes in the **ethical views** and **social awareness** of customers may result in companies purchasing ethically sourced products from fair trade suppliers.
- Changes in **competition** can result in a business losing a lot of its **market share** for particular products — they may need to act to **regain** their market share or **prevent** further losses.

Changes are Vital for a Thriving Business

1) Although change can **create uncertainty** amongst employees and can be **disruptive** to a business, it is **necessary** if the business wants to **grow** and **stay competitive**.
2) Making changes within a business can allow it to take advantage of **new**, **effective** ideas, possibly saving **time** and **money** in the process.
3) People within the business will naturally **resist** change (see p.76) — however, the **advantage** a business gains from implementing a change will often **outweigh** the **disruption caused**.
4) Businesses may be **forced** to change in order to **survive** in a ever-changing market. The **rate** at which technology advances is **speeding up**, so change becomes more and more **essential**. For example, in the car manufacturing industry it is necessary for businesses to be **constantly developing** up-to-date technology for their cars.
5) Without change, a company may **fall behind** its competitors, which could eventually lead to **insolvency** (see p.12).

Graeme was resistant to change — it was the 1992 FA cup final for the tenth night running.

Causes of Change

Change can be Incremental, Disruptive or somewhere In Between

Incremental change is gradual

It's usually the result of a **strategic plan** being put in place, and often attempts to minimise disruption. Managers decide a **timescale** for the necessary changes and then **timetable strategies** for achieving them (e.g. training, closures, product development, promotional activities and all that sort of thing).

Disruptive change is sudden

Disruptive change forces firms to suddenly do things in a different way to usual. They may have to **close or sell off subsidiary companies**, spend heavily on **promotions** to raise customer confidence or **totally restructure** the way the firm's organised.

When you think of disruptive change, you usually think of a **negative event** that makes customers suddenly go elsewhere. However, it's also possible for **customer demand** to **increase** and force the company to expand even though it wasn't planning to.

For example, Coca-Cola® had to change their US recipe after the colouring used was linked to cancer in rodents.

Changes in the **law** can be **incremental** or **disruptive**. Sometimes, the government gives **plenty of notice** that they're going to change the law, so that businesses can **plan ahead** and put a strategy in place. Sometimes governments change the law **suddenly**, e.g. in response to a health scare.

Force Field Analysis is used to analyse Forces For and Against Change

1) **Kurt Lewin** developed a concept called **Force Field Analysis** to help understand **change** in different situations.
2) A **diagram** is drawn (see right) to show the **plan**, the forces **supporting** the plan, and the forces **opposing** the plan.
3) After the forces are written down they are **numbered** to show how significant they are, from 1 (least) to 5 (most).
4) The numbers are added up to show the **total force** for and against the plan.
5) The **analysis** can be used to help decide whether the plan should **go ahead**. Alternatively, it can help managers work out how forces could be **strengthened** or **weakened**.

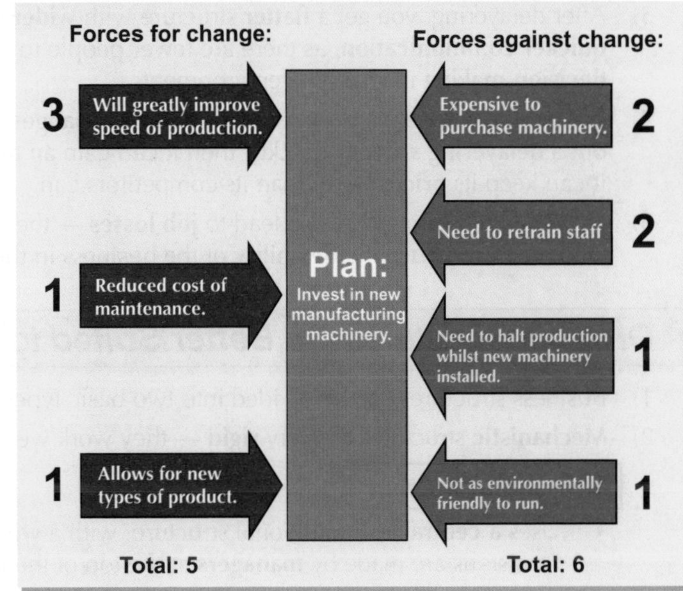

Practice Questions

Q1 Give two examples of internal and external causes of change.

Q2 Give an example of a disruptive change.

Q3 Draw an example force field analysis diagram for a hotel that wishes to build an extension with 20 new rooms.

Exam Question

Q1 A food and soft-drink manufacturer has been growing over time to become one of the UK's leading food and drink producers. To what extent is it inevitable that the business will need to make changes as time goes on? [25 marks]

Accidentally getting your hair dyed green, a classic disruptive change...

Change is a fact of life, and a fact of business too. In general, people prefer stability — change is stressful, and the bigger the change, the more stressful it is. Without change though, things start going to pot — the business could become unprofitable, get into trouble with the law or lose out to competitors. It may never be able to recover.

Managing Change

Change management isn't about the guys who sit in those little money booths in the arcade — it's all about how businesses can adapt to external and internal change. As you'll see, it's important for businesses to be flexible.

Flexible Businesses are able to Restructure frequently

You will have learnt about organisational design in Year 1.

1) Changing the **organisational structure** of a business is known as **restructuring**.
2) Businesses that are able to restructure **quickly** and **efficiently** can adapt their structure in order to keep up with changes in the **external environment** or to implement **new strategy**.
3) The main reason for restructuring is to **maximise** the **efficiency** of **decision-making**, **communication** and **division of tasks** in the business's current situation. Restructuring can also **reduce costs**, which makes the business **more competitive**.
4) Businesses might **decentralise** in **fast-changing environments** to give more **power** and **flexibility** to different departments or sites. E.g. in fashion chains, each **store manager** (rather than head office) might be allowed to choose the stock for their store, because they know what **fashions** the customers in their particular store are likely to be interested in.
5) Having a **flexible organisational structure** is also important in times of **hardship**, e.g. during a recession. Business may need to **quickly** switch to a **centralised structure** as even **small decisions** can become very important to the **success** of the business.

The staff were really embracing the concept of a flexible organisation.

Delayering improves Communication and reduces Costs

1) Delayering means **removing** parts of an organisation's hierarchy — usually a layer of middle-managers.
2) Businesses with flexible structures are able to delayer in order to **reduce** their **costs**, improve **communication** and give **more responsibility** to employees at lower levels of the hierarchy.
3) After delayering, you get a **flatter** structure with **wider** spans of control. Flatter structures usually have **quicker communication**, as there are fewer people to pass messages through. This can help with **decision-making** in **changing** environments.
4) Delayering can help a business to **respond to changes**, such as **difficult economic conditions**. If it can carry out a **delayering strategy** quickly, then it can gain an **advantage** over its **competitors** — by **cutting costs**, it can keep its **prices** lower than its competitors can.
5) However delayering can also lead to **job losses** — the business risks losing some vital **skills** and **experiences**, which could **reduce** the **flexibility** of the business in the future.

Organic Structures are Better Suited to Change than Mechanistic ones

1) Business structures can be divided into two basic types — **mechanistic** and **organic**.
2) **Mechanistic** structures are very **rigid** — they work well for businesses operating in a **stable** environment.

Mechanistic Structure

- Uses a **centralised**, traditional structure, with a well defined hierarchy of power. Decisions are made by **managers** at the top of the hierarchy.
- Uses a **tall structure**, so messages can take a **long time** to travel through the business.
- Suited to businesses that don't need to adapt to change very often. Departments are given tasks which don't vary much so it's easy to assign **resources** efficiently, but it can be **slow** to make **changes** within the business.
- Employees are **specialised** in certain tasks and tend to **work separately** on them. For example, each marketing employee may focus on a **specific market** rather than all of them looking at the whole market.

3) When **flexibility** is **important** to a business they may choose to have an **organic** structure.

Organic Structure

- Uses a **decentralised structure**, meaning employees get more say in **decision-making**.
- Uses a **flat structure**, which allows **fast communication** throughout the business.
- Best suited to an uncertain, **changing environment** as information can be acted upon **quickly**.
- Employees in an organic structure usually **work in teams** to complete tasks, rather than each person having a **strict single role**. These teams can be adapted to suit the situation.

Managing Change

Knowledge and *Information Management* Increases *Flexibility*

1) **Knowledge** and **information management** refers to the **collection**, **organisation**, **distribution** and **application** of knowledge and information within a business.
2) Knowledge can be any **data** gathered by the business, as well as **procedures**, **workers' skills** and **individuals' expertise**. Knowledge can be stored and organised in **specifically designed databases** that allow anyone using them to quickly **sort** and **find** the information that they require.

The most useful data is directly **relevant**, **correct**, **up-to-date** and **easy to analyse.**

3) Businesses should try to get employees to **record** any **specialised knowledge** they have so that if **someone leaves**, the business will still be able to use the **knowledge** gathered from that **employee**.
4) A business can **improve** its **internal communications** by implementing **procedures** to collect and distribute knowledge effectively. For example, if staff share '**lessons learned**' at the end of a project, it allows others to **learn** about the difficulties faced, which should help them **avoid** the **same problems** in the future. A business may also try to **improve communications** within and between **sites** and **departments**, so that staff can contact individuals who have the required expertise **easily**.
5) Having a **wide range** of knowledge and information **easily accessible** by everyone in the business helps a business to be **flexible** and to **respond to change**. If people have information to hand, they can **quickly assess** the current position of the business and **decide** what action to take. It also makes it easier for staff to **change roles** and learn their new responsibilities quickly.
6) Data needs to be **maintained** and **updated** to make sure the most up-to-date information is accessible — large businesses will need to **employ people** just to deal with the day-to-day **management** of information.

Flexible Employment Contracts help a business to *Manage Change*

1) Flexible employment contracts allow businesses to be more **flexible** themselves — so the business is more effective at **managing change**. For example, if a business has a lot of employees on **zero-hours contracts** it can easily cope with increases and decreases in demand.
2) A flexible workforce can be achieved through employing a mixture of **core workers** and **peripheral workers** — core workers can provide a **stable environment** for the change to take place and the peripheral workers can help with any **additional work** during the change.
3) A flexible business is also able to **outsource** some of its work in order to **manage change.** For example, if a business is updating the machinery in its manufacturing department, it might outsource some of the manufacturing while staff are **trained** and get up to speed with the **new processes.**
4) Employing people on flexible contracts can also make it easier for businesses to hold onto **valuable employees** and open up more **job opportunities** for **skilled applicants.** Businesses will then have a wider range of **skilled employees** when it comes to implementing change — they may not even need to **retrain people.**
5) Unfortunately, flexible contracts have **downsides.** Allowing people to work **flexi-time** could result in **poor communication** and **teamwork** between staff who work at **different times.** This could make it a lot **more difficult** to manage change effectively and businesses may need to put a **strategy in place** to deal with it.

Practice Questions

Q1 Give two ways in which a business can change its structure in order to react quicker in fast-moving environments.

Q2 Give two features of a mechanistic structure.

Q3 Give three ways that businesses can use employment contracts to become more flexible.

Exam Question

Q1 Staff at a call centre have recently been moved onto flexible contracts.
To what extent is this likely to affect the performance of the business? [12 marks]

It was 27 °C today, but apparently it's inappropriate to 'de-layer' in the office...

Make sure you learn the difference between mechanistic and organic business structures. Imagine mechanistic structures like a well-oiled machine — a traditional, inflexible system where employees all work on specific, separate tasks. Organic systems are flexible, flat and decentralised, with employees working together as a team.

Overcoming Barriers to Change

Unlike the 100 m hurdles at sports day, you can't just jump over barriers to change — you have to manage them...

Resistance is the most common *Barrier to Change*

1) In order to **manage change** effectively, businesses need to be able to **overcome barriers to change**.
2) Even with the **best plans** and **strategies**, businesses will face some barriers:

- **Organisational structure:** some structures can make it difficult to manage change — e.g. if the business has a **tall structure** it can be difficult to **communicate** the change and the reasons for it to the lower layers.
- **Resources:** businesses need to have the correct resources **in place** before making a change — e.g. a business shouldn't introduce **new machinery** until they employ someone who can **operate it**.
- **Poor management:** when managers are unable to **communicate** effectively and **engage** workers — this is usually the result of a **lack of trust** between the manager and the worker.
- **Passive resistance:** when people carry on with the **old ways** despite being aware of the **new needs** and being shown the **new processes**. Passive resistance is most common in **employees** and **suppliers**.
- **Active resistance:** when people **argue** against the change and **challenge motives** for the change. **Workers** can organise themselves through their **trade union** and **refuse** to carry out tasks. **Customers** can also show active resistance by refusing to make further **purchases** from the company.

3) Businesses need to be able to **communicate effectively** with groups of workers throughout the business. If workers feel **engaged** and are kept **up-to-date** with any changes, they are much **less likely** to resist them.
4) **Good planning** and **strategies** can help businesses to **avoid** some of the barriers to change. For example, a business may have to give staff **better training** before implementing the change.

Kotter and *Schlesinger's Four Reasons* for *Resistance* to change

Managers need to consider which of the following reasons is **most relevant** to the **specific change** in their company.

1) Self-interest

- People are more concerned with their **own situation** rather than the success of the business — if they can't see how the change **directly benefits** them, they will **resist it**.
- People can't see that ultimately a **more successful** business may have **individual benefits** too.
- For example, **organisational change** through delayering may meet resistance from middle-managers who fear **loss of income** or **redundancy** — they can't see that a more successful business might create **new positions** for them even **higher up** the hierarchy.

2) Misunderstanding

- People also resist change when they don't **fully understand** what it means for them. They will usually think that they have **more to lose** than **gain** until they are told otherwise.
- **Poor communication** from management can lead to **incorrect information** being passed down to workers. This breeds **uncertainty** and **confusion** and will **increase anxiety** amongst employees.
- Businesses need to have a **high level of trust** between employees and managers to prevent misunderstandings.

3) Low tolerance of change

- People get used to **completing tasks** the way **they know** — they will resist change if they **fear** that they won't be able to develop the **news skills** required after the change. They may believe that they won't perform as well in the **new situation** and they will lose their **job security**.
- There may also be a **loyalty** to **existing relationships** and **methods** as these are **known** and **established** — e.g. workers may be **comfortable** in their current teams and not want to break up existing work groups.

4) Different assessments of the situation

- The **key stakeholders** may have **strong disagreements** over the reasons for change and therefore there may be an inability to accept the **need for change**.
- They may not be able to see the **advantages** brought about by the change — they may only see the **disadvantages** that the change will bring and everything that could **go wrong**.
- They may **agree** that a change is needed but think that they have a **better idea** of what to change.

Overcoming Barriers to Change

Kotter and *Schlesinger's Six Ways* of *Overcoming Resistance* to change

Once managers have identified the reason for resistance, they can try to **do something about it**.

1) Education and communication

Managers need to **raise awareness** of the reasons for change and how it will be carried out.
The education process usually involves **discussions**, **presentations** and **reports** — they should clearly communicate the **reasons** behind the planned change and identify the **benefits** for the business and individuals.

2) Participation and involvement

Key stakeholders should be **involved** in the **design** and **implementation** of the change. If they **participate** in the decision-making process then they will feel more **engaged** and their ideas form part of the change — if people become **part of the process**, it'll be more **difficult** for them to resist the change.

3) Facilitation and support

Listening to the **concerns** of the workforce by holding **regular meetings** will help workers to adjust as they'll **feel supported** — it can also help the business to meet the needs of the workers.
Support groups can help workers to overcome their **anxiety** about the changes.
Businesses should also provide **training** for workers who will be required to gain **new skills**.

4) Negotiation and agreement

Giving stakeholders opportunities to **negotiate** and compromising over **key sticking points** can lead to full agreement over the proposed change. **Financial** or **non-financial incentives** may need to be offered by the business in order to obtain **full acceptance** of the change. If full agreement can't be made then **voluntary redundancy** or **early retirement** may be offered to employees who are resisting change.

5) Manipulation and Co-option

An employee who is resisting change may be given a **desirable role** in the decision-making process in order to gain their cooperation. This can be a **risky strategy** as these roles often give the worker **little power** and they can feel **tricked** into agreeing to change. Alternatively, a manager may **manipulate** the information regarding the change, e.g. they may **exaggerate** the extent of a financial crisis and state there is no other alternative.
If it's found out that the manager has **manipulated information** they will have **lost the trust** of their workers.

6) Explicit and implicit coercion

As a last resort, in order to speed up the process, a person may be **threatened** to comply with the planned changes or face consequences. The consequences of resistance could be clearly stated or just implied.
These could be **redundancies**, losing out on **promotion opportunities**, or transfers to other departments, etc.

Practice Questions

Q1 Describe two barriers to change for an organisation.

Q2 Outline Kotter and Schlesinger's four reasons for resistance to change.

Q3 Identify Kotter and Schlesinger's six ways of overcoming resistance to change.

Q4 Give one advantage and one disadvantage for using "Facilitation and Support" as a method to overcome resistance to change in an organisation.

Exam Questions

Q1 Discuss two ways of overcoming resistance to change in a multinational organisation. [6 marks]

Q2 A furniture manufacturing company plans to install new technology in order to improve productivity.
Evaluate the strategies it should implement to overcome the likely resistance to change from workers. [16 marks]

Businesses need to overcome resistance or else there'll be friction...

There's loads to learn on these two pages — most of it thought up by those clever chaps Kotter and Schlesinger. Make sure you can identify all the barriers to change that businesses can face and give reasons why they come about. Then it's just a case of learning the six different ways that businesses can deal with any resistance that they might face.

Managing Organisational Culture

A company's organisational culture (or corporate culture) is based on the company's values and objectives.

Organisational Culture is the Way things are Done in a Business

1) **Organisational culture** is the way that people do things in a company, and the way that they expect things to be done. It's an important way to shape the **expectations** and **attitudes** of staff and managers.
2) Because organisational culture **affects staff behaviour** and how they make decisions, it has an effect on **planning**, **objective setting** and **strategy**.
3) Organisational culture is **created** and **reinforced** by company **rules**, **managerial attitudes**, **managerial behaviour** and **recruitment** policies that recruit people who "fit in".
4) Culture is often affected by the way in which employees are **rewarded**. For example, if an employee acts in an **unethical** manner, yet has **high sales**, rewarding them could lead to a culture valuing **short-term profits** over the **company's reputation**.
5) A company's culture can be **identified** by looking at its **heroes** (people who represent the company's values), the **stories** that are told repeatedly within the company, **symbols** that represent the company's values (like staff mottos and sayings), and the **ceremonies** that the business holds (such as office parties).

Organisational Culture can be Strong or Weak

Strong culture

Organisational culture is strong when employees **agree** with the **corporate values** of the company. Having a strong corporate culture has several advantages:

- Employees need **less supervision**, because their behaviour will naturally tend to fit in with the company's values.
- Staff are more **loyal** to the business, so **staff turnover** is lower.
- It increases employees' **motivation**, so they work more productively.

Weak culture

Weak culture is where the employees of a company **don't** share the company's values, and have to be **forced** to comply with them (e.g. through **company policies**).

There are Four Main Types of Organisational Culture

Organisational culture has a big impact on how companies handle change, and whether staff are **open** to change or **resistant** to it. In 1993, Charles Handy identified the following **four main types** of organisational culture:

1) Power culture

- **Power cultures** have a **centralised structure** where decision-making authority is limited to a **small number** of people — perhaps just **one person** in the **centre** (possibly the owner).
- Power cultures may begin to **struggle** if the business **grows** and cannot be run from the **centre**.
- Employees are likely to be **more resistant** to change, because they don't have the opportunity to give their **opinions** on what changes should and shouldn't be made.
- They might also be **resistant to changes** because they don't have enough **faith** in senior managers who they feel are **out of touch** with the day-to-day activities of the business.

2) Role culture

- **Role cultures** are common in **bureaucratic firms** where authority is defined by job title. **Decisions** come from **senior managers**, so employees don't have the **opportunity** to get involved in the **decision-making process**.
- Organisations with role cultures tend to have **poor communication** between departments so they **respond slowly** to change — this could result in them **losing out** to **competitors** in **new** or **expanding** markets where strategies need to be developed and implemented quickly.
- These organisations also tend to **avoid risk** for fear of failure which means that **change** is **quite rare**.
- Any changes that are brought in will meet **resistance** as employees are **not used** to doing things differently.

Managing Organisational Culture

3) Person culture

- **Person culture** is common in loose organisations of **individual workers**, usually **professional partnerships** such as solicitors, accountants, doctors, etc.
- The **objectives** of these firms will be defined by the **personal ambitions** of the individuals involved. The firms have to ensure that the individuals actually have **common goals.**
- **Decisions** are made **jointly**, so all employees are likely to be **comfortable** and **accepting** of any changes that are made because they have agreed to them.
- However, decisions on **change** can be **difficult** to make — individuals will often think about what is **best** for **themselves** rather than thinking about what is **best** for the **organisation.**

4) Task culture

- Organisations with a **task culture** place an emphasis on getting specific **tasks** done.
- Task culture gets **small teams** together to work on a project, then disbands them. There may be **conflict** between teams for **resources** and **budgets**. It can be confusing if a firm has too many **products** or **projects.**
- This culture supports **objectives** which are based around **products** (e.g. make Product X the market leader).
- Task cultures respond well to **management by objectives**, which translates corporate objectives into **specific targets** for each **department** and for each **individual employee.**
- Staff working in a company with a task culture are likely to think that change is normal because they are used to **changing teams** often and working with a variety of people. This means that they are likely to be **less resistant** to change in general.

There are many other types of **organisational cultures**. An example is **entrepreneurial culture**:

Entrepreneurial culture

- Employees are encouraged to look for **new ways** of bringing **revenue** into the company.
- **Change** is a big part of entrepreneurial culture, and **all employees** are responsible for coming up with ideas to **improve** how the business is run.
- If employees are encouraged to be **creative** and **innovative**, they are likely to be much more **open** to change, especially when changes are made based on their **suggestions.**

Vicky was brilliant at managing her change.

Other examples of organisational culture are **customer-focused** culture (which bases its values on customer **feedback** and **satisfaction**), **clan** culture (where the organisation acts more like a **family** with managers as **parent-figures**) and **market** culture (where the focus is on **competition** with **other organisations** and **between employees**).

Practice Questions

Q1 What is organisational culture?

Q2 Give three benefits of an organisation having a strong culture.

Q3 Describe a power culture.

Q4 Why can change be hard to implement in an organisation with a person culture?

Exam Questions

Q1 In which of the following cultures is change least likely to meet resistance from employees?

A weak culture B role culture C power culture D task culture [1 mark]

Q2 MindGadgitz are a company developing new household gadgets for sale to the public.
They have decided to change their organisational culture from a power culture to a task culture.
Analyse how the change may affect the performance of the company. [9 marks]

We always go bowling on Sundays — we have a strong roll culture...

This stuff on organisational culture's pretty interesting I reckon. Remember that the organisational culture of a business affects all sorts of things — from whether they take financial risks, to whether they have office parties. When you get a case study, look for clues about the culture of the business — it can tell you a lot about what's happening and why.

Managing Organisational Culture

Sorry old chap/chappette — there are another two pages of organisational culture...

Corporate Culture *is* ***Important*** *for the* ***Stakeholders*** *of the business*

The **organisational culture** of a business affects stakeholders such as **staff**, **customers** and **shareholders**:

1) **Staff** — Culture affects the **motivation** of the employees. E.g. a **power culture** or **role culture** can **demotivate** creative staff who can see ways to **improve** things but don't have the **power** to put changes into practice.
2) **Customers** — Organisational culture affects **customers' loyalty** to a business. Businesses with a **customer-focused** culture are more likely to have customers loyal to the firm or their brands.
3) **Shareholders** — The level of **risk** that businesses take depends on their organisational culture. Shareholders might get **low returns** on their investment if they invest in a company with a **low-risk culture**, whereas investing in a company with a **high-risk culture** gives shareholders the possibility of **high returns**, but there's also the risk that they'll **lose money**.

Managers might want to ***Change*** *the* ***Organisational Culture***

There are **two** main reasons why the managers of a business might want to **change** the organisational culture:

1) The organisational culture of a business depends on the **preferences** of its **leaders**. When a new manager joins a business, they might change it to make it more **similar** to businesses they have worked in **before**. E.g. if a manager who is used to working in a business with a **role culture** starts working in a business with a **task culture**, they might **force** the business to adopt a role culture because that is what they are used to.
2) A business might change its culture in order to be more **competitive**. E.g. businesses with a **power culture** can be **slow** to spot ways to **save money**, or more **efficient** ways of working, so adopting an **entrepreneurial culture** where all the staff are constantly looking for ways to **improve** the business could make the business more **competitive**.

Changes such as ***Growth*** *can* ***Influence*** *organisational culture*

1) If a business **grows**, it might need to take on **new employees**. New employees may have different **expectations** and **aims**, which could influence the pre-existing culture.
2) A business's **growth** and **success** can lead to it becoming **more corporate**, with a more **rigid structure**. This can sway the business towards a **role culture**.
3) If a business becomes a **multinational**, its culture may be influenced by the culture of the country the business has entered. Companies can use **Hofstede's six dimensions of national culture** (see next page) to analyse the differences between the culture of each country.
4) The **amount** by which a culture is **affected by a change** depends on how **strong** the original culture was (see p.78), how well it was **reinforced** and whether employees **appreciate** its values.

Changing *the* ***Organisational Culture*** *can be* ***Difficult***

1) Employees usually **resist** any kind of change (see p.76), including changes in **organisational culture**. Employees who have worked for the business for a **long time** are **especially likely** to resist changes to the **organisational culture**, because they'll think the way they've **always done** things is better.
2) Changing organisational culture means changing the **attitudes** and **behaviour** of staff, so it's much more **complicated** than changing things like pricing structure. E.g. the managers of a company might want to change from a **person culture** to a **task culture**, but splitting people up into **small teams** and giving them **a project** won't achieve anything if employees just want to work **individually** and in their own **interests**.
3) Changing the organisational culture can also be very **expensive**. It might involve changing the **office layout**, giving **extra training** to staff, devising **new processes**, changing the **company motto** on marketing material, etc. This means that businesses can't always **afford** to **change their culture** as much as they would like to.
4) The **HR department** plays a **big role** in changing the organisational culture of a business — they might need to change their **recruitment** and **induction procedures**, change their **payment and reward system**, etc.

Managing Organisational Culture

The **Dimensions of National Culture** show how cultural values **Differ**

1) **Geert Hofstede** used a large set of data collected from employees across **different countries** to identify **four areas** or '**dimensions**' of national culture. Since then, **two more dimensions** have been added, making a total of **six**.
2) Countries are **scored** on each of the **six dimensions** — these scores allow **businesses** to assess the **cultural differences** when dealing with businesses from **different countries** and plan for any **culture clashes**.

Power Distance
The extent that people accept that power and wealth is distributed **unequally**. Societies with **low power distance** expect **equality**, and societies with **high power distance** (such as Saudi Arabia) accept the **hierarchy** of power without argument. For example, in a country with **high** power distance you would be expected to follow your boss's orders **without question**.

Uncertainty Avoidance
The extent to which people attempt to **minimise uncertainty**. This can be done by **introducing rules** or regulations. People in societies with **low uncertainty avoidance** tend to be **open to change**.

Individualism vs. Collectivism
The extent to which people are expected to **look after themselves** rather than **support each other**. Societies with **high individualism** focus on **personal achievement** and **rights**, and people are expected to look after **themselves** and their **close family**. Collectivist societies, e.g. Pakistan, are made up of **large groups** (such as large extended families) where members are expected to **support** each other in return for **loyalty**.

Masculinity vs. Femininity
Masculine cultures are highly **competitive** and **powerful**, with **contrasting gender roles**. **Feminine** cultures focus on **caring** and **quality of life**. The higher the masculinity, the more focus there is on power and money.

Long-term Orientation
The higher the long-term orientation, the more the society looks to the **future** and accepts new ideas, rather than following **tradition**.

Indulgence vs. Restraint
Indulgent societies allow their people to **satisfy** their desires and impulses, within reason. **Restrained** societies attempt to **regulate** the desires of their people.

Sandra's new-fangled cultural-reality headset let her see in 6D.

3) Businesses can use this model to plan for **communication problems** when **trading** with international suppliers, **expanding** into other countries or during **mergers**, **takeovers** and **joint ventures** (see p.56) with businesses in other countries. It can also help businesses to foresee any **potential issues** when **entering international markets**.
4) The model is also handy for **multinationals** — it allows them to assess how **proposed changes** will affect their employees in **different countries**. They can then adjust the changes to **match the cultures** in different countries.

Practice Questions

Q1 Why is changing organisational culture difficult?

Q2 What are the six dimensions of national culture?

Q3 What is individualism?

Exam Question

Q1 A company has been slowly expanding over the last 20 years, increasing its market share to around 12%. The directors plan for the business to continue growing and to set up factories in different countries. To what extent might this affect the organisational culture of the business? [25 marks]

Organisational Culture Club — an 80s tribute band formed by executives...

Make sure you're confident with the six dimensions of national culture — you'll find them useful when you're writing longer answer questions. You also need to understand how businesses can use them when trading internationally.

Planning Strategy

It's not a great idea to just pluck a strategy out of thin air — there are loads of factors that need to be considered. Strategic planning is the process of analysing and evaluating these factors and working them into a great strategy.

Businesses can go through a *Planning Process* to create a *Strategy*

A business's **strategy** is a **plan** for achieving its **corporate objectives**. For example, if a business's main objective is to grow, it needs a strategy for how it's going to go about growing. One way of deciding on strategy is to go through a **strategic planning process**.

The strategic planning process involves several stages:

- Senior managers set the long-term **corporate objectives** of the business based on its mission.
- They analyse the **internal** position of the business to identify **strengths** and **weaknesses**. They analyse the **external** environment to identify **opportunities** and **threats** (see below for more on analysis).
- They develop possible **strategies** to achieve the corporate objectives, **evaluate** each one and then select the strategy that best **fits** their business.
- They plan out how the strategy will be **implemented**. This will include an outline of **functional objectives** for each department, the resources needed, etc.
- They set up **processes** for **monitoring** and **evaluating** the strategy as it is being implemented.

The key information is written up in a **strategic plan**. This document clearly **defines** a business's corporate objectives and strategy, along with an outline of how the strategy will be **implemented** and **monitored** throughout the business.

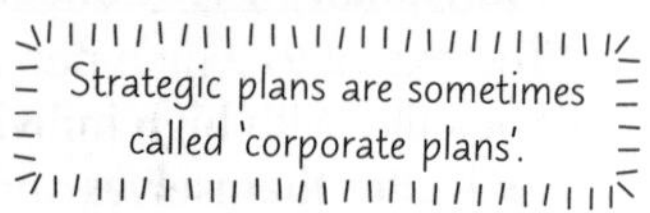

Analysis of *Internal* and *External Factors* influences a *Strategy*

A business needs to look at **many** different **factors** to decide on a **strategy** that will work for it.

1) When **planning** a strategy, a business looks at **internal** factors to determine its **strengths** and **weaknesses**.
2) These can include many different things, such as the **skills** and **motivation** of the staff, the **quality** of the products, the business's **finances**, the **production capacity** and the **core competences**.
3) For example, if a business has the **capacity** for **increased production**, this would be a **strength** in enabling it to **grow**. Or if a business's **strength** is making **high quality** products, it could develop a strategy for building its **brand** around quality.
4) A business will also look at **external** factors to identify any **opportunities** and **threats**.
5) These can include **political**, **legal**, **economic**, **social**, **technological** and **environmental** factors and **competition**.
6) For example, the **growth** of internet shopping might provide an **opportunity** to **increase sales**, or it could be a **threat** to a business that only sells through **physical** channels.
7) There are helpful tools that a business can use to analyse the internal and external factors, such as **SWOT analysis** (p.3), **Porter's five forces** (p.40-41) and the **Balanced Scorecard Model** (p.20).

There's loads more detail on internal factors in Section 2, and on external factors in Section 3.

Risk and *Feasibility* affect *Strategic Decision-Making*

Strategic decisions are **long-term** and **high-risk** — a business needs to weigh up its strategic options carefully.

1) A business needs to assess **risk** and **feasibility** when selecting strategy.
2) A useful **tool** for assessing risk is **sensitivity analysis** (see p.47). This looks at each **assumption** that a strategy relies on, and predicts how well the strategy would still do if these assumptions **change**. For example, could the business cope if the increase in costs is greater than expected. Based on this analysis, the business will **assess** whether the strategy is **worth** the risk.
3) The business could also consider how different **stakeholders** would react to a strategy — they should consider how highly the stakeholder **maps**.
4) **Feasibility** is also an important factor — the business needs access to the **resources** or **skills** necessary to implement the strategy.

You'll have learnt about stakeholder mapping in Year 1.

Planning Strategy

Contingency Plans prepare for Out Of The Ordinary Events

1) Strategic planning can include **contingency planning** — outlining what to do if something **unexpected** happens.
2) Contingency planning can help a business **respond** to lots of different types of **crises**. For example, a **hostile takeover bid,** a **fire** that destroys a factory, **bad news** or **PR** in the media, a sudden **change in demand** for products, or **lost** or **corrupt data** caused by computer network problems.
3) Businesses **can't** plan for **every unforeseen event**. Some adverse events are hard to plan for. Contingency planning is very **expensive**, so it's not worthwhile to plan for every single thing that could possibly go wrong. Managers have to decide **how likely** a particular adverse event is to happen, and how **badly** it would damage the business if it did happen.
4) **Crisis management** is when an unexpected situation **occurs**, and a business has to respond.

- If managers haven't carried out **contingency planning** they're **not prepared**, so they have to make **snap decisions** about what to do. If they've done contingency planning then they've already decided what to do in that situation, which makes crisis management **much more straightforward**.
- Managers need to **act quickly** and **decisively** to **limit** the amount of **damage** caused. This is best achieved through **strong leadership**, e.g. an autocratic leader.

Strategic Planning can Help and Hinder businesses

1) Strategic planning can be **helpful** because a strategic plan gives the business a **clear direction**. It can **communicate** exactly what the business is trying to achieve, so everyone works towards the same goals.
2) Strategic planning makes managers think about the **strengths** and **weaknesses** of the business, and its **external threats** and **opportunities**. This helps managers to spot opportunities that they might not have noticed, and to match strategy to the current situation.
3) However, strategic planning can **restrict** the business's **flexibility** — employees might think that they have to follow the plan even if the situation has **changed** since it was made, or if there's a **better way** of doing things. Also, the plan is based on **analysis**, which may be **inaccurate** — e.g. it's difficult to **predict** long-term trends.
4) Strategic planning is likely to be more **useful** for businesses operating in **stable** markets, rather than more **innovative** businesses that need to respond to change on a regular basis. An innovative business would be more suited to an **emergent strategy** (see page 91).

Practice Questions

Q1 Describe the steps involved in carrying out strategic planning.

Q2 Give two examples of information that could be included in a strategic plan.

Q3 Give three examples of internal factors that might influence a business's strategy.

Q4 Give three examples of external factors that might influence a business's strategy.

Q5 Give three examples of situations that a business might have a contingency plan for.

Exam Question

Q1 Do you think strategic planning is essential for all businesses? Justify your answer. [16 marks]

My contingency plan: hide in a cupboard and hope the problems go away...

These pages are pretty packed... And there you were, hoping for a gentle introduction to the section... There's a lot of important stuff here though, so it's definitely worth taking time to make sure you understand it all — maybe challenge yourself to list as many SWOT factors that influence strategy as you can. That sounds like a fun game, right...?

Implementing Strategy

Implementing strategy effectively is really important in business. I bet you never would've guessed that...

Implementing Strategy** is putting strategy into **Action

If a business has come up with a great **strategy**, it'll also need to come up with an effective way of putting it into **action**. There are a few things that need to be **considered**:

- A business might have to **make big changes** to implement their strategy. So the success of a strategy will depend on how well the business **manages change**.
- The business needs to **plan** and **organise** the **resources** they need — e.g. assign responsibilities to staff, organise training or recruitment, or budget time and finances.
- To effectively implement strategy, there are three main factors that a business needs to get right — **leadership**, **communication**, and **organisational structure**.

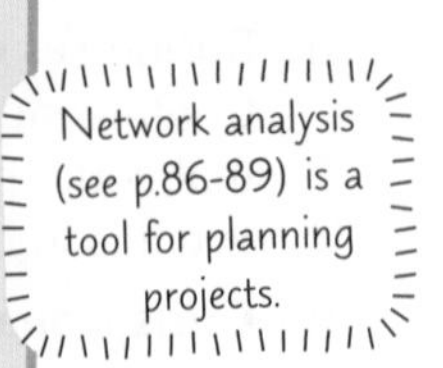

Leadership** is important in **Implementing Strategy

1) Implementing strategy often means a business makes **big changes**. For example, they might change teams around, bring in new technology, move to a new location or alter their product range.
2) A **good leader** can **take action** to make sure the changes go as smoothly as possible:

- A leader should take overall **responsibility** for management of strategic implementation, and **delegate** responsibilities for different elements where necessary.
- The leader should create a **clear** and **inspiring** vision that comes from the top and **sets an example** for everyone in the business.
- They can **motivate** everyone in the business to **engage** with the process. This can be done by creating a **positive** culture, for example by **rewarding** employees for hitting targets.
- Leadership is important in successfully **managing change** — this can be done with clear **communication**, lots of employee **involvement**, and a suitable **leadership style**.

Leaders are usually senior managers.

See p.77 for more on managing change.

3) In times of change, **authoritarian** leadership might make employees more **fearful** of change, and they might be more likely to resist it. **Laissez-faire** leadership can mean that employees don't have **confidence** that changes will work out well, so they won't be **supportive**. The most **suitable** forms of leadership for helping employees cope with change are the **paternalistic** and **democratic** styles. Forms of leadership will have been covered in more detail in Year 1.

Good Communications** are vital in **Implementing Strategy

1) The purpose of communication is to **clearly** pass on **information** and **ideas**, and to **motivate** people.
2) **Senior managers** need to communicate the **functional objectives** to department managers, and the business's **objectives** and **strategy** to all staff so that they know **what** the business is doing and **why**.
3) Different **departments** also need to communicate with **each other** in order to coordinate their activities.
4) Any employee affected by a strategy needs to **told** how it's going to **change** their **role** or **responsibility**.
5) Communication is a **two-way process** — for instance, employees should inform their managers if there are any **issues** with implementing the strategy, and managers should respond to the feedback.

Example Part of a company's strategy is to have a big **publicity launch**.

- **Senior managers** need to **communicate** with **Marketing** and **Operations managers** to inform them of the **work** required from their departments.
- These departments will need to communicate with **HR** to **decide** on the best action to take — for instance, hire **more** people (as either permanent or temporary staff) or ask current employees to work **overtime**.
- **Finance** will also need to be involved, so that they can calculate **costs**, **cash flow**, etc.
- Every decision has **knock-on** effects, and they all need to be **considered** carefully and the outcomes communicated clearly.

Implementing Strategy

A **Business** needs an **Organisational Structure** that suits its **Strategy**

You've already come across different types of organisational design (in Year 1) and general structures (see p.74). Here are **four specific types** of organisational structure a business can use. Depending on the strategy, a business may need to **change** its structure — e.g. by reorganising departments or creating new ones.

Functional Structures organise staff by **Department**

1) Businesses can be organised into several **departments**, which group jobs together by **function**.
2) The main four departments are **finance**, **marketing**, **operations** and **HR**, which are all run **separately**.
3) Each function can work in its own area of **expertise**, which can make **implementing strategy** simpler.
4) However, this could mean each department has its **own culture** and focuses on its own priorities. If communication between departments isn't good, it will be **hard** to **coordinate strategy**.

Product-based Structures organise staff by **Product**

1) In a business that produces **lots** of different **products**, each group of products can be run almost as a **separate business**. Each product division has its **own director**, **marketing** team, **finance** team, etc.
2) This would be an **ideal** structure for implementing certain **strategies** — for example, a business may want to grow the **market share** of one particular product, while keeping another product's market share steady.
3) But there may be **unnecessary duplication** of roles — e.g. instead of each division having its own research team, it might be more **efficient** to have just one research department for the whole company.

Regional Structures organise staff by **Geographical Location**

1) **Regional** structures are based on **location**. A business might have branches all over the country, which are grouped into **regional divisions** that run themselves.
2) A **global** company could have **headquarters** on each continent, which oversee **national divisions**. For example, an Asian HQ oversees the Japanese and Indian divisions.
3) A regional structure tends to suit a **market development strategy** where the business is expanding into **new geographical markets**. If there are **different market demands** in different locations, control can be **decentralised** so each division can run itself independently and adapt to local needs.

Matrix Structures can organise staff by a **Combination** of **Factors**

1) **Matrix** structures organise staff by **two different criteria**.
2) The diagram opposite shows a business organised by **project** and **function**. Each project team has workers from different functions. The red circle shows a **salesperson** working in **Project B** — they **report** to a Sales manager and the manager of Project B.
3) The matrix structure ensures that staff are pursuing **clearly defined objectives**, and it **encourages** departments to build **relationships** with one another.
4) However, this structure could lead to **conflict** — e.g. project managers and department managers might have different ideas about how strategy should be implemented.

Operations | HR | Sales | Finance
Project A
Project B
Project C

Q1 Give three factors that are important in implementing strategy effectively.

Q2 Describe each of the following structures in a few sentences: a) functional
b) regional
c) product-based

Exam Question

Q1 To what extent is communication likely to be the most important factor in implementing strategy effectively? [25 marks]

Take me to your leader...

The key to all this is being able to say what is appropriate for a particular situation — there's no "one structure fits all", so a business needs to figure out which structure will be best for implementing their strategy. Not always easy...

Network Analysis

Network analysis is used to find the most time-efficient way of doing a complex project. It's a really handy tool for working out how best to organise resources and activities when implementing strategy.

Network Analysis works out the Quickest Way to Finish a Set Of Tasks

Network analysis identifies the most **efficient** and **cost-effective** way of completing a complex project — i.e. a project made up of a series of **activities**. Network analysis is sometimes called 'critical path analysis'.

1) The various activities which make up the project are **identified**, and the **order** or **sequence** that these activities must be performed in is worked out.
2) The **duration** (how long each activity will take) is **estimated**.
3) These **activities** are then arranged as a **network** or graph, showing the **whole project** from start to finish, and showing which tasks can be **performed** at the **same time**. For large, **complicated** projects made up of lots of activities, **computer programs** are used to construct the network.
4) The **shortest time** required to get from start to finish can then be identified. The sequence of tasks which have to be done one after another with **no gaps in between**, to get the project done as fast as possible, is called the **critical path**. Activities on the critical path are called **critical activities** — if they're delayed, the **whole project** is delayed.

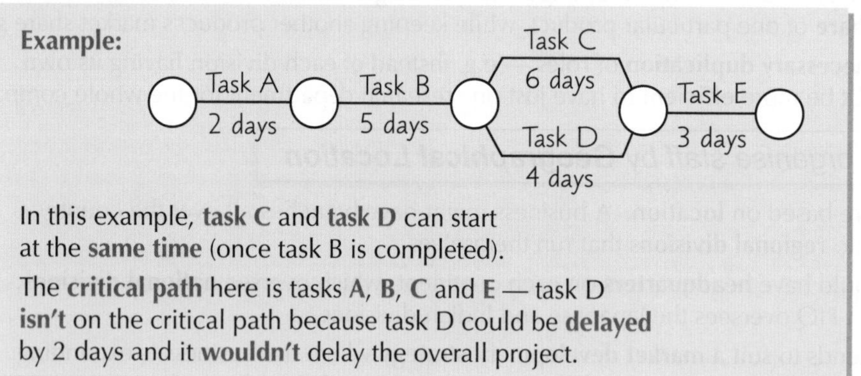

In this example, **task C** and **task D** can start at the **same time** (once task B is completed).
The **critical path** here is tasks **A**, **B**, **C** and **E** — task D **isn't** on the critical path because task D could be **delayed** by 2 days and it **wouldn't** delay the overall project.

"Dearest, we really must get back to the path before we ruin our skirts. It's absolutely critical."

Nodes show when one task Must Finish and when the next task Can Start

1) The **circles** on the network are called **nodes** — they show where one activity **stops** and another activity **begins**.
2) Each node is split into **three** parts. The numbers inside each node show the **number** of the **node**, the **latest** time that the **previous** task can **finish**, and the **earliest** time that the **next** task can **start**:

- The **left** part of the node shows you which **number** node it is.
- The number in the **top right** is the **earliest start time** (EST — see next page) of the activity **following** the node. That's the **earliest** time from the beginning of the project that the activity can **start**, assuming that all the activities before it are completed in as short a time as possible.

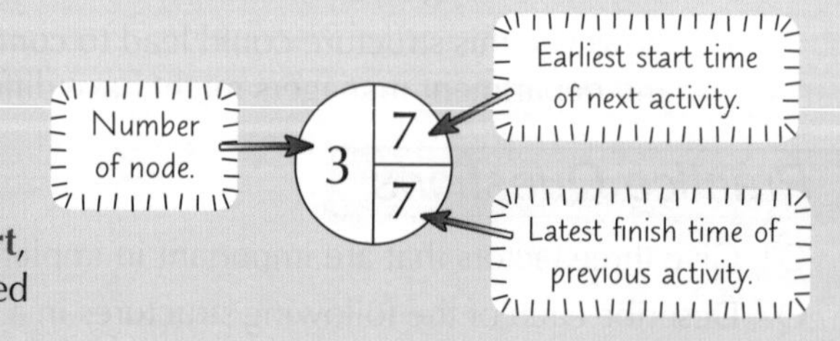

- The number in the **bottom right** of the node is the **latest finishing time** (LFT — see next page) of the activity immediately **before** the node (or the LFT of the activity with the longest duration if there's more than one activity going into the node). That's the **latest** time that the activity can **finish** without having the knock-on effect of making the whole project **late**.
- If the **EST** and the **LFT** are the **same**, then the node is on the **critical path**.

Network Analysis

Networks** include **Start Times, Finishing Times** and **Float Time

It's really important to know the **earliest** and **latest start** and **finishing times** for each activity so that you can make sure the whole project can be completed **on time** — if you **miss** the latest start time of an activity, there's **no way** you can finish the project on time (unless you can do individual activities **more quickly** than you predicted).

1) **EST** = **earliest start time** (in number of e.g. days, weeks, months) since the start of the project. An activity can't start until the activity before it has been completed — e.g. you can't ice a cake before it's baked. EST is worked out by **adding** the **duration** of the **previous activity** to its **EST**. The EST of the first activity is always 0.

   E.g. a business wants to trade internationally. Their strategy involves **opening** a new office (**1 month**), **hiring** new staff (**3 months**), **producing** the product (**6 months**) and **launching** the product in the new market (**2 months**). So, the **EST** (in months) of **producing** is: **0 + 1 + 3 = 4**.

2) **EFT** = **earliest finishing time**. It's the time that an activity will **finish** if it's **started** at the **earliest start time**. You can work out the EFT for an activity by **adding** its **duration** (in months here) to its **EST**.

   Using the same example, the **EFT** of **producing** is: **4 + 6 = 10**

   The EFT isn't shown on the nodes of a network.

3) **LFT** = **latest finishing time**. This is the **latest** time by which the activity can be completed without **holding up** the **completion** of the project. It's **calculated** by working **backwards** from the **final** node. The LFT of the final node is **equal** to the EST of the final node. To work out the LFT of the node before, you subtract the duration of the next activity from its LFT.

   If the business needs the product launched by the end of **month 12**, the **LFT** of **hiring** is: **12 – 2 – 6 = 4**

4) **LST** = **latest start time**. It's the **latest time** an activity can be **started** and still be **finished** by its **LFT**. To calculate LST, **subtract** the **duration** of the activity from its **LFT**.

   The **LST** of **hiring** in the example above is: **4 – 3 = 1**

   The LST isn't shown on the nodes of a network.

5) **Float time** is the **spare time** available for an activity. Only **non-critical** activities have **float time**. **Total float** is the length of **time** you can **delay** an activity without delaying the **completion** of the **project**. You can work it out by:

   total float = LFT – duration – EST

   There's an example of a network on the next page.

Practice Questions

Q1 What is meant by the "critical path"?

Q2 What do the three numbers inside each node show?

Q3 What do the initials EST and LST mean?

Q4 How do you calculate the latest finishing time of an activity?

Q5 Explain the term "total float time".

Exam Question

Q1 Explain how a critical path network is produced. [8 marks]

If you're here to study an online dance craze, that's 'net twerk analysis'...

To be honest, this does all sound a bit confusing. But there's an example on the next page which should make it a lot clearer. If you have a network to show the order of tasks in a project, you can figure out where there's some spare time. Remember that you work forwards to fill in the ESTs, and then backwards to fill in the LFTs.

Network Analysis

These are the last two pages on network analysis, so make the most of it — you'll miss it when it's gone...

Here's an **Example** of **Network Analysis**

A project is made up of **nine separate tasks** — A to I:

- **Task A** takes **4 days** to complete and can be done at the same time as **task G** (5 days).
- **Task B** (7 days) and **task C** (9 days) can be done at the **same time** once **task A** is finished.
- **Task D** (6 days) can start once **task B** is completed.
- **Task E** (5 days) can start once **task B** and **task C** have **both** finished.
  Task E can be done at the **same time** as **task D**.
- **Task F** (3 days) can start once **task D** and **task E** have both finished.
- **Task H** (7 days) can start once **task G** has finished.
- **Task I** (4 days) can start once **task F** and **task H** have both finished.

You can work out the **ESTs** of all the tasks by working **forwards** from the start of the project, and then work out the **LFTs** of the tasks by working **backwards** from the end of the project.

The network looks like this:

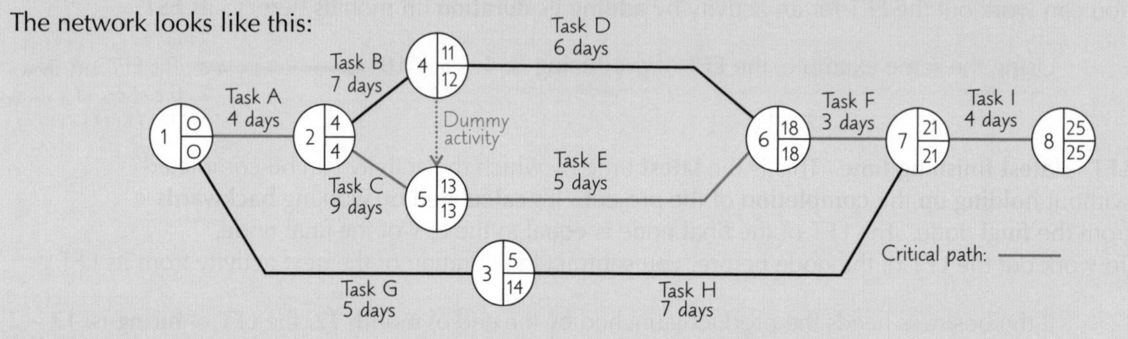

1) The **critical path** (in pink) is task **A**, then task **C**, task **E**, task **F** and finally task **I.**
   If you add up the time taken to do each task, it shows that the project can be completed in 4 + 9 + 5 + 3 + 4 = **25 days** in total. The LFT of task I in the final node is 25 days.
2) In each node on the **critical path**, the **EST** equals the **LFT**.
   For nodes that aren't on the critical path, the **EST** and **LFT** are **different**.
3) **Task B** and **task D** both have a **total float time** of 1 day, and **task G** and **task H** have a total float time of 9 days. These tasks are **non-critical activities** — if there is a **delay** in starting them, it's still possible to complete the project **on time**. E.g. if task G starts on day 5 instead of day 0, it will still be completed before its latest finishing time. If **critical tasks** start **late** or take **longer** than they're expected to, the project **can't** be completed on time.

There is a **dummy activity** between node 4 and node 5. A **dummy activity** is an **imaginary activity** — it just shows that one activity is **dependent** on another. In the example, the dummy activity shows that **task E can't start** until **task B** and **task C** have **both** finished. **Without** the dummy activity it would look as though **task E** was only dependent on **task C**, but having only **one node** between tasks B and C and tasks D and E would imply that **task D** was dependent on **both task B** and **task C**, instead of just **task B**.

Network Analysis can be used for **Time Management** of **Strategies**

1) Network analysis is used when **implementing** a **strategy** or **planning** a **complicated project**, such as the launch of a new product or building a new office block.
2) It allows companies to work out when they'll need **resources** to be **available**, e.g. that a certain **machine** will need to be **free** on Friday or that a **new office** is open and ready to use 15 months into a project.
3) In many cases, it's possible to **shorten** the **critical path** by allocating **additional resources** to an activity. For example, sewing buttons onto a batch of jumpers might be expected to take 5 days, but if the company hired extra machinists, it might be possible to reduce that to 3 days.
4) Some **resources** can be **switched** between activities — e.g. recruiters can be moved from hiring manual labour to hiring managers.
5) Network analysis also helps managers with **decision-making**. Knowing the **latest finish time** of a project makes it easier to decide when to launch an **ad campaign** or when to become a **public company**.

Network Analysis

Network Analysis has several Advantages

1) Network analysis identifies the **critical activities** (activities on the critical path), which need to be supervised closely, to make sure they meet their deadlines.
2) Resources can be transferred from activities with **float time** to **critical activities**, if needed. For example, people packing items could change roles to making them.
3) If different **functions** such as finance, operations, marketing and human resources can start work at the **earliest start time**, then this will make the implementation of **strategy** as speedy as possible. This saves on many **costs**, including the opportunity costs of not working on other projects.
4) Network analysis helps firms forecast their **cash flow** — it gives definite earliest start times when cash will need to be spent by different functions, which allows the firm to budget accurately.
5) Network analysis finds the **shortest time possible** for completing a complex project. This can give a competitive advantage. It's an important element of **time-based management**.
6) It's an excellent **visual aid** to communications, because it shows at a glance which steps take place at the **same time**, and which have any **float time**.
7) Network analysis forces managers to think about the **activities** involved in a strategy. Without the **systematic approach** of network analysis, something might be forgotten.
8) Network analysis can be used to review progress on **individual tasks**, e.g. if a task overruns its float time you can see if it will delay the overall project or just the next activity.
9) If there are changes and modifications to the progress of the project, the network can be **amended** as the project goes on.

Professor "Biddy" Bidness preferred rhyme-based management.

Network Analysis has Disadvantages as well

1) Network analysis relies on **estimates** of how long each task will take. If these aren't accurate, the whole analysis will be wrong.
2) **Constructing** and **amending** the network will require a significant amount of **planning** and **time**.
3) Network analysis sets **tight deadlines**, especially for critical activities. It's tempting for employees to **cut corners** in the rush to meet deadlines, which means that **quality** can suffer.
4) Network analysis can't tell you anything about **costs** — or anything about **how good** the project is.

Practice Questions

Q1 What is a dummy activity?

Q2 Give two examples of projects that managers might use network analysis for.

Q3 Give two advantages to managers of using network analysis.

Q4 Give two disadvantages of network analysis.

Answers on p.103.

Exam Question

Q1 A project contains seven separate activities. Activity A must be completed first, and it has an estimated duration of eight days. Activities B, C and D can take place at the same time — B takes four days, C takes six days and D takes four days. E can only be started once B, C and D are completed and will take seven days. Once E is completed, F and G can take place at the same time — F takes three days and G takes five days.

a) Construct a network to show this data. [9 marks]

b) Find the critical path and state the minimum number of days the project will take to complete. [2 marks]

c) What are the float times for activities B and F? [2 marks]

You take the high road and I'll take the critical path...

Network analysis can seem a bit tricky, but don't be put off by a scary-looking network — just break it down and it'll seem a whole lot simpler. Don't forget to learn the advantages and disadvantages of network analysis too — they could easily come up in the exam. (You could say that one disadvantage is that you need to learn it for the exam...)

Difficulties with Implementing Strategy

It'd be nice if you could just come up with a strategy and then implement it, no hitches. Unfortunately, things aren't usually so simple. Problems can arise at any time, and have to be dealt with.

Strategic Decision-Making involves Risk and Uncertainty

When a business is **deciding** on a strategy, there are usually a large number of factors that have to be **considered**. The more factors there are to consider, the higher the number of potential **problems**.

1) Most strategies will have an element of **risk** involved — when you're trying to plan for the future there will always be **unknowns** that you can't account for. When managers are **making decisions** on strategy, they will need to consider how much risk is involved. However, it can be **difficult** to figure out exactly which parts of a strategy are risky.
2) It is also difficult for a business to judge the **feasibility** of a strategy. Managers need to have **information** about the resources, skills and time available. But even with this information, it can still be hard to **choose** between strategies.
3) The **external environment** is continually **changing**, but strategic decisions can **rely** too much on the **current** environment. This can make implementing the strategy **difficult** if the business faces **changes** from **external factors**.
4) The **internal environment** also **changes** — e.g. a business's resources might change unexpectedly, which can cause issues when trying to implement a strategy. Contingency plans (see p.83) should be included in the strategic decision-making **process**.
5) **Stakeholders** often want **different** things from a business — it's difficult to keep all groups happy all of the time. A business may have to take into account the views of a **group** of stakeholders in its decision-making, and be able to **justify** its **decisions** to other stakeholders.

It's important for a business to **think** about all the **potential problems** when **making decisions** about strategy — otherwise it might make things more difficult when it comes to **implementing** the strategy.

Implementing a strategy isn't Straightforward

There are many **difficulties** that a company needs to **overcome** to ensure the **success** of its strategy.

For example:

1) A lack of **resources** (e.g. money, skills, time) can make implementing a strategy **difficult**, especially if big changes are needed. **Heavy investment** can mean there is **less working capital** available for day-to-day activities.
2) Managers at all levels need to **understand** the strategy being implemented. If it isn't fully understood, this could lead to problems such as **miscommunication** or tasks being **assigned incorrectly**.
3) If managers **don't** provide strong, clear **leadership** and **communication** to manage the change, employees might **not embrace** the changes required.
4) A strategy may rely on **assumptions** about the **amount of resources** needed and the **length of time** tasks will take. **Accurate forecasting** can be very difficult, but any inaccuracies can cause problems.
5) **Changing the structure** of a company can cause difficulties — for example, if a company **delayers** (see p.74), then this will involve making redundancies. A structure change could also lead to a change in the **culture** of the business.
6) If a strategy sets out a **strict** path for the business, it may have difficulty implementing it in the future. A lack of **flexibility** in a strategy could mean that if the **environment** changes, the strategy will no longer be **relevant**.

Valerie's view of the new customer service strategy had taken a sudden downturn.

Difficulties with Implementing Strategy

There are Issues with Planned Strategies

Strategies can be described as **planned** or **emergent** (or somewhere in between).
Planned strategy, as you can probably guess, is **planned out** before action is taken to **implement** it. This sounds sensible **in theory**, but planned strategy has its **disadvantages**.

1) **Planning** a strategy can **cost** a lot of **time** and **money**. It's easy to get caught up in trying to plan the **perfect** strategy, which is practically **impossible**.
2) A planned strategy will gradually become **out of date**. For instance, if strategy is planned every 5 years, then 3 years into the **implementation**, the **environment** could have **changed** a lot from the time of planning. It's difficult to **adapt** a planned strategy to a changing environment.
3) **Senior managers** who plan the strategy could be **out of touch** with what's really going on in the business.
4) Strategic planning could require the **input** of many people, each with a specific **skill set**. There is a chance that these people will only understand their own **contributions**, and not see the **bigger picture**.
5) A planned strategy could be **too detailed** and **theoretical** — the plan might not focus on how to implement the strategy **in practice**.
6) Managers can become too concerned with **analysing data** and making sure that everything is going **exactly** according to the plan. The strategy can become too **rigid**, which stops people being **creative** or **innovating**.
7) Senior managers who implement strategy could be **too busy** to fully **oversee** everything. If tasks are **delegated** down to people without authority, then things could be trickier to implement.

Emergent Strategies solve some of the Problems of Planned Strategies

Emergent strategy develops over time, as a business's actions lead to **patterns of behaviour**.
Emergent strategy can be **adapted** as the business **learns** what works in the **current environment**.
Following an emergent strategy can **solve** many of the **problems** that occur with a planned strategy.

1) **Emergent strategies** save a lot of **time** and **money** that would otherwise have been spent on strategic planning.
2) Emergent strategies stay **relevant**, because they can **adapt** to the **changing environment**.
3) A planned strategy relies on senior managers making a lot of the decisions. An emergent strategy is based more on the decisions of **junior- and middle-managers** — they will often have access to more **up-to-date information** about the business and its environment.
4) Junior- and middle-managers will be more **knowledgeable** about employees — e.g. who would be most **suitable** for different tasks or projects. Emergent strategies also give low-ranking employees a **chance** to **have a say** in some aspects of strategy, instead of all decisions being made by people at the top.

Alligators only occasionally implement an emergent strategy.

Emergent Strategies also have Disadvantages

Of course, not everything about **emergent strategies** is perfect — they have their **downsides** too.

1) With an **emergent strategy**, it might not be clear what the **end** goal is — a **planned strategy** is clearly working towards stated objectives.
2) If the strategy is constantly changing in the **lower ranks** of a company, those at the **top** might have **little idea** about what's going on in their business. This could lead to senior managers believing that the company is following a **particular direction**, but in **reality** it's going in a completely **different** direction.
3) It can be very difficult for **large companies** to implement an emergent strategy because the different parts of the business need to coordinate with each other. Emergent strategies work best in a company that has a flat organisational structure — **communication** is easier and **decisions** can be made more quickly.
4) Some organisations might be affected by certain **requirements** that don't allow for an emergent strategy. For example, the NHS will have a lot of its strategic decisions made for it by the **Government**.

Difficulties with Implementing Strategy

Strategic Drift happens when Strategy and Reality grow Apart

1) **Strategic drift** is what happens when **strategy** becomes **less and less suited** to the business's **environment**. It happens when a business's strategy **doesn't adapt** to keep up with **changes** in the **environment**.
2) Many different **factors** can cause strategic drift to happen. For example, new **technology**, changes in consumer **tastes** and **expectations**, and **legal**, **political** and **economic** factors. A business should **respond** to these changes, especially if **competitors** are benefiting from them.
3) Managers might react to poor results simply by **improving** the way the strategy is being **implemented**. If that doesn't work, managers may make **small alterations** to strategy, sticking mainly to what the business **knows** and does already. They may think it's too **risky** to introduce big changes, or there might be **resistance** to change, e.g. from employees, or managers worried about their own positions.
4) Small changes might work in the **short-term**, but as external change increases, **strategic drift** will **increase**. At this point, managers will be required to step out of their comfort zones to implement **big** strategic change — there will be lots of uncertainty as they try to decide what direction the business should go in. This **transformational change** will be needed for the business to survive.

Divorce Between Ownership and Control causes Conflicting Interests

1) In **small** firms, the **owner** often **manages** the firm on a day-to-day basis.
2) As a firm **grows**, the owner can raise finance by **selling shares**. The new shareholders become **part owners**, and the firm will be run by **directors**, who are appointed to **control** the business in the shareholders' interests.
3) This is known as the **divorce between ownership and control** — the owner(s) of the firm are **no longer** in day-to-day control. In large firms, much of the control will pass down to managers.
4) So there will be **different groups** with **ideas** and **influences** — e.g. the original owners, new shareholders, directors and managers might all have **different views** on **objectives** and **strategy**.

- **Corporate governance** describes the **power structure** of a business. It lays out how decisions should be made, the influence that different groups of stakeholders have on strategy, and the information that should be available to each group.
- When ownership and control are separate, a company could have internal and external **stakeholders** with many **different interests** competing for **influence** on strategy.
- For example, the **board of directors** might decide strategy, but shareholders appoint the board, so **shareholders** can also influence strategy by choosing board members who represent **their own interests**.
- **External stakeholders** can influence strategy by influencing **internal stakeholders**. For example, if a company has a lot of union members as employees, the **union** can call for strike action. Or if a **bank** funds a company, the bank can cut off funding and force the company to adopt a strategy that the bank prefers.
- Different groups of stakeholders **competing** for their own interests to be **represented** in a strategy can make it **difficult** to make **strategic decisions**.

Practice Questions

Q1 Give three examples for each of the following: a) difficulties in the strategic decision-making process, b) difficulties in the implementation of strategy.

Q2 What is strategic drift?

Q3 How does divorce between ownership and control affect corporate governance?

Exam Question

Q1 Evaluate the advantages and disadvantages of following an emergent strategy. [20 marks]

In my divorce, I got the TV — but I lost ownership of the control...

It was dreadful. I had to get up and press buttons actually on the actual television set, can you believe. But then my armchair strategically drifted towards the telly, so I don't have to get up anymore. Look who's laughing now, Sandra.

Evaluating Strategy

Just one little page left now — and it's all about figuring out how well a strategy is working.

Strategies** must be continually **Checked** and **Reviewed

A business must **evaluate** whether its **strategy is working** — and whether it's on track to meet its overall objectives.

1) The managers who devise a strategy must **monitor** whether all parts of the firm are **meeting** their targets for implementing the **strategic changes**. They need to check that each **department** is **sticking** to its **timescale** and budgeted **resources**.
2) Plans include a series of deadlines by which certain **objectives** should be met. When each deadline is reached, **actual** performance should be measured against the **objectives** in the plan.
3) The **competitive environment** also needs to be monitored so that any **external factors** that could lead to **strategic drift** are **spotted** and **acted on**.
4) If **targets** or **objectives** are not being met, it's crucial to find out **why**. For example, it could be because a department isn't implementing the strategy **effectively**, or that a strategy is no longer **suitable** for the environment. **Action must be taken** to get back on track.

*Businesses use **Various Techniques** to **Monitor** how the strategy is going*

Businesses use **market analysis** and **management information systems** to measure the **performance** of the business and to monitor the progress of the strategy towards the business's objectives.

Market analysis shows if assumptions about the **market** are correct.

1) Firms use both primary and secondary **market research** to check how the strategy is proceeding.
2) They **audit sales levels**, concentrating particularly on the **target markets**. If there is a big **difference** between **expected** sales and **actual** sales, then the business will want to know why.

Management information systems provide most of the information.

1) **Management information systems** are computer systems that constantly **collect** and **process** routine departmental data, to give a picture of the **current state** of the business. One example of this is **Enterprise Resource Planning** (see p.71 for more). This data is used to see if the business is on course to meet its **objectives**.
2) Managers use **mathematical techniques** such as extrapolating trends to interpret the data.

Picture of the currant state.*

Practice Questions

Q1 Explain why a business needs to monitor its strategic performance.

Q2 Explain how management information systems can be used to monitor the progress of a strategy.

Exam Questions

Q1 Which of the following is not part of the process of evaluating strategic performance? [1 mark]

A Monitoring departmental targets.

B Measuring performance against objectives.

C Conducting network analysis.

D Monitoring the external environment.

Q2 A business plans a strategy for the next five years. To what extent do you agree that the strategy should only be evaluated at the end of the five-year period? [8 marks]

My strategy is so out of date, I get it evaluated on Antiques Roadshow...

This evaluating stuff is really important to a business — there's no point coming up with a brilliant strategy and then not checking it's working. And now all I've got left to say is 'Congrats!' for making it all the way to the end of the section.

*It's Wyoming, made of raisins... Obviously...

Maths Skills

There are loads of statistics involved in running a business, so you need to be able to understand what they all mean.

Businesses produce lots of **Statistics**

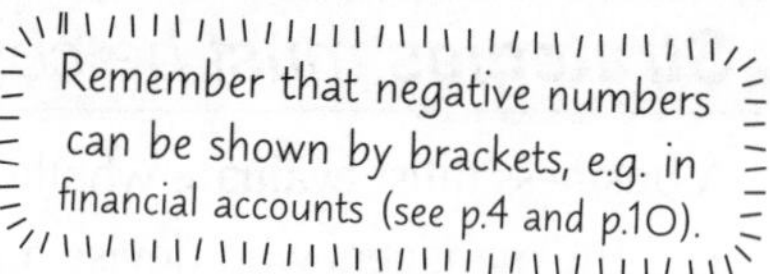

1) Businesses have a lot of **figures** — e.g. figures for sales, costs, revenues and profit, and market research data.
2) Businesses need to understand what their figures **mean** so that they know how well the business is **performing**, and can forecast how well it will perform in the **future**. In order to understand the data and be able to use it, they present it in a way that makes it **easy** to understand.

Diagrams make data **Easier** to **Understand**

1) **Pie charts** can be used to show **market share**. Each **1% share** is represented by a **3.6°** section of the pie (because there's 360° in a circle and 360 ÷ 100 = 3.6). Pie charts are **simple to use** and **easy** to **understand**. They can be created quickly using **spreadsheets**.

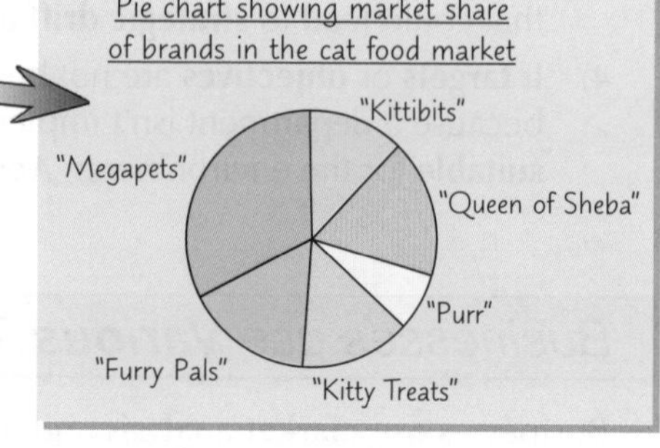

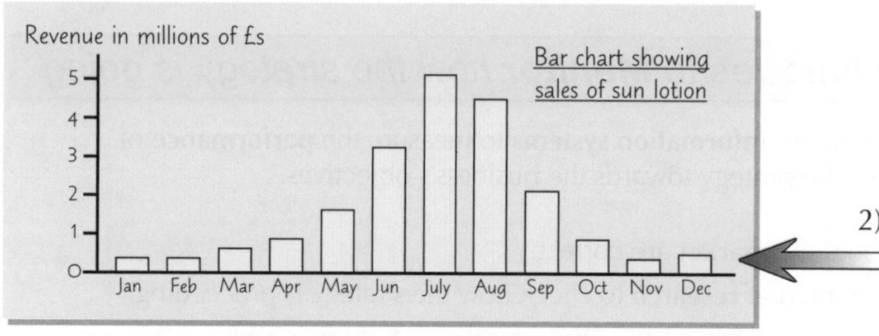

2) **Bar charts** show different values for a **single variable**. They're **easy** to **construct**, easy to **interpret** and they have **high visual impact**.
3) A **histogram** looks quite similar to a bar chart. However, in a histogram the **area** of each block is proportional to the value of the variable measured (not just the height), and there are no gaps between the blocks. So a histogram is different from a bar chart because the bars can vary in both **width** and **height**. Histograms are suitable for comparing variables with **large ranges**.
4) A **pictogram** is a bar chart or histogram where the bars are **pictures** — logos or images. Pictograms are often used in **corporate brochures** — e.g. Cadbury might use pictures of their choccie bars in their sales charts.
5) **Line graphs** plot one variable against another — e.g. sales against time. **More than one line** can be shown to make comparisons — they should be in different colours to keep the graph easy to read.

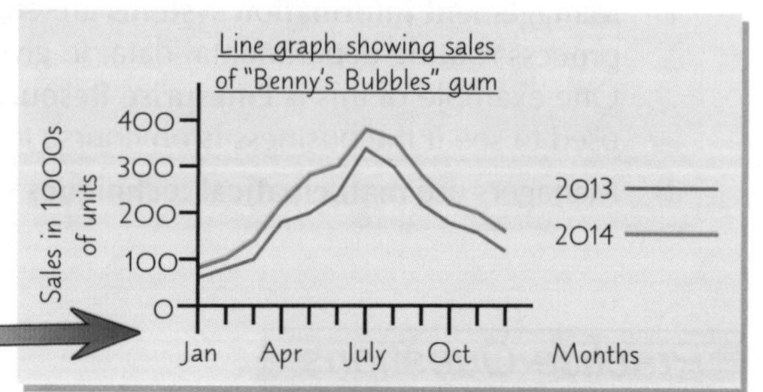

Diagrams can be **Misleading**

1) Graphs and charts can sometimes give a **false impression** of what is actually going on.
2) If the scales on a graph don't start at **zero**, it can be difficult to see what they show and the meaning can be distorted — e.g. the graph on the right seems to show that the profit has **tripled** between 2010 and 2013, but actually it has only gone up by **10%**.

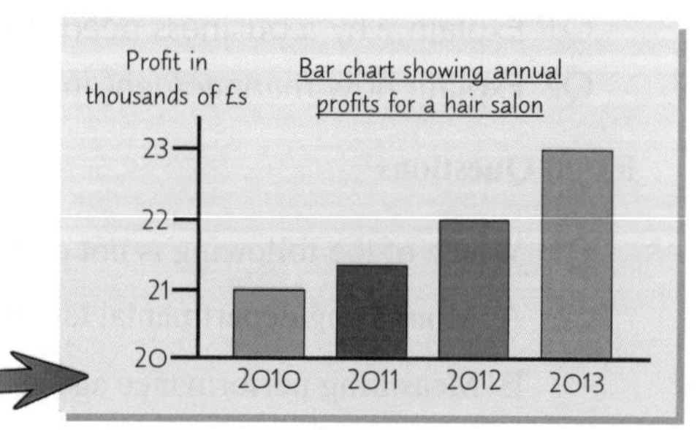

You need to be able to **Analyse Data** and **Graphs**

- As well as being able to read graphs and charts, you need to be able to **analyse** them.
- This means you need to be able to say what you think is the **important bit** of the chart — e.g. an upward trend in sales, or a big market share.
- You need to be able to say what you think is **causing** it, and what the potential **effects** might be — e.g. a **decrease** in market share might have been caused by the arrival of a new **competitor**, so the **marketing** budget will have to be **increased** to try to get the market share back.

Maths Skills

Data is clustered around an *Average* — *Mean*, *Median* or *Mode*

1) The **mean** is found by **adding together** all numbers in a data set and **dividing** the total by the **number of values** in the data set. Shops could calculate the mean spend per customer:

> **Example:** 5 customers spend £5.90, £27.97, £13.62, £24.95 and £78.81
>
> $$\text{Mean spend} = \frac{5.9 + 27.97 + 13.62 + 24.95 + 78.81}{5} = \frac{151.25}{5} = £30.25$$

2) The **median** is the **middle** value in a data set once all the values are put in **ascending order** — e.g. a business might rank all salespeople by the revenue they've generated over the past month, then identify the **median** and pay everyone above this position a bonus for good performance.
3) The **mode** is the **most common number** in a data set. E.g. Marks & Spencer might check the modal dress size when planning their shop displays so that the mannequins would reflect the most common body size among British women.
4) The **range** is the **difference** between the **largest** and the **smallest** in a group of numbers. It's not an average, but it's often used alongside averages.
5) A **confidence interval** is a range of values used to show the **uncertainty** of an **estimate**. E.g. if a business estimates sales of 2200 units, they might say that they are **95% confident** that the actual sales will be **between** 2000 and 2400. Luckily you don't have to calculate confidence intervals, you just need to know what they mean.

You should have covered confidence intervals in Year 1.

Index Numbers show *Changes* in data over time

1) **Index numbers** are a simple way of showing percentage changes in a set of data over time.
2) Businesses take a set of data showing revenue/profits etc. over a number of years, and make the earliest year the **base year** — the value for the base year is set as 100, and the figures for the following years are shown as a **percentage** of this figure. E.g. the table below shows the index numbers for revenue for an Italian restaurant:

Year	Total Revenue	Revenue Index (2010 = 100)
2010	£17 000	100
2011	£19 550	115
2012	£21 250	125
2013	£22 440	132
2014	£24 650	145

To work out the revenue index for any year, take the total revenue from that year, divide it by the total revenue in the base year and multiply it by 100, e.g. for 2013:

$$\frac{22\,440}{17\,000} \times 100 = 132$$

3) The main advantage of indexing is that it makes it easy to see trends within the business.

Rearrange Formulas to get them into the Form you Want

Sometimes you'll have to **rearrange** a formula before you put the numbers in. Rearrange so that the value you're trying to find is on one side of the formula, and everything else is on the other side.

> **Example:** A company selling novelty doorbells has fixed costs of £6000 and the variable cost per unit is £15. They have to sell 1500 units to break even. What is the selling price per unit?
>
> Use the formula: **Contribution per unit = selling price per unit – variable costs per unit**
>
> Rearrange to get the value you're looking for on its own:
>
> **Selling price per unit = contribution per unit + variable costs per unit**
>
> You'll have seen these formulas in Year 1.
>
> But you don't know the contribution per unit, so you'll need another formula to work this out:
>
> $$\textbf{Break-even output} = \frac{\textbf{fixed costs}}{\textbf{contribution per unit}}$$
>
> Rearrange to get contribution per unit on its own: $\textbf{Contribution per unit} = \dfrac{\textbf{fixed costs}}{\textbf{break-even output}}$
>
> $$\text{So: } \textbf{Selling price per unit} = \frac{\textbf{fixed costs}}{\textbf{break-even output}} + \textbf{variable costs per unit}$$
>
> $$= \frac{6000}{1500} + 15 = 4 + 15 = \mathbf{19}.$$ So each novelty doorbell must sell for **£19**.

Maths Skills

Businesses use Percentage Changes to Analyse Figures

1) Businesses work out **percentage** increases or decreases in figures like sales volume, revenue, profit and market share in order to see how performance is **progressing** over time. By looking at percentage changes over a number of months or years, they can see **trends** in the business's performance.

2) The **formula** for working out percentage change is:

$$\textbf{Percentage change} = \frac{\textbf{new figure} - \textbf{previous figure}}{\textbf{previous figure}} \times 100$$

E.g. if sales of hats have gone up from 9000 to 11 000, the percentage increase in sales is (11 000 – 9000) ÷ 9000 × 100 = 22.2%.

3) By rearranging the formula, you can **increase a figure** by a **percentage**:

$$\textbf{New figure} = \frac{\textbf{percentage change} \times \textbf{previous figure}}{100} + \textbf{previous figure}$$

E.g. if a business's profit was £40 000 in 2013 and it increased by 20% in 2014, then the 2014 profit was (20 × 40 000) ÷ 100 + 40 000 = 8000 + 40 000 = £48 000.

Related: 100 percentages that will restore your faith in humanity (#148 BLEW MY MIND)

Percentages, Fractions and Ratios are all Related

You could be given data about a company or a product in a few different ways, and you should be able to convert between them.

To get from **fractions to percentages**, times by 100. And to get from **percentages to fractions**, divide by 100 and simplify.

For example, if $\frac{1}{4}$ of a company's total revenue is profit, then $\frac{1}{4} \times 100 =$ **25%** of its total revenue is profit.

You can also convert from **fractions to ratios** — a ratio is a way of comparing one amount to another. Here, there is 1 part profit to 4 parts revenue, so the ratio of **total revenue to profit** is 4 : 1. This means that for every £4 of revenue, the company makes £1 of profit.

Example: During one year, the average number of employees at a company is 100, and 20 employees leave the company. Calculate the labour turnover as a percentage and as a fraction, and find the ratio of the number of employees leaving to the average number of employees.

$$\textbf{Labour Turnover (\%)} = \frac{\textbf{Number of staff leaving}}{\textbf{Average number of staff employed}} \times 100$$

Labour turnover was covered in Year 1.

Labour Turnover (%) = $\frac{20}{100} \times 100 =$ **20%**, so labour turnover as a **fraction** is simply $\frac{20}{100} = \frac{1}{5}$.

The **ratio** of the number of employees leaving to the average number of employees is 20 : 100 or **1 : 5**.

Practice Questions

Q1 Why can graphs and charts sometimes be misleading?

Q2 Explain the difference between the "mean", "median" and "mode" of a set of data.

Q3 What do index numbers show?

Exam Questions

Q1 Discuss how statistics can hinder as well as help decision-making. [8 marks]

Answer on p.103.

Q2 Look back at the revenue table for the Italian restaurant on page 95. The restaurant owners now decide to take 2012 as their base year. Calculate the new revenue index for 2014. [2 marks]

Ladies and gentlemen, you have been warned — maths kills...

All this maths stuff can be very helpful, but it can also be biased. If you're given a table or graph as part of an exam question, watch out for things like how the axes are labelled, whether the axes start at zero, and whether important info is left out. Businesses often use graphs and charts to put their facts and figures in as good a light as possible.

The A-Level Exams

This page will get you familiar with how the A-level exams are set out, so there'll be no nasty surprises on the day.

A-Level Business has Three Exam Papers

This book covers all of the material from **Year 2** of your course. Make sure you revise your Year 1 notes to cover the rest of the A-level course.

1) A-level Business is made up of **three exams** — Paper 1 (Business 1), Paper 2 (Business 2) and Paper 3 (Business 3).
2) All three exams test the **whole A-level course** — that's **everything** in this book, plus everything you learnt in **Year 1**. They also test your **maths skills** — calculating and interpreting data crops up in different topics, and there are some more general maths skills you need as well (see Section 9).

At least 10% of the exam marks will be for maths skills.

3) Each exam lasts for **2 hours** and is worth **100 marks**. Allowing for reading time, that means you need to achieve a **mark almost every minute**. Each paper counts for **33.333...%** of your A-level.
4) Each paper tests the same four **assessment objectives** (AOs). These are AO1 (**showing knowledge**), AO2 (**applying knowledge**), AO3 (**analysis**) and AO4 (**evaluation**) — there's more detail on each AO on the next page. The AOs have **different weightings** on each paper (see below).

Paper 1 has Four Different Sections

Paper 1 is made up of **four different sections** — Section A is worth **15 marks**, Section B is worth **35 marks** and Sections C and D are worth **25 marks each**. Each section is made up of different **types** of question.

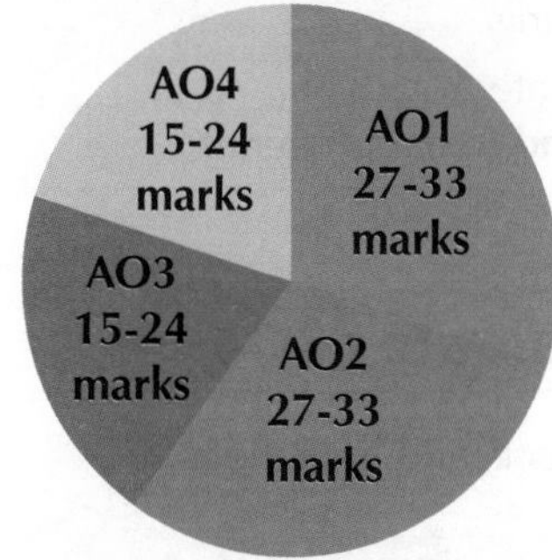

1) Section **A** is made up of **15 multiple choice questions**, worth **1 mark** each. There are 4 options to choose from for each question.
2) Section **B** is made up of **short-answer questions** that could be worth up to **9 marks** each. You'll need to **cover a few points** in these answers, or show a few steps of working in **calculation** questions.
3) In Sections **C** and **D**, you'll be given a **choice** of two questions — and you'll only have to answer **one** for each section. Each question is worth **25 marks**, so you'll have to write an **essay** to get all the marks.

Paper 2 has Three Case Studies

For Paper 2, you'll be given three mini **case studies** and asked **questions** about them (these are known as **data response questions**).

1) In each **case study**, you'll be given some **written information** or some **data** given in **graphs** and **tables** (e.g. costs or profits) — or a mix of both.
2) You'll be asked roughly **3 or 4 questions** on each case study, ranging from **short-answer questions** (worth around **3-4 marks**) to **extended-answer questions** (worth **16** or **20 marks**).
3) Some of the questions will involve **calculations** and **interpretation** based on the data you've been given.

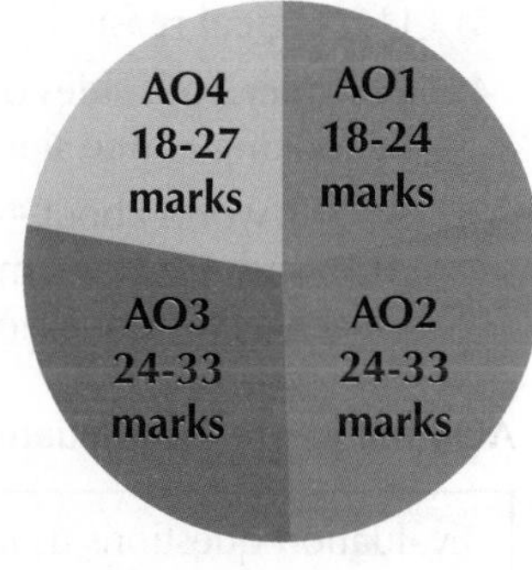

Paper 3 has One Case Study

For Paper 3, you'll be given one extended **case study** and asked **questions** about it.

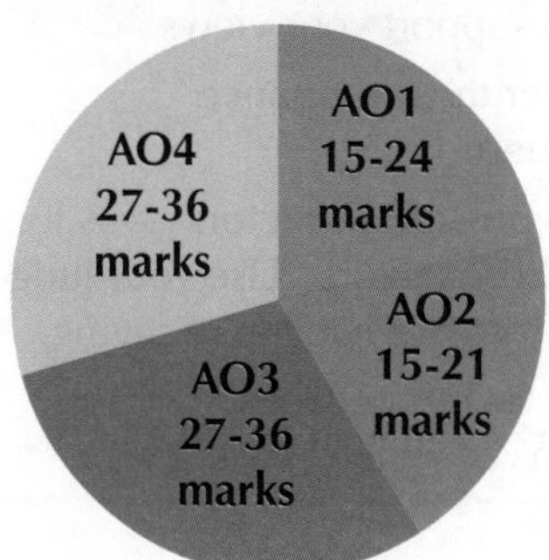

1) You'll be given a lot of information about a business, including **written information** and **data** for calculations.
2) You'll be asked about **6 questions** on the case study, ranging from **12 to 24 marks** each — they all require **longer answers**.
3) Even if the question doesn't ask you to do any **specific** calculations, you might need to do some calculations to **back up** your answer with **evidence**.

There are some **worked examples** of different types of question on pages 100-102.

Get Marks in Your A-Level Exams

These pages explain how the exams are marked. Basically, the marks are divided up into four different skills — AO1, AO2, AO3 and AO4. So to get all the marks, you need to demonstrate all the skills.

You get marks for **Showing Knowledge (AO1)** and **Applying Knowledge (AO2)**

AO1 and AO2 questions usually start with words like "**Describe**", "**Explain**" or "**Calculate**".

"**Describe**" questions ask you to say what something **shows** or **means**, "**explain**" means you have to **give reasons** for something and "**calculate**" means you have to **work something out**.

1) **AO1** marks are for **knowledge** of e.g. **terms**, **methods** and **theories**.
2) This means things like knowing the **proper definitions** for **business terms** (this is often what you're asked for in **multiple choice** questions).
3) For a multiple choice question, you'll get **1 mark** for AO1. For longer questions, you'll usually get between **2-5 marks** for AO1, whether the question is a **short-answer** one worth 4 marks, or an **extended-answer** one worth 16, 24 or 25 marks.

To make sure you get these marks, always give definitions of terms you're using, or formulas if you're doing a calculation.

1) **AO2** marks are for **application** — applying your knowledge to a situation. This means thinking about the **type of business** in the **question**, the product or service it's selling, and the type of market it's in.
2) Numerical **calculations** and **interpretation** are also awarded **application** marks.
3) AO2 is usually worth **2-3 marks**, but questions which want you to demonstrate AO2 will be expecting you to demonstrate **AO1** too, so they'll be worth between **3 and 6 marks** overall.

You'll get more marks when you **Analyse (AO3)** and **Evaluate (AO4)**

AO3 marks are for **analysis** — thinking about benefits, drawbacks, influences, effects and limitations.

Analysis questions often start with the word "**Analyse**".

1) Use your knowledge to **explain** your answer and give **reasons**.
2) If there's data, say what the figures **mean**, talk about what might have **caused** them and say what **effect** you think they will have on the business in the **future**.
3) Use **logical reasoning** to link **influences**, **actions** and their **effects** together.
4) Consider **both sides** of the **argument** — you can only get **limited** analysis **marks** by looking at **one side**.
5) AO3 is worth about **4-6 marks** — but the questions will expect you to demonstrate **AO1** and **AO2** (and maybe even **AO4**) as well. AO3 marks are usually given for **longer-answer** questions (worth **9**, **12**, **16** or **20 marks**).

Lucinda, Tarquin, Jemima and Angelica were experts at demonstrating AOs 1-4.

AO4 marks are for **evaluation** — using your **judgement**.

Evaluation questions usually start with words like "**Evaluate**", "**Justify**" or "**To what extent**".

1) **Weigh up** both sides of the argument — consider the **advantages** and **disadvantages** and say which **side** of the argument you think is **strongest**.
2) Make sure you **justify** your opinions — you should always give **evidence** to support your views.
3) Remember to consider **all** the factors involved when you're asked to consider the importance of a **particular factor**. This is essential when answering "**to what extent**" questions.
4) You don't always need a **definite** answer. You can point out that it **depends** on various factors — as long as you say **what the factors are**, and say **why** your answer would depend on those factors. Use your judgement to say what the **most important factors** are. The most important thing is to **justify** what you're saying.
5) AO4 is usually worth **7-10 marks**. It's tested in **extended-answer** questions (worth between **16** and **25 marks**) and you'll have to demonstrate **AOs 1-3** in these questions as well.

Get Marks in Your A-Level Exams

*Make sure you write **Clearly** and **Structure** your answers well*

1) You have to use the **right style** of writing and **arrange relevant information clearly** — write in **full sentences** and **link** your points together. Don't just write a list of bullet points. You need to use **specialist vocabulary** when it's appropriate, so it's well worth **learning** the **fancy terms** used in this book.
2) You have to write **neatly** enough for the examiner to be able to read it. You also need to use good **spelling**, **grammar** and **punctuation** to make your meaning **crystal clear**. Don't worry, you won't lose marks for spelling errors — but if your handwriting, grammar, spelling and punctuation are **so** far up the spout that the examiner **can't understand** what you've written, then it's a **problem**.
3) You won't get any marks for **written communication** — but you might **lose marks** if the examiner can't **read** or **understand** your writing.

Jotting down a quick plan will help with extended-answer questions or essay questions.

Dudley got no marks for his "Boston Matrix in Mime".

*The **Examiner** will try to show you **How Much to Write***

1) The examiner does try to help you by telling you how many **marks** each question is worth and by giving you an idea of how **much** you need to write. The **more lines** there are for an answer, the **more** you're expected to **write**.
2) Remember, you're aiming to score **a mark a minute** — so if a question is worth **5 marks**, you should spend about **5 minutes** on it.
3) Generally, if the question is worth **2 or 3 marks** then you just need to show your business **knowledge**. Give a **short answer** and move on quickly.
4) For a question worth **16 or more marks**, you need to show **analysis** and **evaluation**. You'll have to write much more for these questions. They usually expect you to make a **decision**, or have an **opinion** and be able to **justify** it. There's rarely a right or wrong answer to this sort of question, so just **convince** the examiner that your opinion is **valid** by **explaining** your reasons (based on your business knowledge).

*Don't forget to include **All** the **Skills** in **Extended-Answer Questions***

1) When you come up against a long question (worth, say, 16 marks), **don't jump** straight to the **evaluation** stage. The examiner will be looking for **evidence** of the **other skills**, too.
2) Remember, a question testing **AO4** will also be testing **AOs 1-3** — so you need to demonstrate **all** of the assessment objectives (see previous page).
3) So, if they ask you how a business can increase its profits, and you think it should either decrease its **operating expenses** or make some staff **redundant**, you need to:

    1) **Define** what is meant by operating expenses and redundancy (this will get you your **AO1** marks).
    2) Explain how operating expenses/redundancy are **relevant** to the type of **business** in the question (for **AO2** marks).
    3) Give the **advantages** and **disadvantages** of each method of increasing profits (for **AO3** marks).
    4) Finally, for the **AO4** marks, **weigh up** both sides of the argument and **decide** if the business should decrease its operating expenses or make some staff redundant (you might decide it needs to do both).

For examples of extended answers, which demonstrate all the skills, see p.101-102.

It's exam time — let's get down to business...

These pages should take some of the surprise out of your exams. You don't need to know this upside down and back to front like you do the actual business stuff. What you do need to know is what the examiners actually want to see from you — not just that you know the facts, but also that you understand and can use what you've learnt.

Worked Exam Questions

Here's an example of the kind of case study and questions you might get in Paper 2 or Paper 3.

This case study covers topics from **Year 1** of your course.

Crinkle Cakes Ltd

Crinkle Cakes Ltd is a business that makes cakes, set up by Janet Jones, who made cakes in her own kitchen to sell to family and friends. Over eight years, it has grown from a sole trader business to a medium-sized private limited company. Although Ms Jones still plays an important day-to-day role in the business, it is no longer based in her kitchen. The business now operates out of premises equipped with machinery which allows them to produce 50 cakes per hour. Crinkle Cakes employs 40 staff on both full-time and part-time contracts.

The business operates in a very competitive market which is dominated by two national bakeries. It also faces competition from a long-established local firm, which has an excellent reputation in the area. In order to ensure the long-term survival of the business, Crinkle Cakes needs to compete more effectively and achieve its objective of increasing both sales and market share. Money is tight though, since the machinery was obtained using a bank loan which is still being paid off.

Crinkle Cakes aims to sell its products in the big supermarkets, but so far has been unable to secure a deal to supply any of the major chains. The main reasons the supermarkets gave for not stocking Crinkle Cakes products were that they had a very narrow product range (selling only whole cakes rather than multi-pack slices or individual portions), and that their cakes were priced higher than competing bakeries.

The marketing manager has been looking at ways to expand the product range. He did some market research into the types of cakes consumers buy, and the results are displayed below (see Table 1). He also examined the prices of the cakes in their market. Crinkle Cakes had originally aimed to charge prices that could compete with the local competitor, but the reality is that Crinkle Cakes's prices are on average 10% higher than their local competitor's and approximately 30% higher than the national competitors'. The marketing manager wants to decrease the price of their cakes, but to do this the company will have to cut costs.

The operations manager has been looking at ways to cut costs. She has discovered that one problem is the rising cost of ingredients from their suppliers. Table 2 shows the expenditure budget and their actual expenditure for a typical month.

Table 1
Results from Market Research (Percentage of People Asked)

Product	Purchased weekly	Purchased monthly	Purchased rarely	Never purchased
Whole cakes	2	8	62	28
Multi-pack, e.g. slices	55	23	14	8
Individual portions	67	17	10	6

Table 2
Expenditure Budget

	Budget	Actual	Variance
Raw materials	£20k	£30k	£10k (A)
Staff costs	£50k	£48k	£2k (F)
Marketing	£5k	£8k	£3k (A)
Insurance & utility bills	£10k	£8k	£2k (F)
Other	£5k	£4k	£1k (F)

*An **Example Short Question and Answer** to give you some tips:*

Q1 Crinkle Cakes Ltd is a private limited company.
Explain **two** features of the legal structure of Crinkle Cakes Ltd. [4 marks]

Crinkle Cakes is owned by its shareholders, who have bought shares privately. The shares cannot be bought by the public and won't be quoted on a stock exchange.

The shareholders of Crinkle Cakes have limited liability, which means that they are not personally responsible for the debts of the business. The only money they can lose is the money they have invested in the company.

Other points that could have been made include the fact that Crinkle Cakes doesn't have a minimum share capital requirement and that a shareholder will need the agreement of other shareholders to sell their shares.

Worked Exam Questions

*An **Example Extended Question and Answer** to give you some tips:*

Q2 Crinkle Cakes Ltd are considering changing their marketing mix to make the business more competitive. To what extent do you think that the product is the most important element of the mix to change? [16 marks]

The marketing mix is all the factors a business has to take into account when marketing a product. This is more commonly referred to as "the seven Ps" of product, price, place, promotion, people, physical environment and process. In order to adapt a marketing mix it is necessary to examine each of these factors in turn.

There are a number of ways in which Crinkle Cakes could make changes to the product. At present they produce mainly whole cakes, which 28% of customers never buy according to the research findings in Table 1. This has meant that few supermarkets have shown a willingness to sell Crinkle Cakes' products. Based on this, one change would be to make a wider range of cake sizes. In addition to the whole cakes, they could introduce a multi-pack containing cake slices, aimed at families, and single-slice packs, perhaps aimed at single people or impulse buyers. This would increase the market segments they appeal to and increase the likelihood of sales to the big supermarkets. Another alteration that Crinkle Cakes could make to their products is to target niche markets (e.g. by making gluten-free products), which would reduce their competition and would mean that they could charge higher prices and still be competitive. However, this may require further market research.

Another element of the marketing mix is price. The case study states that Crinkle Cakes charges higher prices than its competitors, but that this is necessary because of costs, e.g. of ingredients. Table 2 shows that they are paying £10K per month more for their raw materials than budgeted, which will impact on costs and the prices they can charge. To be able to charge more competitive prices, Crinkle Cakes could cut costs, e.g. by negotiating a better deal with their supplier, or by changing suppliers. Lower prices would make the cakes more appealing to consumers and especially the big supermarkets. Or, instead of trying to reduce prices, the company could market the cakes as a luxury item (or aimed at a particular niche market) to justify the prices.

As far as place is concerned, Crinkle Cakes could take steps to get their products into the major supermarkets, which should be possible if they make the changes to the product size already discussed. Crinkle Cakes could also attempt to supply high-end bakeries if they decide to sell luxury cakes.

The case study does not give any detail about what promotion has taken place. The company could reposition their brand as a luxury cake company in order to differentiate themselves from their competitors. They could also consider promoting their products through a company website or social media to increase awareness and demand.

There is very little information in the case study about the people, physical environment and process of Crinkle Cakes, so it is not possible to recommend how to improve these factors.

In conclusion, adapting the product is very important to the continued success of Crinkle Cakes, but there are other factors that need to change too.

Stating knowledge is fine, but don't waste too much time on it

AO1: Refers to, and defines, marketing mix

AO2: Links knowledge about marketing mix to business in question

Make use of information in the case study

AO3: Identifies problems and suggests solutions

Apply your suggestions to the business in question

AO4: Evaluates the impact of changes to the product

AO2: Links issue of price to business in question

Make use of information in the case study

AO3: Identifies problems and suggests solutions

AO4: Evaluates the impact of changes to the price

This is a little vague

AO3: Links marketing decisions with actions

Here you could refer to Table 2, which shows an adverse variance for marketing costs that could limit changes to promotion

This is too brief

AO4: Makes vague attempt at overall analysis

- This is a reasonably good answer and would get about **12 marks**. It considers a range of changes to the marketing mix and applies them to the business in the case study. This answer has been set out sensibly with a separate paragraph for each aspect of the marketing mix.
- However, it doesn't use the information given in Table 2 when talking about promotion, and the last three Ps have been skimmed over. Although there isn't much information in the case study, it would have been good to make **suggestions** on how to use these factors to increase competitiveness.
- The **conclusion** is poor and doesn't add anything to the answer. It doesn't really answer the question, and doesn't cover the 'to what extent' element of the question.

Worked Exam Questions

An **Essay Question and Answer** to give you some tips:

Q3 To what extent is product development a good choice of a marketing growth strategy for a multi-product business? [25 marks]

States knowledge but doesn't spend too long on it

AO1: Describes Ansoff's growth strategies

The main marketing growth strategies that a company should consider, as outlined by Ansoff, are market penetration, product development, market development and diversification. The multi-product business should assess all these options before deciding on the best course of action.

Product development means a business tries to sell new products in the market it currently operates in. So for a cleaning product business, it would need to develop a new cleaning product to sell to its existing customers. This is a good strategy in a market with growth potential, but much less effective in a saturated market. This strategy also depends on the research and development department and their ability to produce innovative new products; however, as the business already offers a number of products, it can be assumed that developing a new one is within their capabilities. A multi-product business will also benefit from economies of scope. This is a good strategy to pursue if the business already has a high market share.

Comes up with an example business to help illustrate point

AO3: Suggests a potential problem and gives reasons why it might not matter

Could do with explaining how this links to the question.

Market penetration is when a business tries to increase its market share in the market it currently operates in. As the business has multiple products, its market share may vary for its different products. One product could have a high market share in its individual market, whereas another's market share might be quite low. The business must decide whether it wants to try to increase its market share for all its products, or just to focus on one or two. Before choosing this strategy, the business must consider the condition of its market. If the market is growing, then this is a good strategy, as demand is still growing. However, if the market is saturated, market penetration is not a good strategy for them, as they will struggle to increase their market share.

AO2: Links knowledge to business in question

Could do with recommending which option to take

AO4: Evaluates other factors and makes recommendation

Market development is when a business tries to sell to a new market or segment. This can be done by repositioning the products to appeal to different consumers, or by adapting the product slightly to meet different needs. To do this, a business needs to carry out market research and come up with a new marketing campaign. An example of market development is if the cleaning product company targeted the industrial sector of the market, rather than individual consumers.

Could also evaluate the cost of this strategy

AO3: Considers other action that may be needed

Explains how the company could pursue this strategy

Considers each strategy in turn

Finally, a business could consider diversification. Diversification is trying to sell a new product to a new market, and is the most risky and most expensive strategy, as the business probably won't have any knowledge or experience of the market they're moving into. The research and development team would need to develop a new product, taking into account their existing capabilities. Diversification is a good strategy when high profits are likely, or when a business does not want to rely too heavily on a limited range of products; however in the case of a multi-product business, this is probably not a concern, so diversification is unlikely to be the best strategy.

AO4: Makes recommendation and justifies it

In conclusion, product development is probably the best strategy for a multi-product business to take. The business already has a number of products, so adding another product to the range is a sensible and realistic option. However, they must take the state of the market, the economy and their own financial position into account before pursuing any strategic decision.

AO4: Good conclusion that answers the question with justification

Conclusion is related to the business in the question

- This is a **pretty good** answer and would get you **most** of the marks. It **considers** all four of Ansoff's marketing growth strategies, and **examines** each one in context of the company.
- It has a clear **conclusion** which **answers the question** — with a **recommendation** as to which strategy is the best for this company (but also takes into account **other factors** that might influence the decision).

Answers to Numerical Questions

Section Two

Page 10 — Exam Question

Q1 E.g.

Revenue	£1 500 000
Cost of sales	(£500 000)
Gross profit	**£1 000 000**
Operating expenses	(£250 000)
Operating profit	**£750 000**
Other expenses	(£100 000)
Profit before tax	**£650 000**
Tax	(£130 000)
Profit after tax	**£520 000**
Dividends	(£250 000)
Retained profit	**£270 000**

[16 marks available — 1 mark for correctly writing the revenue and expenses, 1 mark for naming the five measures of profit, 1 mark for ordering the five profits correctly, 1 mark for each correctly calculated profit, 8 marks for a suitable analysis]

Page 14 — Exam Questions

Q1 $\text{ROCE} = \frac{\text{operating profit}}{\text{total equity + non-current liabilities}} \times 100$

$= \frac{£50\,000}{£130\,000 + £30\,000} \times 100$

$= 31.25\%$

So answer C is correct ***[1 mark]***

Q3 a) $\text{Current ratio} = \frac{\text{current assets}}{\text{current liabilities}}$

$= \frac{£40\,000}{£50\,000}$ ***[1 mark]***

$= 0.8$ ***[1 mark]***

b) Inventory turnover

$= \frac{\text{cost of sales}}{\text{cost of average stock held}}$

$= \frac{£120\,000}{£80\,000}$ ***[1 mark]***

$= 1.5$ ***[1 mark]***

Page 16 — Exam Questions

Q1 Gearing (%)

$= \frac{\text{non-current liabilities}}{\text{total equity + non-current liabilities}} \times 100$

$= \frac{£20\,000}{£30\,000 + £20\,000} \times 100$ ***[1 mark]***

$= \frac{£20\,000}{£50\,000} \times 100$ ***[1 mark]***

$= 0.4 \times 100 = 40\%$ ***[1 mark]***

Section Three

Page 31 — Practice Questions

Q4 £0.49 = $1

80 ÷ 0.49 = 163.265..., so £80 = $163.27

Section Four

Page 43 — Exam Questions

Q1 Overall net return =

£320 000 – £40 000 – £200 000 = £80 000 ***[1 mark]***.

$\text{Average net return} = \frac{£80\,000}{8} = £10\,000$ ***[1 mark]***

$\text{ARR} = \frac{\text{average net return}}{\text{investment}} \times 100$

$\text{So ARR} = \frac{£10\,000}{£200\,000} \times 100 = 5\%$ ***[1 mark]***

Q2 $\text{Payback period} = \frac{\text{amount invested}}{\text{annual net return}} = \frac{£11000}{£3000} = 3.67$ years (or 3 years and 8 months).

[1 mark for working, 1 mark for answer]

Section Eight

Page 89 — Exam Question

Q1 a)

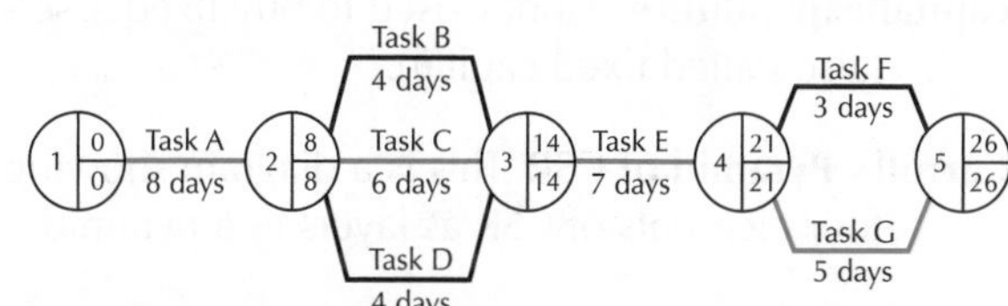

[9 marks available — 3 marks for putting (A), (B, C and D), (E), and (F and G) in the right order, or 2 marks for 1 error, or 1 mark for 2 errors. 1 mark for B, C and D as simultaneous, 1 mark for F and G as simultaneous. 1 mark per node (2, 3, 4 and 5) fully correct.]

b) ***[1 mark for the critical path (the thick pink line on the diagram), 1 mark for the total time — 26 days]***

c) Float times for B and F are both 2 days. ***[1 mark for each]***

Section Nine

Page 96 — Exam Questions

Q2 Divide revenue of 2014 by the revenue of the base year (2012) and multiply by 100:

$\frac{24650}{21250} \times 100$ ***[1 mark]*** = 116 ***[1 mark]***

Glossary

Ansoff's matrix Shows the strategies that a firm can use to expand, according to how risky they are.

asset Anything that a business owns.

balance sheet A snapshot of a firm's finances at a particular time.

barrier to entry An obstacle that makes it harder for companies to enter a market.

benchmarking Identifying how to improve your business by comparing its performance, products and processes against those of another firm.

big data A term used to describe the vast quantities of data that can be collected from various sources.

Bowman's strategic clock Shows positioning strategies based on different combinations of price and perceived added value/benefits.

break-even analysis Identifies the point where a company's total revenues equal its total costs.

budget Forecasts future earnings and future spending.

capacity utilisation How much of its maximum capacity a business is using.

capital A company's wealth in the form of money or other assets.

capital expenditure Money used to buy fixed assets (also called fixed capital).

Carroll's Pyramid of CSR This is a diagram showing four elements of CSR as layers in a pyramid.

cash flow Money that moves in and out of a business over a set period of time.

centralisation A way to structure a business where all decisions come from a few key people.

channel of distribution The route a product takes from the producer to the consumer.

competitive advantage The way that a company offers customers better value than competitors do — generally either lower prices or more product features.

confidence interval A range in which you can say, with a certain level of confidence, that a value lies.

Consumer Price Index This measures changes in prices of a sample of consumer goods and services. It measures inflation.

contingency plan A plan preparing for an event that's unlikely to happen, just in case it does.

contribution The difference between the selling price and the variable costs of a product.

core competence A unique feature of a business that gives it a competitive advantage.

corporate objective A goal of a business as a whole.

corporate social responsibility (CSR) A company's contribution to society.

correlation The relationship between two variables.

cost-push inflation When rising costs (e.g. for raw materials or labour) push up prices.

creditor Someone who a business owes money to.

critical path In network analysis, the series of activities that is critical in the timing of the overall project.

current ratio A liquidity ratio that compares current assets to current liabilities.

debt capital The capital raised by borrowing (also called loan capital).

debtor Someone who owes money to a business.

decentralisation A way to structure a business where decisions are shared across the company.

delayering Reducing the number of levels in the hierarchy of an organisation.

demand-pull inflation When a rise in disposable income means there's too much demand for too few goods, leading to businesses increasing prices.

demographic change A change in the structure of a population.

depreciation Loss of value over time — fixed assets often depreciate.

developed country A relatively rich country with a high GDP.

developing country A relatively poor country with a low GDP.

dimensions of national culture A model used to compare the differences in cultural values between different countries.

director A person responsible for running a company.

discrimination When one group of people is unfairly treated differently to others, e.g. due to race, age or gender.

Glossary

diversification Selling new products to new markets.

divorce between ownership and control When the owners of a company no longer have total control.

earliest start time (EST) In network analysis, the earliest time that an activity can possibly start.

economic growth The rate of increase in GDP.

economies of scale When the cost of producing each item decreases as the scale of production increases.

economies of scope When a single company can make two or more products more cheaply than they can be made by separate companies.

elasticity of demand Shows the relationship between changes in demand for a product and the change in another variable (such as price or income).

Elkington's Triple Bottom Line model A model that assesses performance by considering three overlapping areas: profit, people and planet.

embargo A ban on trade with particular countries.

emergent strategy A form of strategy that develops over time, based on experience and changes in the environment.

emerging economy A developing country with a fast growing, but not yet fully developed, economy.

employment tribunal A type of court which hears disputes between employers and employees.

ethical Morally and professionally acceptable.

exchange rate The value of one currency in terms of another, e.g. £1 = €1.36.

fiscal policy The government's method of adjusting tax rates and its spending to control the economy.

fixed asset An asset that a business keeps long-term or uses repeatedly — e.g. property, equipment, land, computers.

fixed cost A cost that stays the same — no matter how much or how little a firm produces.

flat structure An organisational structure that has few layers of management.

float time The amount of time a non-critical activity can be delayed without delaying the completion of the entire project.

force field analysis A technique used to analyse forces for and against change.

forecasting Trying to predict what will happen in the future.

franchising An agreement which allows one business to use the name, knowledge and processes of an established business.

functional objective An objective of an individual department or business function.

gearing The proportion of a business financed through debt rather than equity or reserves.

globalisation The increase in how interconnected the world is.

gross domestic product (GDP) The total market value of goods and services produced within a nation over a period of time (usually a year).

income statement Statement showing how much money's gone into and out of a company over a period of time.

inflation An increase in the price of goods and services.

infrastructure The basic facilities such as roads, railways, power lines, water pipes and communication networks that allow society to function.

innovation Coming up with new ideas, products and processes.

insolvent Unable to pay debts.

interest rate The fee paid for borrowing.

inventory A business's entire stock.

inventory turnover ratio How many times a year a business sells and replaces all its stock.

just-in-time (JIT) production Manufacturing process that operates with very small amounts of stock.

kaizen A lean production method that involves encouraging everyone to constantly improve quality.

Kaplan and Norton's Balanced Scorecard model A model that assesses performance using four different perspectives: financial, internal business process, learning and growth, and customers.

labour retention The proportion of staff that stay at a company for a given period.

Glossary

labour turnover The proportion of staff that leave a company during a given period.

latest finishing time (LFT) In network analysis, the latest time that an activity can finish without delaying the completion of the entire project.

liability A debt a business owes.

liquidity ratio A ratio that shows whether a business has enough liquid assets (e.g. money) to pay its short-term liabilities.

living wage The amount of money thought to be enough to allow an acceptable standard of living.

market development (or market extension) Selling existing products to new markets.

marketing mix The seven Ps firms use to market their products — the four traditional Ps (price, product, promotion, place) and the three extra Ps (people, physical environment, process).

market penetration Trying to increase market share in your existing market.

market share The percentage of sales in a market made by one firm or brand.

mass customisation This combines aspects of bespoke production with the low costs of mass production.

matrix structure A way of organising staff by two different criteria, e.g. into a combination of departments and teams.

merger Where two companies agree to join together into one business.

migration The movement of people from one place to another.

minimum wage The lowest amount that someone can legally be paid.

monetary policy The government's method of controlling inflation, exchange rates and the economy by adjusting interest rates.

monopoly When one business has complete control over the market. Lack of competition can lead to high prices and low quality.

multinational A business with its headquarters in one country and bases in other countries.

net realisable value The amount a company could get by selling its stock in its current state.

network analysis A method of calculating the most efficient order in which to carry out a series of activities.

new product development Selling new products to existing markets.

node A feature of networks that shows where activities start or finish.

objective A medium- to long-term target.

offshoring When a firm has one or several of its activities carried out abroad.

opportunity cost The idea that money or time spent doing one thing means missing out on doing something else.

organic growth When a business grows from within, also know as internal growth.

organisational culture The way things are done within a business, in relation to expectations, attitudes and how staff make decisions.

organisational design The structure or hierarchy of a company.

outsourcing When a firm has one or several of its activities carried out by another specialist company.

payable Money that a business owes.

payables days ratio The number of days it takes a firm to pay for goods bought on credit.

planned strategy A form of strategy that involves all strategic planning being done before it is implemented.

Porter's Five Forces Model A framework for analysing competition within an industry and judging how attractive the market is.

Porter's strategic matrix Identifies a competitive strategy, based on competitive advantage and market scope.

Porter's three generic strategies Three different strategies that can be used to gain a competitive advantage: cost leadership, differentiation and focus.

privatisation When state-owned firms are sold to private companies.

product A good or a service.

productivity The output per worker in a given time period.

Glossary

profit The difference between total revenue and total costs.

protected characteristic The Equality Act 2010 makes it illegal to discriminate against people based on a protected characteristic, such as age, disability, pregnancy or religion.

protectionist policy A policy designed to protect domestic businesses from foreign competition, (e.g. by using subsidies, tariffs or quotas).

quota A limit on the quantity of a product that can be imported or produced.

re-shoring When a firm brings activities back to the country it is based in.

receivable Money owed to a business.

receivables days ratio The number of days a business has to wait to be paid for goods it supplies on credit.

recession A temporary decline in a country's economic activity.

regional structure A way of organising a business based on geographical location.

regulation Government rules that apply to all firms in a particular industry.

retrenchment When a business decreases in size.

return on capital employed (ROCE) Shows you how much money is made by the business compared to how much money's been put into the business.

return on investment (ROI) A calculation of how efficient an investment is.

revenue The value of sales (also called sales or turnover).

sanction A restriction on trade with a particular country.

shareholder A person that owns a share of a company.

single market The countries in a single market have few trade barriers between them. This means goods and labour can move freely within the single market.

sole trader A self-employed individual who trades under his or her own name, or under a suitable trading name.

stakeholder Anyone with an interest in a business, including workers, shareholders and customers.

strategic drift When a business's strategy doesn't adapt to changes in the environment.

strategy A medium to long-term plan for achieving a business's objectives.

SWOT analysis A method of assessing a business's current situation — it looks at the strengths, weaknesses, opportunities and threats facing the business.

tactics Short-term plans for implementing strategy.

takeover Where one firm buys over 50% of the shares of another firm, giving them a controlling interest.

tall structure An organisational structure that has many layers of management, with a strict hierarchy.

tariff A tax on imports or exports that is put in place to restrict trade.

total equity The total money that's been put into a business by shareholders.

trade bloc A group of countries with few trade barriers between them.

trade union A group that acts on behalf of a group of employees in negotiations with employers.

urbanisation An increase in the proportion of a population that lives in towns and cities.

variable cost A cost that varies, depending on how much business a firm does.

wage-price spiral A cycle in which wage increases cause price increases, which then cause further wage increases, and so on.

working capital Money available for day-to-day spending.

World Trade Organisation (WTO) An international organisation which encourages trade between member countries. It deals with trade rules and negotiations.

Index

A

active resistance 76
aged receivables analysis 14
aged stock analysis 13
alliances 63
analysing data 94
analysing overall performance 18, 19
Ansoff's matrix 49
assets 4-8, 12
average rate of return (ARR) 42
averages 95

B

backwards vertical integration 40, 56
bad debts 5
Balanced Scorecard Model 20
balance sheets 4-8, 11
Bank of England Monetary Policy Committee 33
bar charts 94
barriers to change 76
barriers to entry 40
Bartlett and Ghoshal 68
base cases 47
base years 95
benchmarking 18, 60
big data 71
bloggers 36
booms 29
Bowman's strategic clock 51
brain drain 36
brand loyalty 50
business enterprise policies 26
business growth 52-57
business rates 32
buyer power 40
buying groups 40

C

capital 4-6, 8
  employed 12
  expenditure 6
Carroll's Pyramid of CSR 38
change
  causes of 72, 73
  demographic 36
  management 74, 75
circular economy 27
collectivism 81
communication 74, 75, 77, 84
competition 22
Competition Act 22
Competition and Markets Authority (CMA) 22
competition law 22, 40
competitive advantage 19, 50, 51
competitive environment 40, 41
conglomerate mergers 56
Consumer Price Index 30
Consumer Protection Act 23
contingency plans 83
contractionary fiscal policy 32
copyright 61
core competences 19
corporate governance 92
corporate image 46
corporate objectives 2
corporate social responsibility (CSR) 37, 38
cost leadership 50, 51
cost of sales 9, 10, 13
cost-push inflation 30
costs 9, 10, 50
creditor days ratio 13
creditors 5, 13
critical path 86
cultural barriers 35
currency conversions 31
current assets 4-6, 8, 12
current liabilities 4-6, 8
current ratio 12
customer perspective 20

D

debtor days ratio 14
debtors 5, 6, 12, 14
debts 5, 6
decision-making 2, 82
deflation 30
delayering 74
demand-pull inflation 30
demographics 36
depreciation 5, 7
development stage 59
diagrams (statistical) 94
differentiation strategies 50, 51
digital technology 39, 70, 71
dimensions of national culture 81
direct discrimination 24
direct investment 63
discounted cash flow (DCF) 45
discount factors 44
discounting 44
discrimination 24
diseconomies of scale 53
disruptive change 73
diversification 48, 49
dividends 4, 5, 9, 10
divorce between ownership and control 92
dominant position 22

E

economic growth 28
economic performance 28
economies of scale 40, 52
economies of scope 53
economy 28, 29
efficiency ratios 13
Elkington's Triple Bottom Line model 21
embargoes 27
emergent strategies 91
emerging economies 34-36
Emissions Trading System 27
employment
  allowance 26
  contracts 25, 75
  laws 24
Enterprise Investment Scheme 26
Enterprise Resource Planning (ERP) 39, 71, 93
entrepreneurial culture 79
entrepreneurs 26
Environment Agency 23, 27
environmental laws 27
environmentally friendly 37
Equality Act 24
equity 15
EU Common Agricultural Policy 33
EU competition law 40
EU directives 23-25, 27
European Single Market 22
European Union (EU) 27
exchange rates 31, 33
expansionary fiscal policies 32
expenses 9

Index

experience curve 52
exporting goods 28, 31, 33, 62, 63
extrapolation 19

F

feasibility of strategies 82
feminine cultures 81
financial perspective 20
fiscal policy 32
fixed assets 4-6
fixed capital 6
flexibility 74, 75
float time 87-89
focus strategy 50, 51
force field analysis 73
forecasting 19
forward vertical integration 40, 56
fractions 96
franchising 55
free trade 33, 34
free trade agreements 27
functional decisions 2
functional objectives 2
functional structures 85
future value of money 44

G

GDP (gross domestic product) 28
gearing 15, 16
global finance market 34
globalisation 34
global recessions 29
global strategy 68
global upswings 29
government policies 26, 32
graphs 94
green subsidy schemes 27
Greiner's model of growth 55
gross profit 9, 10
growth
  business 52-57
  economic 28

H

harmonisation 67
histograms 94
Hofstede's dimensions of national culture 81
horizontal integration 56

I

implementing strategies 84, 85
importing goods 28, 63
income statements 9-11
incremental changes 73
index numbers 95
indirect discrimination 24
individualism 81
indulgent societies 81
industrial relations 46
inflation 6, 9, 30, 33, 44
infrastructure 26
innovation 58-61
interest rates 30, 33
internal business process perspective 20
international business strategies 68, 69
internationalisation 62, 63
international markets 62, 63
international strategy 68
intrapreneurship 60
inventories 5, 6, 12
inventory turnover ratio 13
investment 5, 42-47
  criteria 46
  decisions 46

J

joint ventures 56

K

kaizen 60
Kaplan and Norton's Balanced Scorecard model 20
knowledge and information management 75
Kotter and Schlesinger 76, 77

L

labour turnover 18, 96
learning and growth perspective 20
Lewin's force field analysis 73
liabilities 4-6, 8, 12, 15
licensing 63
line graphs 94
liquidity 8, 12
  ratios 12
living wage 25
locating abroad 64, 65
long-term loans 8

M

management information systems 93
managing change 74, 75
market
  analysis 93
  development 48, 49
  extension 48, 49
  penetration 48, 49
  research 58, 59, 93
marketing strategies 48-51
masculine cultures 81
matrix structures 85
mean (average) 95
mechanistic structures 74
median (average) 95
mergers 56, 57, 63
migration 36
minimum wage 25
mission 2, 48
mode (average) 95
monetary policy 33
Monetary Policy Committee 33
monopolies 22, 26, 51
mortgages 8
multidomestic strategies 68
multinationals 66-68

N

National Infrastructure Plan 26
national living wage 25
national minimum wage 25
natural monopolies 26
net assets 4
net cash flow 42, 45
net current assets 6, 8
net present value (NPV) 45
net realisable value 7
net return 42
network analysis 86-89
new product development 48, 49, 59
niche markets 48, 50, 51

O

objectives 2
offshoring 64
open trade 33
operating expenses 9, 10
operating profit 9, 10, 12

Index

opportunity costs 44
organic growth 54
organic structures 74
organisational cultures 78-81
organisational structures 74, 85
overdrafts 8
overtrading 6, 54
ownership 2

P

passive resistance 76
patents 40, 61
payables 5
payables days ratio 13
payback period 43
pensions 25
percentages 96
performance measures 18
person culture 79
philanthropic responsibilities 38
pictograms 94
pie charts 94
planned strategies 91
Porter's Five Forces model 40, 41
Porter's strategic matrix 51
Porter's three generic strategies 50
positioning strategies 50, 51
power culture 78
predatory pricing 22, 40
price
- fixing 22
- wars 40

privatisation 26
process innovation 58
product-based structures 85
product
- development 48, 49, 59
- differentiation 50, 51
- innovation 58

profit
- after tax 9, 10
- before tax 9, 10
- gross 9, 10
- operating 9, 10, 12
- ratio 12
- retained 9, 10

protected characteristics 24
protectionism 27, 33
public limited companies (PLCs) 9

Q

qualitative factors 46
quotas 27

R

Race Relations Act 24
ratio analysis 17
ratios 12-17, 96
re-shoring 64
realisable value 7
rearranging formulas 95
receivables 5, 6, 12, 14
receivables days ratio 14
recession 28, 29
recycling 23
regional structures 85
regulation of industries 26
repositioning 48
reserves 15
resistance to change 76, 77
responsibilities of businesses 38
restrained societies 81
retained profit 9, 10
retrenchment 53
return on capital employed (ROCE) 12
return on investment 12
revenue 9, 10
rivalry 41
role culture 78

S

sales acts 23
sanctions 27
sensitivity analysis 47
Sex Discrimination Act 24
share capital 15
shareholders 38, 92
short-termism 2
short-term objectives 2
slump 29
social media 71
stakeholders 38, 80, 82, 92
state pension 25
statistics 94
stock 5-7, 12
stock turnover ratio 13
strategic decisions 2, 82, 90
strategic direction 48
strategic drift 92
strategic planning 82, 83
strategies 2, 3, 48-51
strong organisational culture 78
supplier power 40
sweatshops 66
SWOT analysis 3, 82

T

tactics 2
takeovers 56, 63
tariffs 27, 33
task culture 79
taxation 32
technology 39, 70, 71
test marketing 59
threat of substitutes 41
time management 88
total equity 4, 12, 15
trade blocs 34
Trade Descriptions Act 23
trademarks 61
transfer pricing 67
transnational strategy 68
trends 8, 19
tribunals 24

U

uncertainty 46
unit cost 52, 53
urbanisation 36

V

value analysis 59
VAT 32
ventures 56
vertical integration 56

W

wage-price spiral 30
weak organisational culture 78
what-if analysis 47
working capital 4, 6, 8, 12, 14
World Trade Organisation (WTO) 27, 33